WRITE OF THE LIVING DEAD

A Writing Guide for Your Dark Side

WRITE OF THE LIVING DEAD

A Writing Guide for Your Dark Side

Araminta Star Matthews, MFA

Rachel Lee, MA

Stan Swanson

dark moon

DARK MOON BOOKS

an imprint of Stony Meadow Publishing
Largo, Florida

Write of the Living Dead
A Writing Guide for Your Dark Side

ISBN: 978-0-9834335-8-3

Library of Congress Control Number: 2012933416

dark moon
www.darkmoonbooks.com

Cover Design by Stan Swanson

ACKNOWLEDGEMENTS

Araminta Star Matthews would like to recognize the many influences that helped her with her part in *Write of the Living Dead*. In addition to the support of her long-time friend and co-author, Rachel Lee, and her favorite publisher, friend, and co-author, Stan Swanson, Araminta would like to also thank her partner, Abner Goodwin for putting up with late nights and keeping their whippet, Devo, out of her office while she clattered away at the keyboard. This book also would not have been possible without the mentors of Araminta's educational career, particularly Eva Giles and William Grant of Lewiston Adult Education for supporting her professional development as an English teacher, and Dawn Walker-Elders for her continuing willingness to talk grammar between classes. Colleagues and mentors, Michael Matzinger and Lucinda Coombs of Central Maine Community College, along with all the other members of her department, have offered tremendous insight, discussion, and support around composition matters. In addition, her colleagues at CMMC CONHP and The Maine Educator Consortium have expanded her professional knowledge of teaching writing and composition. She would also like to thank all of her past and present students of both adult education and college writing courses—she really does learn as much from them as she hopes they learn from her. Lastly, she must acknowledge her parents, Crystal and Michael, for inspiring a lifelong love of reading, writing, and learning.

Rachel Lee thanks the many mentors in her life who have shared her passion for reading, nourished her love of writing, and have shaped her growth as a writing instructor and tutor (especially her partners-in-crime, Araminta Star Matthews and Stan Swanson). She is also deeply indebted to generations of writers whose bewitching prose and dark stories have kept her awake deep into the night, endlessly curious about what happens next.

Stan Swanson would like to thank the hordes of zombies, vampires, and other monsters who scared him just enough over the years to make him hunger for more. He would also like to thank his co-authors, Araminta Star Matthews, who has been his friend and cohort from the very beginning of the journey of *Dark Moon Digest* and Dark Moon Books, and Rachel Lee, whose special attention to detail and editing has put a lasting shine on this tome. He would also like to thank all of the past and present staff associated with Dark Moon as well as the many authors he has befriended during this grand publishing adventure. And, of course, a special thanks goes to his wife, Joy, who has always been a source of inspiration and encouragement. Life would certainly be much darker and more sinister without her.

CONTENTS

Write *night* OF THE LIVING DEAD

FOREWORD

Rocky Wood

There is a fifth dimension beyond that which is known to the average writer. It is a dimension as vast as the blank page and as timeless as story itself. It is the middle ground between light and shadow, between science and superstition, and it lies between the pit of man's fears and the summit of his knowledge. This is the dimension of imagination. It is an area which they call Write of the Living Dead.

(With sincere apologies to Rod Serling who, if he is not shambling the earth seeking the flesh of the living, will be rolling in his grave.)

But you are indeed about to enter *The Twilight Zone*–at least for books that purport to give you all manner of instructions about "How to Write" (drum roll). I will wager you have *never* seen a book like this–one part humor, one part homage to the horror genre, and it is all layered over a solid foundation of serious instruction.

One could spend one's entire time reading such instructional tomes, and never actually write. Your choice, I know, will be different–you will choose to actually write stories, poetry and essays implementing the skills and tips you find here. There are many books on how to write, such as Stephen King's instant classic, *On Writing* (where I learned some Rules that I almost always remember to apply, such as "the adverb is not your friend"). And that one is almost certain to be in the reference books by your computer if you're a horror writer, King holding the place in the horror literary firmament he does (he was once described as Jupiter to our lesser satellites). King's work and a handy list of many other manuals can be found in the "Works Referenced or Consulted" section at the end of this book.

But books about writing in the oldest genre on Earth? (I guarantee you the first caveman to tell a tale around the fire related horror and fear to his eager audience.) Not so much. Surely you have the Horror Writers Association's standard text, *On Writing Horror* edited by Mort Castle? And the Michael Knost edited, *Writers Workshop of Horror*? It is filled with essays by professional horror writers, most members of the genre's leading body, the Horror Writers Association. Both those books won the Bram Stoker Award™ for Superior Achievement in Non-Fiction, presumably indicating horror writers do appreciate a good writing manual!

But it is rare indeed to find a book on how to write *horror*, in this case one from horror aficionados–author and publisher Stan Swanson, Araminta Star Matthews (who spookily enough grew up in the same town where Stephen King attended high school and which features in his latest novel, *11/22/63*) and Rachel Lee. Not to mention, but I will, the many guest authors who appear in the book–my favorite in reading the manuscript was the inimitable and debonair Dr. Abraham Van Helsing, whose name might raise the hackles of the odd vampire (do vampires *have* hackles?).

Horror writing is a community (some say we are a "ghetto"–and I think they who declare such are proud of that, but I'm more one for describing it as self-sustaining and close-knit) and it is to that community this book is squarely directed. There are literally hundreds of horror culture references for you to savor, as you take in the writing lessons. And in the humor of much of what you'll read is a lesson: learning need not be boring, and writing need not be staid. It can be fun, and that fun certainly pours across the pages you're about to read, as blood flows from Dexter Morgan's victims.

Writing is a very personal matter–in the end there is nothing but you and the blank space on the paper/computer screen. No one can really help you but yourself, but everyone needs the best possible tool kit in building their writing skills and, in books like *Write of the Living Dead*, even the most experienced writers will find new advice, and reminders of the basics that we often tend to neglect.

One final note–Stephen King says, "If you don't have time to read, you don't have the time (or the tools) to write. Simple as that." And how right he is–I am astounded by the number of people who tell me they are writing a book, but that they don't read. Read widely–in horror, in other genres, non-fiction, high literature, popular novels, and short stories. You should be learning from everything you read–even Dan Brown can teach you something (generally how not to write, although I'm sure his bank manager disagrees with me). Of course, don't use reading as a reason to procrastinate and not write; there is a good balance, and the best writers achieve it.

So, shamble over to your favorite writing spot, flex your fingers (if you still can), train a half-undead eye on the space where you words will flow, and use what brain you have left to . . . write!

Rocky Wood is President of the Horror Writers Association. He is author of the Bram Stoker Award nominated books *Stephen King: Uncollected, Unpublished* (now out in a revised Fourth Edition) and *Stephen King: The Non-Fiction*, as well as *Stephen King: A Literary Companion*. When not dissecting the literary worlds created by King, he writes graphic novels, including *Horrors! Great Stories of Fear and Their Creators* (illustrated by Glenn Chadbourne) and *Witch-Hunts: A Graphic History of the Burning Times* (with Lisa Morton, illustrated by Greg Chapman).

PREFACE FROM THE AUTHORS
or
"There's a Light on Over at the Frankenstein Place"

THEY'D BEEN SAYING it all along. The zombie apocalypse is coming and we're all going to be food for the dead. Even the Centers for Disease Control announced the impending zombie invasion, asking that all United States citizens put together a disaster preparedness kit. Lucky for us, Rachel had some organizational skills and started stockpiling canned goods and bottled water in her apartment. Not so lucky for us? This publishing contract deadline. Everybody knows publishers and agents accept no excuses for late submissions—even when the whole world is becoming populated by the undead.

"We're being eaten alive up here," Rachel was telling Stan as he barreled into her apartment during the first wave of zombies to sweep the city.

"Doesn't matter. Zombies will read anything. We need to get this book out on time before the market is saturated with blood. A contract's a contract," he had responded. Of course, that was before the electricity was cut and we had nothing but Araminta's solar-powered backpack to recharge the dying laptop battery. And, oh yeah, someone forgot the can opener.

Training for this eventuality his whole life (or, at least since *The Zombie Survival Guide* came out), Stan used his sledgehammer to destroy the stairs leading to the lower floors in order to block any wandering flesh-eaters from making their way upstairs. Rachel papered most of the windows so that any creatures wandering outside wouldn't see the blue glow of the laptop screen from the street. And Araminta arranged the canned goods into a kind of Feng Shui tower to both increase the flow of chi into our writing space and also to create a sad and dysfunctional barricade against any zombies that might find their way inside.

Together, we took turns tapping away at the keyboard or soliciting submissions from the undead. We even managed to get a few flashy celebrities to contribute, including Frankenstein's monster. Impressed?

At any rate, the book is almost finished now. Just in time, too, since we can hear the wrought iron fire escape ladder clanging against the metal frame bolted to the building. The zombies have found us and, whether it will be in minutes, hours, or days, they'll eventually make their way into the apartment and tear the living flesh from our bones.

We don't know how they found us. We took every precaution. Maybe it was the sheet we hung out the window with our submission guidelines painted across it. Maybe one of the monsters tracked our IP address. Or maybe they could smell us. It *has* been a couple months without running water, if you know what we mean. It is surprising you can't smell us. Right now. Through the pages.

As the zombie horde ascends the fire escape and bombards our safe haven, it occurs to us that the decision to take out the stairs may have been a bit hasty—we now have no means of escape. At least we have a little time to finish the final edits and layout of this book before we send it off to the printer.

Just in time, too. The light on the laptop is dying, and the sun is setting over the road to the Western Lands. And there's still so much left to do. Will we make it?

Araminta Star Matthews
Rachel Lee
Stan Swanson

—1—

THE BASICS OF WRITING

or

The Human Skeleton Has 206 Bones, Each With a Unique Nutritional Purpose

The following chapter was composed by the late Reginald Spittoon, a famous author from before the Death Eating swept the world, wiping out more than 90% of its population. From the scraps of bar napkins, notebook pages, and even the bar's ink-scrawled countertop, we have been able to piece together the last moments of his life, giving us a better idea of how long it might take for the zombie virus to seize control of an otherwise healthy, mortal brain. Incidentally, it also afforded us some great tips on composition.

IT'S DARK OUTSIDE.

I can't see through the grime-covered window of the bar to know that for a fact, but the bartender just flipped the switch to the neon sign hanging in the dirt-streaked window. It flickers occasionally, trying in vain to attract the attention of passersby on the street. The evidence of its failure reveals itself in the few people scattered about the seedy hole-in-the-wall joint.

The name of the guy at the bar drinking the Bloody Mary is Eric. (Don't know his last name.) And just for your information, that isn't tomato juice in his glass. More likely it is AB-Positive. Once it gets a little darker outside, I imagine he will disappear into the night in search of the real stuff instead of the refrigerated junk stored below the bar sink.

I'm not sure of the name of the girl sitting alone in the corner. (I think it's Spice.) She is usually out plying her trade as evening approaches, but not tonight. It's that time of the month. Yep, full moon. You can already see the length of her fingernails increasing and small tufts of hair sprouting from the backs of her hands.

The girl at the window is trying to clear the grime from the glass so she can gaze into the outside world. Her name is Misty. She was killed in a robbery attempt at this establishment three years ago. She still hasn't realized that she's dead. Her ghostly hand swipes in vain at the pane of glass and leaves no trace of its touch.

Bub, the elderly man sitting on the floor near the bathroom (and apparently not minding the smell), simply rattles the chain tethering him to the bar railing and moans now and again. The bartender (ever the loving son) throws him a raw steak every night to keep him under control. He died several weeks ago, but walked (or maybe crawled would be the correct term) out of the local mortuary the next day, his pale flesh already peeling away from his face to reveal the jawbone beneath.

I am sitting here at the moment sipping my VooDoo Spiced Rum, jotting down words on napkins that have already turned yellow with age. (I told you this wasn't a popular bar. Bub probably purchased these 20 years ago, long before he turned the bar over to his son.)

I guess I feel an obligation to scribble these words. You see, I'm supposed to be the keynote speaker at a writer's convention this weekend. I figured that the least I could do was write down some notes in case someone wants to read them on my behalf Saturday night.

I won't be able to.

You see, being a horror writer, I had come to love this little bar. I get all kinds of ideas from the patrons that frequent the place. Humans don't usually last long in here, but being famous has its advantages. Eric has never tried to draw blood from my neck with his fangs and Spice has never attacked me during a full moon. (Maybe that is my loss. Now I'll never know.)

But Bub—well, I guess I can't really blame him for what happened. He doesn't have much left in the thought-processing department. And it really is my fault for being careless on my unsteady voyage to the john. It didn't hurt much when he grabbed me

If you need gasoline and matches to spark your inspiration, you might not be doing it right.

and nipped my arm; there wasn't even much blood. But we all know what's going to happen next, don't we?

So, I will see that someone gets these notes for the convention.

My first word of advice for writers? Write, write, and then write some more. It doesn't matter what you write, when you write it, or where you write it. Fiction? Non-fiction? Poetry? It all requires the same thing: putting pen to paper. Or perhaps fingers to keyboard in this day and age. I still love to write in longhand myself. I guess it makes me feel a closer connection to the muse.

Writing is like painting, in a way. Like magic. You wave your wand over the tapestry you wish to bespell, conjuring up new ideas and breathing life into broomsticks and golems with the mere muttering of a few carefully chosen words. Or you can twitch your nose and bring a paint roller to life to fill in the cracks of an existing structure. It doesn't matter what tools you use. It doesn't matter, really, what language you use. Make up a language, if you must (full of slithy toves and mome raths, such as in the brilliant, made-up language of Jabberwocky). The bottom line is this:

You. Must. Write.

I could stop right there and that might be the best advice on writing you'd ever receive, but I'll continue. After all, I am a writer, and what else can I do now but scribble these final words? What was it Isaac Asimov said of writing? I think it was in *Yours, Isaac Asimov: A Lifetime of Letters*. "I write for the same reason I breathe—because if I didn't, I would die."

It holds true, too. I can already feel my insides turning cold, my vision blurring. And a terrible hunger claws at the inside of my stomach. Must focus, now. Must try to write. Must process . . .

The Writing Process

Most people will tell you that the writing process has a tried and true method. *Five out of six writers agree.* (And, at least two or three of them are probably human, just like yourself.) Real writers like me will tell you that the writing process is whatever you want it to be. If you start in the middle and work backwards, fine. If you pull a Tolkien and write the end scene, then spend ten years or more writing all the stuff that comes before it, great. If you start with a meticulous outline and adorn your workspace with color-coded sticky notes, so be it. Whatever works for you won't necessarily work for everyone, but the important thing is that it works for you. So, pretend there's a zombie chasing you and run with that.

At the same time, there is a three-step process that many people employ when they write. This method begins with preparations (like any good camping trip to a secluded cabin in the middle of the woods), moves on to the actual draft (a practice-run, like a *Bride of Frankenstein* wedding rehearsal), and then rethinks the preparations and the process to make sure the trip will go off without being attacked by Jason Vorhees, a band of inbred hillbillies, or a swarm of Deadites. In the world of composition and rhetoric, they refer to it as such:

- Prewriting
- Writing
- Revising

Prewriting consists of gathering resources, planning out ideas, or just breaking down writer's block to get the ball rolling. Writing is the actual drafting phase in which the words find their way onto the page. Revising is where you throw those words in the blender, mix them with a raw egg and a pint of blood, and then pour the concoction back onto the page to see what it creates. The truth is that these steps aren't always final steps and you will almost always find yourself bouncing back and forth between the steps ad infinitum (for eternity) as you write, constantly gathering new resources or ideas, inserting new concepts, and changing things as you go. In fact, sometimes the challenge is knowing when it is time to stop editing and declare the work finished. Remember, the blood in that mixture can coagulate.

I remember creating a character for one of my many screenplays. He was a necromancer who used his words to change worlds. His writing was a ritual, using words penned in the blood of virgins that were gathered with great care by the light of the moon. Writing is, after all, a powerful magic. Written language makes things *happen*. It is performative.

Writing can be a powerful magic regardless of your belief in witches, demons, or other nefarious spellcasting types.

It can change your name. It makes you married or unmarried. It can make you giggle with joy or shiver as you read into the late evening hours. It conjures new ideas into the world.

Writing *well*, however, takes discipline, practice, and commitment, as any good illusionist will tell you. The practice of writing should be a writer's daily ritual, with time and space devoted to the process of writing. A routine of writing, no matter the weather, your feelings, how hungry you are, or the surge of zombies at your door—or in my case, the zombie stirring within—must become part of your regimen, no different than eating your Count Chocula in the morning, talking to your zombie workmates around the water cooler at work, or feeding the dog (who is hopefully not your spouse during a full moon). Remember the story about someone asking pianist Arthur Rubinstein something like "Pardon me, sir, but how do I get to Carnegie Hall?" and Rubinstein replying with something like "Practice, practice, practice"? Nothing could be closer to the truth for the writer in all of us.

To bring words to your page, some writers find it helpful to make a ritual out of it, while others will find words spilling from their guts like blood onto bar napkins. Whichever angle you take, you should know that practice is the deciding factor. An often unrecognized aspect of that practice is being alone when you write. The great

American poet Wesley McNair once told a fledgling writer friend of mine, Araminta, that in order to be a good writer, she'd have to be very good at being alone. And it's true. Apart from collaborative writing and think tanks, real writing happens inside the quiet recesses of your mind. And for that reason, you must realize that writers need space (and, perhaps more importantly, you'll need to convince your roommates, family, or significant others to buy into this as well).

Writers need, as Virginia Woolf was well aware, a room of their own—or at the very least, a space of their own. Where does writing happen in your life? The coffee shop with free Wi-Fi? The hushed silence of the library? The kitchen table? Some writers need total silence, while others thrive working against the low hum of public spaces. Some writers prefer total isolation in a cobwebbed crypt, while others welcome the chance to people-watch and stalk their living prey while working. Some need coffee; others need blood. Writing is a bloody task, after all. It is the act of spilling your thoughts onto paper (or monitor) as if you've cut open your own skin and bled out the words. Not exactly the kind of thing you do over tea and crumpets. Figure out the environment that works best for you and determine what you need on hand to do your best work.

Creating time to write is equally important as devoting space to it. It's easy to procrastinate when it comes to writing, especially when you are writing on your own, with no looming deadline or a teacher or editor impatiently tapping their fingers. It's easy not to write. Why? Because it's hard work—much harder than most non-writers would envision. Of course, it is not so easy for me here and now, but it's not quite the

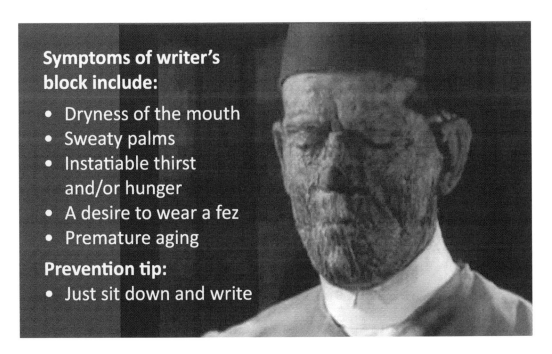

Symptoms of writer's block include:

- Dryness of the mouth
- Sweaty palms
- Instatiable thirst and/or hunger
- A desire to wear a fez
- Premature aging

Prevention tip:
- Just sit down and write

same thing. These are my dying words. I used to think I'd have all the time in the world to write them. Now I can only watch as minutes evaporate like the mist in a bad horror movie and my vision slowly clouds with my own black blood. I must devote this time to this act, or these words will never see the light of day.

That's why it's essential to schedule your writing time. Consider it a sacred space on your calendar that cannot be postponed or cancelled or skipped even just this one time. If you do that once, you'll do it twice and then—well, you get the idea. Ideally, you might be able to schedule your writing to coincide with your mental peak. What time of day are you at your best? When can you devote time to writing during the week? As you think about scheduling time to write, be mindful of how much time you give yourself. Ideally, a writing session should end when you still have something to say. That way, you can jot down notes and ideas for your next session, which will set you up with the proper tools to plunge right back into a productive writing session the next time around. It also keeps your brain on active duty and looking forward to the process instead of dreading it. If you simply write until you have nothing left to say or stop because you don't know what to do next, then your next session will loom as a task rather than something you anticipate with eagerness.

As novelist and Nobel Laureate Thomas Mann put it, "A writer is somebody for whom writing is more difficult than it is for other people." At some point, all writers must face the blank page, that empty space whose pale glow is just as bad as any nightmare terror, and the impossibly clean slate whose insistent, blinking cursor is more demanding than the hungriest, brainless zombie.

We all know it as writer's block: that terrible condition of having something to say, but not being able to say it. The terror of total silence.

Many things contribute to writer's block, but a common thread is fear: the fear of being wrong, sounding stupid, or not being able to actually *write* the poem, story, or essay that exists perfectly in your imagination. As with any creature of the night, one way to battle the fear of failure is to face it head on—to arm yourself with whatever you have and go after the creature before it gets you. In other words, start writing. The sooner you can convert your ideas into language, experiment with writing, and get feedback from readers, the closer you get to accomplishing your goals. Writing is hard work—all writers make mistakes. But the sooner you start making mistakes, the sooner you can learn from them. And having a ritual of writing can help ease the passage through these dark moments.

Prewriting

There are no right answers in prewriting and lots of choices. Informal writing—writing which helps you plan and think—can help you figure out what your choices are, what works, and what doesn't. Freewriting, webbing, creating, generating, and outlining are all ways to avoid that terror-filled silence represented by the blank page.

They are techniques for snapping your brain out of writer's block. (Assuming you still have a brain and it hasn't been eaten by yours truly.)

Let's say I want to write a novel about a vampire who was buried thirteen feet underground. Two hundred years later, a family builds a house over her grave. But, apart from this basic concept, I'm utterly stuck about where to go from there. Every time I sit at my desk, pen and page in hand—or sit before my laptop, it's cursed cursor blinking steadily at me—I freeze up. No words come. I can picture the story in my head, but I simply can't write it.

Chances are, I can't write because I'm afraid that the second I start putting words out into the universe, they'll be "wrong" or "judged" or "not good enough." Maybe I don't know where to start because I don't know a blessed (or unblessed) thing about vampires. Whatever the case may be, I can overcome my problem, or at least make progress, by experimenting with some informal prewriting.

Freewriting

Freewriting is a method for undoing writer's block as well as a method of prewriting. It works in several ways. For one thing, it gives you permission to fail. That permission to fail allows you to take the initial leap necessary to bleed those first inky words onto the page. Sometimes you might be afraid to write because you are fearful that your writing will be mundane or something akin to the rotting intestines dragging along the floor behind a zombie. Good news, my friend: freewriting is meant to be thrown away. It isn't meant to be your beautiful masterpiece's first draft, so it doesn't matter what you commit to paper. No one else ever has to see it.

> **Freewriting is satisfying for the simple reason that it gets the creative juices flowing, and no one ever has to see it.**

Secondly, it gets your writing juices flowing. Simply moving your hand across a page or fingers along a keyboard is like a trigger switching your brain to "it's time to write" mode.

Lastly, freewriting typically consists of non-stop writing for a short burst of time. That means you set an egg-timer and start writing. You don't stop to think or waste time going back to correct anything. Your task is simply to keep the words flowing until the timer runs out. Not your proverbial life timer, of course, like what is happening to me. I'm referring to the egg-timer. If you get stuck, you simply repeat the same word over and over until a new word pops into your head, or you could actually use the time to write about being "stuck." There really are no rules. The goal of freewriting is to set the tone for the work you are about to create. It tells your brain that this is important (important enough that you can't take a break), and it reinforces that trigger effect I wrote of before. Here is an example of freewriting for my vampire novel. I set the timer for five minutes and here is what I wrote:

Vampire lives in southern part of England maybe but is found out by villagers and linched by a mob of pitch-fork and torch-wielding maniacs in the middle of the night. They bury her in the ground under thirteen feet of hallowed earth and a priest reads rites over the soul but for some reason they cant cut off her head or stake her before burying her? Maybe it was too hard she put up too much of a fite tried to bite them they were too scared. She's buried now and starving naturally and can't get out. Maybe rats burrow in and insects insects insects insects insects bugs bugs larvae and she maintains herself by eating the vermin that crawls in but it isn't enough so shes gastly looking and desperate for a human meal. Flash forward 200 years and a family in the early 1900s decides to buy a previously protected plot of land and build a house there-might be unlikely for England as there is a land shortage there. Could this work in Canada? America? China? Think other cultural implications—They build the house over the burial plot unknowing. When they break ground, they shorten the gap between the basement floor and the vampires coffin. Then, shortly after moving in a water main breaks or some such and they have to dig up part of the floor. That's how the vampire escapes and she begins to

Notice how the piece is unfinished and jumps around a lot? Notice that it also has misspelled words and missing punctuation? In one section, it even repeats a few words over and over again, demonstrating moments where I myself got stuck on what to write next. This is an example of freewriting. It is meant as an exercise to get the creative juices flowing and help ideas begin to take shape. This piece of writing will never appear in a book (at least not *my* vampire novel), but at least it helped me get started. Now I'm ready to start writing the actual novel because, not only have I removed the drivel that was cluttering my mind and causing a kind of paralysis that kept me from writing, it has also actually started me *writing*. It matters little what I wrote—only that I was, in fact, writing. It tells my brain that it is time to write and, well, you can't write if you don't *write*. Right?

Webbing

Webbing is a way of organizing your thoughts into a visual context—and no, I'm not talking about the gargantuan spider that has cocooned all the small rodents in your basement with her fateful web. In the context of writing, webbing is more about crafting visual connections between the ideas bouncing about in your skull. By creating a visual connection, you can sometimes see relationships, structure, and organization in a different way. (I would say a "new light," but that might scare off some of the vampire-types who might be reading this.) Occasionally, this prewriting tactic helps writers evoke new concepts, see emerging patterns, or simply get all the gunk out so they can begin writing.

Using the same story concept, here is an example of a web:

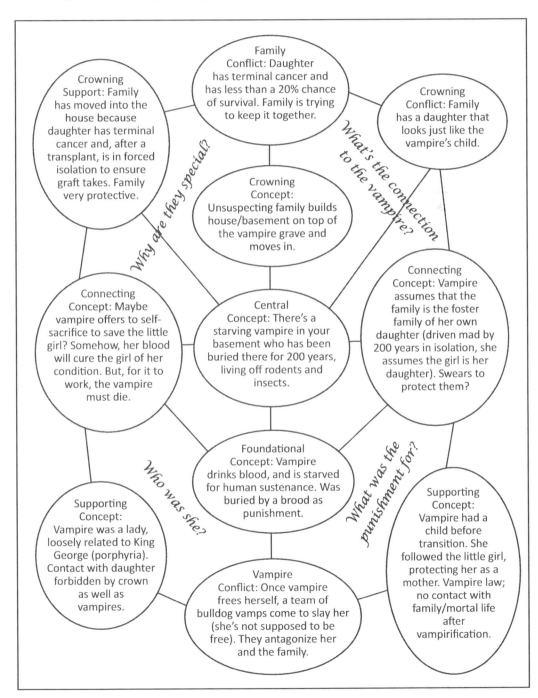

As this example of webbing demonstrates, when the original story concept is documented into this visual context, new ideas—and connections *between* ideas—have developed. The story is beginning to take shape—as if layering flesh onto a skeleton—before it even hits the page. We now have a back story for the major players in the tale, and the questions (inserted between the web strings) have helped to clarify relationships between the different concepts playing a role in the storyline.

Creating

Another way to start hacking away at word craft is to actually start the process by creating something completely (or loosely) unrelated to words at all. The act of creating (whether an academic, business, or fictional work) is a similar process across the spectrum. Engineers will collaboratively powerhouse concepts in a room together, brainstorming a list of possibilities (whether practical or not) to solve problems completely unrelated to the project at hand just to get the ideas flowing. Artists produce thumbnails, concept boards, layouts, or sometimes just doodle in the margins while they gibber on the phone. Sculptors make collages or write in their journals to record the different construction media and concepts that flitter through their brains. These same concepts work for writers as well. We, too, can jog the old creative noodles by engaging in alternative methods of conceptualization before actually putting pen to paper.

One way to get started is to draw a picture of the ideas in your head. And you certainly don't have to be a talented artist to do this—you just might not want to place these scribbles on the front of your fridge for display. By drawing an image of your

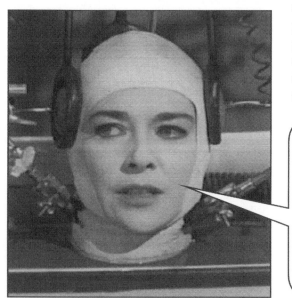

story, you'll begin to see the major patterns and themes emerge. A picture, after all, forces you to hone in on at least a thousand words, requiring you to pick one specific thing to focus on. Whatever you pick

I have no trouble picturing things in my head, but creating the body of my work seems difficult for some reason.

might inadvertently tell you what the most important part of your book really is. Either way, the actual drawing that comes from this is an act of creation which should get you in the mood to begin assembling words. This method works whether you are writing a poem, a business report, or an academic paper, and it doesn't require artistic skill. The simple act of drawing (even stick figures) will cause patterns, ideas, and concepts to begin forming.

If drawing isn't your thing, try sculpting. Grab a wad of clay or wax. Whittle some wooden stakes (these might come in handy at a later time, anyway). Use your hands to shape the story's ideas—literally. By moving clay around, you are not only shaping concepts that may appear in your story, but you are also distracting the anxious (or fearful) parts of your brain with activity so the calm and lucid parts of your brain can start working out the important details of the story.

Another way to create words is to act them out theatrically. One of the authors of this book, Araminta Star Matthews—the one who roped me into this gig—told me once that she acts out every fictional scene she writes. (Incidentally, the other authors of this book told me they think she should record a video of this so they can upload it to the web.) If her characters are scared, she brings fear to the surface of her mind, then pays attention to what her body does: raised shoulders and eyelids, vibration in the neck muscles, gasping, heaving chest, trembling, and the like. If a scene requires a complex fighting maneuver, she tucks and rolls around her floor to "see" and "feel" what the characters might be going through.

This method can work for other types of writing, as well. "Play-acting" and "role reversal" are quite common in the business world and academia. A business owner might act out the role of a customer reacting to a sales pitch. An interviewee might act out how she'll respond to tough interview questions, or imagine the role of the interviewer and how he might react to certain statements in her cover letter. A student might enact scenes from a piece of literature to better understand it when writing a literary analysis, or she can even act out statements from her research to see the relationship it will have to her own original writing and thus weave it into her paper in a fluid way. Acting is a great way to improve understanding and to create.

Creating word art or collages are additional ways to start a writing process. Try snipping images from magazines (which, incidentally, will be extra impressive if they happen to be the current issues of *Fangoria* or *Cemetery Dance*) and gluing them to posterboard to either create a pattern of your writing concepts, or perhaps to create images of your characters and their settings. Consider a few key words that pop into your head before you write and draw them in blank letters on a posterboard. Fill the letters in with snippets of magazine clippings, doodles, or even just paint. The movement and the action of creating is what is important here—not the end product. Get your blood flowing and the vampire muse will come. (Or, if you are human, perhaps the vampire will simply arrive at your doorstep. Whatever you do, do not invite him in. And if you do, at least have those stakes you were whittling earlier close at hand.)

Generating (Ideas, Prompts, Starters)

Sometimes writer's block can be overcome preemptively—like eliminating the zombie threat with a strategically deployed nuclear bomb. (Just look out for the acid rain, my friends.) If you have some idea of what you want to write about, you can create a list of ideas in advance.

For instance, let's say you are a student and know you need to write a research paper for your Necrology class, an argumentative essay for Latin, and a business plan for your Mortuary 101 class. Hopefully you will know your upcoming assignments long before you have to start preparing for them, so why not generate a few lists of ideas now, before the real pressure begins? Try to create a list of ideas for any given assignment so that when the time comes to start writing, you can simply check your list and pick the topic that appeals to you the most. (As a bonus, you have also created a list for future class assignments.)

Prompts and starters are ways to get the ideas tumbling out once you've decided what you want to write (or simply, *that* you want to write). There are hundreds of story prompts and generators on the web that will give you randomized story starters or research paper ideas or business models or résumé and cover letter samples. These generators can help take the pressure off of having to create your own ideas from scratch. Just be certain that you don't plagiarize someone else's concept or intellectual

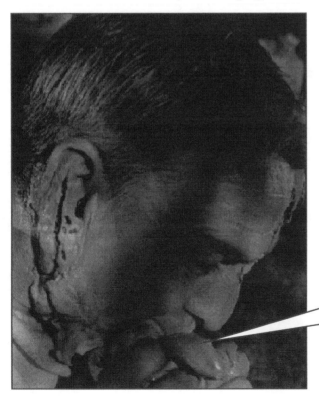

property when you consider using a prompt. Whatever you write has to be of your own devising. And never get too reliant on these "story starters"—reserve them for times when you need to kick-start your creative synapses into action. Prompts and starters are simply tools to get you started writing.

You can make your own prompts and starters, too. One of

Lend me an ear, my friend, and I'll explain our desire for brains. Come closer now. A little closer.

the problems I always found when I would use idea-generating tools made by other people was that other people were interested in things I didn't care a lick about. (Although, more and more, licking all kinds of things—or, more accurately, gnawing things, is beginning to appeal to me. Brains are starting to sound especially delicious. Maybe I'll attend that writer's convention after all. Creative types are bound to have yummy brains, don't you think?)

Where was I? (Need to concentrate and ignore my complaining stomach.) Oh, yeah. So, one day, I just started making my own prompts. I began small. Just a paper sack full of random numbers and a bookcase filled with books. I would draw a number and then find that page in a random book to see if I could work a prompt out of anything on the page. Another time I took a couple of small paper bags and labeled one "characters," another "settings," and another "conflicts." Then, I started writing little strips of paper that fit into those categories. When I was stuck, I'd just pull one or two out of each paper bag. One time, I got "Poltergeists," "Indie Record Store," and "everyone's teeth keep falling out for no medical reason." That was an interesting story starter. Try making your own and see what happens. If the paper version isn't your speed, then start a spreadsheet or make a web tool. You can always pick random numbers or use a number generator to get the items from the spreadsheet, and the web tool can work all on its own.

Outlining

Outlining is the chief method taught by elementary school teachers all over the world. It involves a complex procedure of Roman Numerals, uppercase and lowercase lettering, and numbers to help you organize your thoughts. Outlines are great for linear thinkers as they help people put their thoughts onto paper in a way that integrates structure (and thus organizational flow) into concepts, which allows the drafting phase to commence a little more smoothly. The trouble is, I have yet to meet a creative writer who is a linear thinker—and many analytical or critical writers think associatively or visually as well. That's why this one is last, I suppose. (Although a method that is a cousin to outlining is one I use occasionally. It involves creating a list of bullet points and then simply rearranging them until they fall into a linear format. As writers, we all eventually find what works best for ourselves. And, of course, you don't have to rely on the same method of organizing your ideas each and every time.)

Still, I suppose if I were drafting a linear document—say, a cookbook or a feasibility report—I might consider an outline a helpful tool to process my ideas. Let's say, though, that I am a linear thinker—my rapidly deteriorating mind, now hell-bent on devouring your living flesh, thinks in rigid, somewhat mathematical constructs—and I still want to write that outline for my vampire story. It might look something like this (and, I'd better do this quickly while I still remember what an outline is):

I. Back story: vampire woman (name?) is caught brushing her six year old mortal daughter's hair.
   A. Vampire stalks midnight Parisian street
       1. Spies girl through bakery shop window
           a. Girl is playing with bread dough
       2. Breath doesn't steam window even though it's cold
       3. Moves toward the door—is she going to kill the girl?
   B. Paragraph Two: vampire moves into the shop
       1. Girl startles, drops dough
           a. After a moment, not afraid. It's mom
       2. Vampire runs to embrace the child
   C. Vampire begins to brush girls hair, taking care
       1. In bursts a team of vampires
       2. They destroy the place
           a. Seize the vampire
           b. Kill the girl in front of her
   D. Vampire is put to trial by league of vampire elite
       1. Sentenced to be buried alive
           a. Survives for 200 years on rodents and insects that burrow into her casket.
II. Flash Forward: Family of four moves into a newly built house (which they commissioned themselves).

As you can see, this method of prewriting also allows for the overall arc of the story to be ordered sequentially. There is still room to go back into the outline and add details or plot lines, but the overall gist of an outline provides structure—or if you prefer, a skeleton to which you can add flesh like putty. The skeleton is simply the structure provided by the outline; the quickly rendered sketch comprises the bones, while the flesh itself forms the details that lift words off the page and give them life. That's what the term "fleshing out" refers to. When it comes time to tackle those details and put flesh to bones, remember that your back story can either appear in flashbacks, in a prologue or perhaps not at all. It is simply a tool. Whether any of it appears in your manuscript is a decision you will make during the writing process itself.

Outlining is a good tool if you feel like you might get off track while writing and also a great tool for first-time novelists. A short story will likely not require a writer to remember details across large chasms of time. Novels, on the other hand, are more complex and require a great deal of information to be held in the forefront of a writer's mind. You can't, for instance, say that Sally has red hair on page 12 and then mention she has brown hair on page 79 because you forgot what color it was during the 67 pages that came between. And be forewarned—readers have a keen eye for such details. An outline is the kind of tool that helps make sure that details are not forgotten along the way.

Whichever method of prewriting you choose, it is important that you select one that works for you. Prewriting is about gathering provisions for a journey. Your journey is going to be unique to you and you alone. If the methods outlined in this chapter don't work for you, tweak them. Play with them. Create something new. The goal is simply to get started. After you've begun the process, that's when it comes time to actually start writing a draft.

Drafting

After you've gathered your resources and decided upon your desired destination, it's time to start writing. Unfortunately, I've seen many an amateur scribes assume their writing is going to be this bloody brilliant work the second it hits the page. An equally flawed notion is that with little thought or editing, they can zip this first draft off to a publisher and have it accepted for publication within a few short weeks. Experienced writers know that things almost never work that way.

A manuscript doesn't spring fully formed from the writer's brain into the world like a Greek god. Rather, writing is an organic, continuous process which includes many types of activities: reading, research, thinking, mapping, outlining, brainstorming, talking, informal writing, and editing. An author friend of mine once told me he is either in "input" mode or "output" mode. You need to take time to do both. Create a space in your process for informal, pre-writing activities and use this space to be messy, imperfect, and experimental. Write for yourself before you think about writing for others. If you don't expect everything you write to be perfect, then you open yourself up to the process of writing as an act of discovery, making you more receptive to new observations and ideas.

Once you have created your "masterpiece," you can go back and begin making changes. You need words on a page before you can make sense of them. Words can be reordered, and paragraphs can be moved. It is important to remember this: no piece of writing needs to be finished until you feel like it truly is—this holds true even after a work is published because you can always go back to the editing phase in case the story is ever reprinted. Don't expect your writing to be perfect when you finish your first draft. (In fact, no piece of writing is ever really "perfect.") Be prepared to revise and edit the piece to within an inch of its teeth (however bloody they might be by then) before submitting it for publication. Most writers will tell you that they hate the tedium of editing because it is a less fun than the writing itself, but that doesn't mean that this process can be skipped. In fact, it might be the most important step in the entire scheme of things. So, as you embark on the drafting of a story or essay, keep forever in the corners of your juicy brain that you will have to revise it before it's ready for publication. An actor, after all, wouldn't dream of performing without a rehearsal—so writers shouldn't dream of seeing their work in print without editing and revising.

The drafting process is where you can get a little messy. Given that you've already resigned yourself to the fact that you will need to revise your manuscript, you now have permission to play and, yes, even to fail. "Playtime" is often where the best writing emerges, because when we play, we step outside of our usual haunts and start mucking about in the mud. It's that glob of clay that eventually turns into something recognizable. Sometimes playing will only yield a few nibblets of tripe. Other times, it will give you the real, blood-filled liver cutlets and steak tips (although for the record, whether your preference is for cooked or raw meat does not matter).

Audience and Purpose

Two important things writers should keep in the back of their minds during the drafting phrase are *audience* and *purpose*. Audience and purpose are inextricably linked in the world of writing. The audience for which you are writing dictates a lot about the way it should be written stylistically. The purpose of your writing also dictates the way you will write it, creating a target the writer should continually aim for while crafting meaning. Your purpose many times dictates your audience and vice versa. Audience is a fancy, writerly way of describing the readers who may read your words. Purpose is the reason you are writing in the first place. In my current situation, my audience is certainly not a vampire, a werewolf, a zombie and a ghost. My audience—assuming these notes eventually make it to their intended destination—will be the gaggle of writers (a wrangle of writers? A murder of authors? That sounds more accurate) who will be attending Saturday's conference. My purpose is to provide techniques to help improve the quality of their writing.

Let's say you are a teacher creating a lesson for your kindergarten class. Your purpose, of course, is to teach them something. Knowing that purpose helps you formulate the important points you will need to tailor into your message. The fact that your audience is a bunch of five year olds also tells you which words will (and won't) help get your message across to them. You wouldn't wax prolific about existentialism with the tikes because "wax," "prolific," and "existentialism" are really big words and your purpose will be lost on them. But you might talk what's special about being alive. You achieve the same purpose, but the words are now appropriately tailored for the audience.

Many new writers forget the importance of their audience. They think that just writing the story is enough; why should the question of who will read it come into consideration? The simplest example of the importance of audience comes when you consider the use of jargon and slang. If you are writing for an audience that you anticipate will be in their late seventies, having one of your characters state "this party is sick" will have your audience scratching their heads thinking you meant that the party was disgusting. Conversely, if you anticipate your audience will be a room full of teenagers, and you say "the vampire had great gams," your adolescent audience will roll their eyes, thinking you misspelled the word "yams" and it's a vampire Thanksgiving dinner, not knowing that gams is an old slang term for legs. (And, don't give much thought to the menu for the vampire Thanksgiving gathering—unless you're on it.)

Jargon, too, can cause these hiccups with your audience. If I'm writing a story about New England during the frosty month of January and I say that my characters struck a frost heave in the road, toppling the car onto its roof, my California- and Florida-based readers probably won't know what I mean. (Incidentally, a frost heave is a bump in the road caused by snow melting when the sun is out. The water then pools under the pavement and freezes overnight when the sun goes down which causes the tar to swell and crack.) Knowing your audience helps keep them engaged and ensures that what you're trying to convey isn't lost on them.

The Structure of Writing

There are many ways to structure your writing. For non-creative writing, you should choose patterns of organization that both support your objectives as a writer and meets the needs of your reader. Most non-creative writing will have a similar structure in the drafting phase to that of a formal speech. As the old adage suggests, "tell them what you're going to tell them, tell them, then tell them what you told them." The basic format for non-creative pursuits is: an introduction or hook, the body, and then the conclusion.

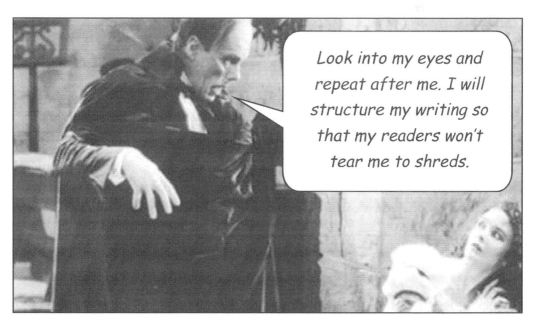

To picture the structure for non-creative writing, try to imagine your work as a mortuary which has been constructed for a particular use, audience, and purpose. Mortuaries have doors—points of entry that enable people to enter the space and flow in the direction they need to go. This is the job of the introduction. Mortuaries also contain numerous rooms, many of which have separate functions (a viewing area filled with coffins versus an embalming room, for instance). Together, they create a cohesive structure. Written paragraphs need to function like the rooms of a building—they have separate functions, but need to work together.

Creative structure can be a bit different, depending on what you are writing. For example, fiction and poetry can be "anything goes." You can start in the middle, flashback, flash forward, then flash back again. You can even start at the end. As long as you remember to transition and follow your instincts, you should do all right with creative structure. Just don't get lost yourself. If you lose your way, your reader will as well. And that's just what the zombie hordes desire.

Patterns of Organization

Patterns of organization are similar to a blueprint. Thinking about structure as you draft may help you build an effective piece of writing, but don't feel limited to the patterns discussed here, and don't think you need a clear blueprint before you begin writing. While some writers may find it useful to finalize their blueprint before they begin writing, other wordsmiths draft first and then go back during revision to clarify organizational structure.

These are some of the common patterns for organizing writing, which might help you blueprint an entire paper or plan individual sections and paragraphs.

Chronological: This organizational style lists the order in which things occur, from beginning to end. It is one of the easiest systems to follow. To structure an entire piece chronologically is to follow the order of time. Different points in time need to be marked clearly for the reader along the way. Here's this pattern in paragraph form:

The scientists watched in amazement as the evolution from cadaver to zombie took place. First, undead eyes popped open as if seeing the world for the first time. Then the nose twitched as the creature caught the scent of meat. When the undead thing rose, the scientists were too enthralled by the spectacle to move. It wasn't long before they became part of their own experiment.

Cause and Effect: This organizational style first states a cause or reason before leading the reader to the desired effect or end result. Depending on the topic, you might choose to begin your writing with an overview of the central conclusion before presenting causes. Here's an example of this pattern in paragraph form:

As science and history have merged, the idea that vampires are unable to exist in daylight is now just the whim of a fairy tale. It is the emergence of scientific research and not legends of magical rings and potions that have enabled the undead to finally watch the sun rise over the horizon.

Problem and Solution: In this style of organizing information, the problem is presented up front, followed by a solution. The solution doesn't have to be singular, a proven theory, or even conclusive, but if you pose a problem, you should provide an answer for your reader. (In academic writing, sometimes it's enough to argue persuasively that a problem *exists* without having to offer a particular solution.) Here's a paragraph demonstrating this structure:

Many demon slayers meet their doom for the simple reason that they go into battle improperly armed. You cannot approach demons in the same manner that you stake vampires, burn witches and destroy the brains of zombies. The solution is to go into battle knowing your opponent is more powerful on almost all fronts. The secret is that all demons have a weakness and that is what you must exploit.

Increasing Complexity: In this pattern, you first present basic information before moving on to more complex concepts. You might begin with information that will *not* challenge your reader before moving on to present ideas in a new way that will challenge your reader to either accept a different position about a topic or to think more deeply about a subject. This is a good strategy to use if you are writing about controversial topics, since it can build both trust and rapport with your reader. Here's a paragraph which demonstrates increasing complexity:

Vampires are an idea. They are a concept in the imaginations of people who used stories of them to frighten little children into behaving: "Don't skip washing your ears, little Neville. Everyone knows vampires love the smell of ear wax." We know that vampires have existed as a concept for millennia, crossing geographic, linguistic, and cultural boundaries. Sometimes vampires are the living dead, and other times they are of the psychic variety which prey on hope and passion. What few people realize, though, is that vampires are more than just a concept. Vampires are quite real, and they are among us even today. Not just in fairy tales and folklore anymore, vampires have come out of the coffin and roam the streets of the world at night when your misbehaving children are sleeping. Perhaps you've even met one.

Climactic: Climactic style takes the reader from the least important ideas to the most important. Papers written in this style might save the best ideas or examples for the end. This pattern also works to structure paragraphs and even sentences, where the new or most important pieces of information come last. Here's a paragraph written in this style:

> *As our boat cleared the reef, the clouds parted and we saw land off our bow. The remaining survivors cheered as I brought the spyglass to eye level. The mist cleared and I saw figures on the shore. They beckoned us to safety. How were we to know at the time they were Sirens?*

Patterns of organization might offer a blueprint for individual sentences, paragraphs, or an entire piece of wiring. They can even be used in combination. While knowing your audience and purpose might help you choose which patterns might work best for a piece of writing, don't be afraid to experiment to see what works.

The Introductory Paragraph

Regardless of how you've decided to organize the structure of your writing, it will need to start somewhere. The introduction is the door leading into the space of your writing—what kind of space is your reader entering? How will you invite them in? A good lead paragraph will grab your reader's attention and refuse to let go. There are several approaches you can use when writing your introductory paragraph for nonfiction.

Open with a question: Opening with a question will make your readers curious enough to read more. There is nothing more engaging than creating a question that demands you read on to find the answer.

> *Have you ever wondered if, with the scientific knowledge we possess today, a laboratory could actually create a Frankenstein-type "monster" using modern medical technology?*

Open with an announcement: By using this approach, you give the reader some insight about what's to come. Just enough to tease them, but never so simple and obvious as to insult their intelligence.

> *Anticipating that there will eventually be a zombie apocalypse is not enough to ensure the safety of you and your family. Just like those who live in areas affected by hurricanes and put together a hurricane kit and an evacuation plan, we must also hone our skills and knowledge for combating an uprising of the undead.*

Open with an opinion: By giving your opinion on a subject at the outset, you are letting readers know where you stand. They will want to read on regardless of their position on the subject to either see whether your arguments agree with their perspective or to discover why they think you are wrong.

> *Vampires should not be allowed to feast upon human blood unless said participant has signed a waiver in advance.*

Open with a riddle: We're not talking about a "what's red and gray and splashes?" type of humorous riddle (by the way, the answer is a zombie baby playing in a puddle of brains). It's similar to asking a question, but takes things a step further. You can either answer the riddle up front or save it for your conclusion.

> *What holiday is celebrated worldwide as a religious event, and yet also celebrated by non-religious persons, more than any other day of the year? If you guessed Halloween, then take off your mask and celebrate.*

Open with a challenge: Similar to making an announcement, a challenge is a technique to make readers disagree with your opening statement. It may be what you actually feel and you are using it to first, get their interest and second, possibly change their mind. It can also be used to present an argument that is in complete disagreement with the facts you will present—but whether your reader is in agreement with you or not, the objective is to keep them reading.

> *The hunting and slaying of vampires is inhuman and should be outlawed. According to existing laws, there is nothing wrong with taking a sharp wooden stake and pounding it cruelly through the heart of creatures that, in many cases, possess more intelligence than their living brethren.*

Open with a definition: Make the subject matter of your topic plain and simple for all to see. You can either use a definition straight from a dictionary or comparable resource, or provide a definition of your own. Also, remember always to give credit if you quote directly from a reference resource. There are many different ways, or "styles," we use to demonstrate proper credit when credit is due. In this example, you'll see the citation as a page number in parentheses following the section taken from *The Maleus Maleficarum* in MLA format.

> *Witches are defined by the very real (albeit dated) Catholic document,* The Malleus Maleficarum *(or "Hammer Against the Witches") as creatures imbued with evil, magical energy from Satan and his demonic minions. The book, used to help inquisitors determine who should be burned, reports that the effects of their spells are not imaginary nor phantasmical (51) as*

skeptics suggest, but are very real threats to humanity and the Christian faith.

Open with a personal experience: Another way to catch the reader's attention is to give them a glimpse of who you are and something that happened in your life to validate your subject matter expertise. A variation on this theme is to give them a glimpse of why it is not only important to you, but also why it should be important to them as well.

I was ten years old when my father was attacked and killed by a zombie before my very eyes. What made the experience even worse was when I was forced to kill him again after he rose from the dead and cornered me in that dark, damp cellar. It is also why I feel every human being needs to know the truth about zombies.

Open using figurative language: Although similes, metaphors, and personification are frowned upon in some forms of writing (or for certain audiences), the use of figurative language in your opening paragraph can create an air of familiarity with your reader.

The smell of the undead was so heavy in the air that I stooped under the weight of it. It was as though I could dog-paddle through the density of stench as overpowering as a swamp full of dead gators or my teenage son's bedroom. My stomach twisted like a wrung out dishrag and seemed to force its way into my mouth. I was as sick as a werewolf during a full moon.

Open using a quotation: A quote from a well-known person—whether it be Hannibal Lecter or the infamous leader of the local vampire clan—can go a long way towards defining your work.

In culture after culture, people believe that the soul lives on after death, that rituals can change the physical world and divine the truth, and that illness and misfortune are caused and alleviated by spirits, ghosts, saints . . . and gods. (Steven Pinker, How The Mind Works*)*

Open using an overview of your points: If you begin your work with this method, you must give two or three ideas which are general in purpose without getting too specific. You will leave the details to the paragraphs that follow.

Becoming a good ghost hunter requires many different skills. The most important tool in your skill set is to keep an open mind. Simply believing in ghosts does not preclude you from knowing that there are possibly other things in our spiritual universe that may not resemble Casper the Friendly Ghost. But don't forget about logic, and that bringing along a buddy or two doesn't hurt either.

Open with a problem or question that you want to answer in the form of a thesis: In academic writing, readers expect to see your thesis statement in the introduction. If your goal is to present a thesis (that is, a debatable claim *about* something), then the introduction needs to set up the question or problem that your thesis addresses. Even if the question is not directly stated in the introduction, your motivating question or problem statement should be clear from the thesis. Your thesis statement must be clearly understandable and leave no question about where you will lead your reader. It should work like a road map, pointing the way to the argument you present in the body paragraphs but not listing all of the details.

> ***Weak Example:*** *Vampire hunters hate vampires and kill them to save other people.*

This thesis is weak because it seems more like a statement of fact, rather than a debatable assertion about vampire hunters. The question seems to be one of intent ("why do vampire hunters kill vampires?"), but without specific examples, it seems less interesting and hard to argue.

> ***Strong Example:*** *While individual vampires might lose the battle to their human hunters, vampire hunting ultimately makes the vampiric breed more successful since they must either adapt or die.*

This thesis is stronger because it's saying something about vampire hunting that other, reasonable people might disagree with—it's debatable. In addition, it also offers a conclusion that readers don't expect. The writer is attempting to answer a question about causality: "What is the effect of vampire hunting on vampires?" Even if this topic is new to the reader, it's clear that it probably has a complex answer. Complex questions and surprising conclusions make a reader curious and interested in your writing.

Again, don't be afraid to experiment or combine these strategies. And don't forget the power you have as a writer—while the reader must start at the beginning, you don't have to. Many writers write the introduction last—it's only after they draft the entire piece that they can sit back and see what would be the best starting point for their reader. Other writers begin with the introduction, but plan on revising it (or even re-writing it entirely) once they complete their first draft.

Paragraphs

In nonfiction, each paragraph should focus on one main idea. Paragraphs offer important visual clues to your reader—just by glancing at a page of writing, readers can determine how many main ideas or separate pieces of information will be presented. There are no rules about how long paragraphs should be, but readers tend to get lost in long paragraphs that present multiple ideas or pieces of research, and a series of short paragraphs can make the writing feel choppy and uneven. Strive for cohesive, well-organized paragraphs that work together to build your writing.

Background: This type of paragraph gives the reader background information—things they need to know before moving on to the rest of your paper. For example, a reader might need to know history, definitions of key terms, statistical data, or a plot summary. Background paragraphs often show up towards the beginning of the paper, usually right after the introduction.

Frankenstein; or, The Modern Prometheus is a novel about a questionably successful experiment to create a living creature from the parts of cadavers. It was written by Mary Shelley who started writing the story when she was eighteen. Little did she know the effect her creation (both the novel and the monster) would have on the world or the works it would inspire generations later.

Descriptive: In non-fiction writing, descriptive paragraphs might describe a painting, or a scene in a play for analysis, or describe the steps of a process or experiment. At its best, this style simply takes the reader on a visual journey.

The storm raged from the east and the crashing of waves on the rocks nearly hid the advance of the skeleton army. They marched from the dark water like matchstick figures with rusty swords clanking against yellowed bone. The coward next to me screamed and dropped his musket to the sand before disappearing into the shadows. I stood in place, my trigger finger slippery with ocean spray, sweat, and tears.

Directions: This is the style that most instruction manuals and "how-to" articles utilize, describing step-by-step actions needed to reach a final goal—whether it's learning how to cook or create a magic potion.

The first step to creating your stew is to gather all of your ingredients from food items to implements. Bringing the contents to a rapid boil and simmering for an hour will usually bring out the best taste in a human brain. Just take care not to use too much salt.

Paragraphs are the building blocks of your writing; they present unique main ideas or pieces of information, but they also need to work together. Effective paragraphs often have a topic sentence, which clearly announces the main idea. Following sentences, sometimes called support sentences, expand on this idea by offering new information, details, and/or evidence. The concluding sentence in a paragraph wraps things up before the reader moves on to the next paragraph—the next main idea in your writing.

The Closing Paragraph

And finally, readers must exit the space of your nonfiction writing. Do not simply restate your opening paragraph. The closing paragraph gives you the opportunity to tie all of your ideas together and make sure you get your point across to the reader. Too many writers let their work die at the end. This is the time to make sure your reader remembers your main point and concurs with your conclusion. A good conclusion might even leave your reader hungry for more—an interesting quote or provocative example that sticks in their mind. Food for thought, whether it be a pint of blood for the vampire at the bar or brains for the zombie in the corner.

In conclusion, we find that salt deteriorates the taste of human flesh. Partly because it preserves meats, that lovely bouquet created by decaying guts is lost in the fury of salt and the flavor is, ironically, more bland as a result. Therefore, it is fruitless to use salt to enhance the taste of a fresh-served corpse. Zombies, like carrion, prefer it raw and stinking.

When drafting, especially when it comes to non-fiction or academic writing, it's very common for the conclusion of an early draft to become the introduction in the next draft. For some writers, the process of writing that first draft is a process of discovering new ideas. In an early draft, that "aha!" moment of finally figuring out what the idea is often happens in the conclusion—writers "arrive" at their purpose, thesis, or idea only after writing their way there. During revision, don't be afraid to use your "old" conclusion as a new starting point—it may create a better door *into* your writing than an exit out of it.

Transitions, Cohesiveness, and Flow

Transitions are a vital component in writing because your audience isn't you. That's obvious, right? And yet the number one mistake writers make is assuming that everyone thinks the way they do. You know exactly what you are writing about whether you are debating that vampires actually exist or that believing in ghosts is a bunch of "hooey." Even if you are writing a short biography about Bram Stoker, you need to presume that your reader has no idea who he was. That poses a problem if the writer jumps to a new idea without explaining to the reader the connection or relationship with the old idea.

Compare it to the process of a deceased person turning into a zombie. If I told you I was going to the supermarket to buy some cheese, and then in the very next line I told you I was biting into the fleshy cheek of the store clerk, you would be a little lost. How did I go from mundane cheese-shopping to pulse-racing people-eating? This is an extreme example, but the key here is to note that I skipped a few steps. Rather than walk my reader through my transition from being mortal to a member of the living dead, I just assumed he or she knew this had transpired.

And you know what they say about assume, right?

Vampires know a little something about transitions. For example. I transitioned from living to dead. You transitioned from friend to food. Very simple, you see.

Transitions happen in two places: in the body of a paragraph to create *cohesiveness* and between paragraphs to create *flow*. These words can either bring your reader back to focus or get them interested in your next subtopic. Words like "however," "nevertheless," "in addition," and "consequently" can reinforce your entire work. Use teaser words like "first" and "secondly" to lead your reader forward so they know something else is coming. Transition words are like the teenage cheerleader's scent for the werewolf or the droplets of blood leading the vampire toward his prey in a darkened alley.

Cohesiveness in Paragraphs

Paragraphs typically need to introduce one topic, flesh it out, and then close up shop. Kind of like a zombie dining experience—pounce, eat, digest. There is a certain amount of intuition that comes with keeping a paragraph cohesive. You can usually tell where transition words are needed when you look at your expectations about the text. Each sentence of a paragraph should intuitively or logically lead you to the next.

In other words, I should be able to make a reasonable prediction about what the next sentence will say and have my prediction be correct. If it isn't correct, then the paragraph is probably lacking transitions or needs to be re-organized around a central idea.

Consider the following example:

My eyelids fluttered open. The guy lay yelping in a pool of blood trying helplessly to hold his guts in as they spilled through his fingers. I looked around the room. He screamed at me as I bit into the soft flesh behind his elbow. My vision was blurry and bloodshot. I rose clunkily from the bar stool and walked toward a man leaning over a pool table. It appeared I was sitting in a bar, a pile of scribbled napkins cluttered around me. I reached into the man's stomach and ripped out his small intestine with one quick punch.

The sentences in this paragraph are confusing because one does not lead logically to another. There are no clear transitions between ideas and, frankly, the sentences feel out of order. If you were to dissect this paragraph sentence by sentence, making predictions about what was to come next, you'd feel derailed at every corner because each sentence goes in an unexpected direction.

Consider the following revision:

*My eyelids fluttered open. **Though** my vision was blurry and bloodshot, I looked around the room. It appeared that I was sitting in a bar, a pile of scribbled napkins cluttered around me. **Blinking,** I rose clunkily from the bar stool and walked toward a man leaning over a pool table. **Spinning him around,** I reached into the man's stomach and ripped out his small intestine with one quick punch. **I saw that** the guy lay yelping in a pool of blood, helplessly trying to hold in his guts as they spilled through his fingers. **Leaning forward, I did not hear his screaming** as I bit into the juicy flesh above his elbow.*

Notice how a little restructuring and a few well-placed transition words made this paragraph more cohesive? The revised paragraph reads like it moves in one direction rather than jerking about like a zombie in the full throes of rigor mortis. Transition words assist with the smoothness of a paragraph, but they can also be used to set up or lead into new paragraphs as well, to improve the flow.

Flow Between Paragraphs

Flow is a buzzword in writing, and while everyone knows they need it, not everyone knows how to execute it. It's not as simple as executing a zombie with a shotgun blast to the skull, but it's not as hard as you might think. Flow is perhaps best demonstrated between paragraphs. It is the way a writer creates a relationship between one idea or topic and the next. You can mark your reader's path through your text by using transitional words and phrases, by repeating a few key terms or important ideas, or by crafting a more organic relationship between ideas. Let's look at the preceding example as a paragraph about to lead into a new paragraph.

My eyelids fluttered open. Though my vision was blurry and bloodshot, I looked around the room. It appeared that I was sitting in a bar, a pile of scribbled napkins cluttered around me. Blinking, I rose clunkily from the bar stool and walked toward a man leaning over a pool table. Spinning him around, I reached into the man's stomach and ripped out his small intestine with one quick punch. I saw that the guy lay yelping in a pool of blood, helplessly trying to hold his guts as they spilled through his fingers. Leaning forward, I did not hear his screaming as I bit into the juicy flesh above his elbow.

It was cold outside, but I didn't feel it. My muscles were already draining of fluid and my joints moved against each other like unlubricated gears. It was zen-like, this new state of being. I had no fear of what was to come. I had no worries about finances or jobs or whether to further my education. All that mattered was eating. The hunt. Consuming living flesh. It was my only desire now, and it was so simple.

Now, consider how these two paragraphs are disjointed. It's like walking through a post-apocalyptic zombie scene surrounded by abandoned cars and desiccated (and digested) bodies. The dead litter the streets and you are pondering your next move when you suddenly find yourself in the Land of Oz. You blink, glance around the yellow brick road, glare at the Lollipop Guild, and wonder how the heck you got there. There's no relationship between the paragraphs, so it feels like you are leaping from one idea (or place) to the next.

Crafting a transition between these paragraphs can happen either in the last sentence of the first paragraph, the first sentence of the new paragraph, or in both places to neatly tie it all together. Let's look at a revision of this example:

My eyelids fluttered open. Though my vision was blurry and bloodshot, I looked around the room. It appeared I was sitting in a bar, a pile of scribbled napkins cluttered around me. Blinking, I rose clunkily from the bar stool and walked toward a man leaning over a pool table. Spinning him around, I reached into the man's stomach and ripped out his small intestine with one quick punch. I saw that the guy lay yelping in a pool of blood, helplessly trying to hold his guts in as they spilled through his fingers. Leaning forward, I did not hear his screaming as I bit into the juicy flesh above his elbow **before rising to my clumsy feet and lunging toward the pub door**.

Still chewing on his fleshy elbow, I began to realize i*t was cold outside, but I didn't feel it. My muscles were already draining of fluid and my joints moved against each other like unlubricated gears. It was kind of zen, this new state of being. I had no fear of what was to come. I had no worries about finances or jobs or whether to further my education. All that mattered was eating. The hunt. Consuming living flesh. It was my only desire now, and it was so simple.*

Now the reader has no trouble seeing how you went from eating his elbow to wandering outside into the cold. The first paragraph leads neatly into the new paragraph. The new paragraph plants the reader back into the moment by reminding him or her of the chewy elbow bits in the narrator's mouth.

Transitions, cohesiveness, and flow can be part of the drafting stage (something you pay attention to *as* you write) or part of revision (something to pay attention to *after* you write). It doesn't really matter when during the process you use transitions (and other strategies) to develop cohesiveness and flow in your writing, as long as you do at some point. Some writers prefer to write to themselves first, and then use the process of revision to "translate" that draft into writing that will make sense to someone else's brain. Other writers (writers like me, growing hungrier by the minute) always have the reader's brain in mind.

> **"Elbows? Well, we prefer brains, but we'll eat anything with a bit of living flesh on it—though we draw the line at prosthetics. A healthy zombie avoids harmful plastics."**
> **–Zed the Zombie**

Voice and Tone

Voice and tone are also important things to consider during the drafting phase. Because all writing is composed of sounds, words have "a voice" and voices carry tone. Consider the voice and tone of the following excerpt from Edgar Allen Poe's immortal poem, "The Raven":

Ah, distinctly I remember it was in the bleak December,
And each separate dying ember wrought its ghost upon the floor.
Eagerly I wished the morrow; - vainly I had sought to borrow

From my books surcease of sorrow - sorrow for the lost Lenore -
For the rare and radiant maiden whom the angels named Lenore -
Nameless here for evermore.

And the silken sad uncertain rustling of each purple curtain
Thrilled me - filled me with fantastic terrors never felt before;
So that now, to still the beating of my heart, I stood repeating
`Tis some visitor entreating entrance at my chamber door -
Some late visitor entreating entrance at my chamber door; -
This it is, and nothing more.

Consider the choice of words here—words chosen very carefully by Mr. Poe, according to his own essay on the composition of this poem. Consider the way the words are strung together. Consider the level of vocabulary these words possess. Consider the education required to wield them. Consider, too, the anachronistic language no longer used by today's society—words like "'tis" and "chamber."

As you read this excerpt, were you envisioning a man? Why exactly? How is it that a gender identity can be read through the words on a page? Something subtle in the way we speak, in different patterns, perhaps? This subtlety of engendered language is explored by innovative, postmodern writers like Jeanette Winterson and Tom Robbins (Virginia Woolf's *Orlando* also played with the gender of English words) as they toyed with different voices and gender identities in their work. Whatever it is within us that makes us "hear" or "assign" a gender identity, most people (not all, of course) "hear" a man's voice when they read this passage.

Also, the man is old—or, at least, older—based on the way he weaves his words along with the words he chooses. Words like "chamber" and "'tis" inform us that this

It's time for Ghoul Scout cookies again? Egads! I still have 13 boxes left over from last year.

speaker is not of our generation. The level of vocabulary this speaker employs is a bit higher than your average high school student, so he's probably been to college. Perhaps he reads those types of books all the time and has picked up his words from them.

This poem clearly has a voice. We can "hear" and "see" the person speaking the words. The poem also has a tone. The tone this voice takes in speaking is punctuated by facial expressions and body language. In writing, it works more subtly than that. Most people will hear a depressing, somber tone here. Words like "bleak," "wrought," "sorrow," "lost," "sad," and "uncertain" all paint a grey color over the scene created by these words.

In addition, the tone carries with it fear. Part of that is in the pulse of the words—look how quickly the words move in the second stanza. "And the silken sad uncertain rustling of each

> **Tone can carry the feeling of fear. It slithers out quickly like a snake in the grass.**

purple curtain." It slithers out quickly like a snake in the grass. The speed quickens the pulse, so that by the time we reach "beating of my heart," our own hearts are beating faster. This carries the tone of terror on top of the somber tone. You can hear him. He's panicked as he repeats himself.

Voice and tone, then, create mood and character in the mind's eye and ear. If you were writing a business report, you would not want a casual, devil-may-care tone—that won't impress your partners or instill pride and trust in your consumers. If you are writing an academic paper, you certainly wouldn't include your texting-language, with all your lol's and brb's—at least, not if you expected to pass the course. And if you are writing a text to your best friend, you probably are not talking like our friend, Mr. Poe, are you?

Thus, audience and purpose also have a role in determining what voice and tone you use. In addition to that, when writing fiction, characterization and psychology also play a role in voice and tone. You do not want your modern-day teen characters to sound like they came straight out of Victorian England (unless they are supposed to sound that way). And, you don't want your zombies to sound like comic book supergenius Lex Luthors (again, unless that's the point—or your *purpose*). Keep voice and tone consistent with your purpose and you can't go wrong.

The Tools of Writing

Everyone writes differently. Before computers were invented, Jack Kerouac supposedly wrote his drafts on an endless spool of paper threaded through his stainless steel typewriter. Jane Austen (you know, of *Pride and Prejudice and Zombies* fame) penned all her manuscripts by hand using a quill pen. And nowadays, writers can literally write and publish their work simultaneously in things like blogs and online periodicals. Whatever tools you use to write are entirely up to you, and it's important to understand the advantages and disadvantages of whatever tools you choose.

For instance, you know I write by hand. (And quite a lot, actually. There's a mountain of napkins below the bar stool now.) Some people say that's a waste of time; if I just typed it up, I'd have it all right there ready to revise and edit at a whim. Sure, I would eventually have to type out my handwritten draft, but the advantage is that, by going from longhand to keyboard, I actually use different parts of my brain. That means when I write by hand, I see things one way; and when I type, I see them differently. Thus, if I draft by hand then revise by computer, I get the benefit of seeing the same text through two (or more) different lenses.

Still, there is something to be said for word processing software and the speed of typing. I am only able to write about 30 words a minute by hand, but I can type almost a hundred. If you want to be a writer, one of the best things you can do is improve your typing proficiency. You see, as a writer, ideas and thoughts come quickly. The muse is fickle. When she shows up, she expects to be taken out to dinner and a movie on the turn of dime. If I don't catch her right away, she's out the door and the next writer down the street will be the lucky recipient of her company.

Typing allows me to write as fast as I think (sometimes faster), and this means little is lost in the process. I can always go back and take things out later if I find I've overwritten something. (And I have found it is usually better to overwrite than the opposite.) The point is, at least I've captured and documented my ideas for later consideration.

Although, my necromancer friend (introduced below) might have a few different things to say about it. He's fairly opinionated (like I am) about the importance of writing ideas and concepts by hand. Then again, I suppose as a wizard of the darkest arts, he knows that it is much easier to draft a handwritten contract in blood ink versus a laser printer.

To Write by Hand, or by Keyboard? That is the question . . .

A note from my friend and character, the necromancer Nigel Scruplestone, on the importance of handwriting.

There has been a rumor circulating of late that the great officials of our countries plan to do away with the instruction regarding penmanship. Indeed, our young and blossoming minds shall be taught the tenets of printed block writing, but the quicker cursive writing shall disintegrate like the burning embers of the great fires that consumed the libraries at Alexandria. They tell us it is for the speed by which we chat and message and email and type that we must destroy the elderly cursive writing and send him to an early retirement, but I know the real reason. If our young cannot write in cursive, then they shall not be able to read in it either—and what does that mean? It means our sacred texts and historical documents are safe from their interpretations. Only the elite and highly educated shall know the secrets they possess. Only we few necromancers of language shall know how to resurrect the words from the page and the lot of you shall be cornered, for you'll be forced to trust that we speak the truth when we tell you what the scrawling inky trails are trying to say.

Why bother bringing up cursive writing at all in a discourse dedicated to the basics of writing? Surely this technological age has done away with the archaic need to write things by hand? Cannot people simply spill their words onto the cloud where it can be muted and transformed at the touch of a button? For one thing, our brains work differently when engaged in longhand writing than when engaged in pushing buttons. We remember more of what we write when we write it by hand. We create stronger pathways inside our minds when we put pen to paper than when we tap a few keys faster than our minds are capable of forming lasting memory. What does that mean to your writing? It means one way is great for quantity over quality, but the other way is better for quality over quantity. It creates a conundrum of great debate which may rage for decades. (Or until the time your very thought can be transformed into word without using a muscle in your body.)

In other words, if you wanted to write an entire novel, you'd probably start by entering it into a document on your computer. By typing, you allow yourself to create a quick series of workable sentences, paragraphs, and chapters that can then be manipulated like the limbs of a corpse into whatever position you desire with the mere click of a mouse. Writing by hand forces you to type it up after you've written it. (Most people do not accept handwritten anything these days—even receipts for your organ donations. The nerve.) But while writing by hand may take longer to fully process, it also allows your mind to think more clearly about how your words fit together. Therefore, if I were writing a paper for a college class or an application for a grant to fund my new wax museum of horror, I'd start my first draft in handwriting before moving to a type-written version of it.

Drafting also has its place in the structure of writing as a whole. Never should you assume that the first fleshy bits of your writing should all stay on the page when you serve it up to friends and family. It is like trying to gulp down the heart of a virgin in one swallow. You scarcely can savor the gamey, bloody delight because you expect to eat it so fast that it barely glances off your tongue. You want to feel the texture of the ventricles as they slide, rubbery and cord-like against the saliva-slippery smoothness of your inner cheeks, don't you? Well, then you have to make sure that you take your time with it. Prepare the thing properly. Don't just cut it out with a butcher knife and slap it on a plate. Take your time. Pierce the flesh slowly, severing the meaty bits until the rich, velvety mass frees itself almost willingly in your palm. Season it appropriately. Garnish it with, perhaps, a pair of eyeballs or a sprig of wolfsbane. Serve it on your finest china. Eat your heart out. (Or rather her heart . . .)

You can't do that if you rush headlong into it. You have to learn to think about your words. That means, you write something, and then you revise and edit until it becomes the perfect dish.

Revision

Finally, and perhaps most importantly, we come to the last step in the writing process: revision. I won't lie to you. I loathe revision with a passion. Drafting is where the joy is. It's where the creation happens, and my monster takes shape on the slab with hasty stitches and piecemeal flesh. Revision, though, is where all the heavy-lifting takes place. It's where I'm forced to face my creature head-on and see all the mistakes I've made and pieces I've left out and need to stitch anew. I have to go through my work with painstaking detail, meticulously pouring over every piece to make sure I've gotten it all just right.

Without doubt, revision is the longest step in the writing process. Believe me.

At the same time, revision is the single most important thing I will ever do with my work. It's the polish on the stone. The presentation in a carefully wrapped box. The liver and spleen accoutrements on a plate full of delectable brains.

In general, the process of revision should move from big-picture things (like your purpose or the organization of ideas) to smaller things (like word choice). After all, it doesn't make sense to revise and rewrite a sentence if you ultimately decide you should delete the whole paragraph. After you've revisited the global aspects of your work (such as the structure of your writing, the organization of ideas, or gaps you need to fill in), then move onto your sentences.

One of the most important things you can do as a writer is speak with a reader. Have someone read your work and describe it back to you. Ask them questions and listen carefully to their answers. Before you can make informed decisions about how to revise, what to cut, and what to keep, you should know exactly how your words affect someone else. The best, and only, way to do this is to ask.

You need to be as ruthless as a mad scientist experimenting on a corpse when you revise. Cut the things that don't matter. Add the things that do. Get messy with your writing—print it out, use highlighters, purple pens, a pair of scissors. Dismember it and put it back together in a different way.

Revision is a good time to focus on language. Choose strong words and verbs, eliminate useless references and fluff, and cut the fat out of those blasted clichés. Use strong words that convey a picture. I call these "power words." Sometimes it calls for simple substitution of a single word. Consider: "The ugly zombie walked toward me." versus "The horrific creature shambled forward." Use your draft just to get your ideas onto paper and revise to make your prose polished and more precise.

Also consider wordiness. Don't use five adjectives to describe an object when one (or even none) might suffice. "Vampire" is a pretty powerful image in itself. Why use phrases like "undead blood-thirsty vampire." It's sort of a given, isn't it? Work through each sentence, asking yourself if every word is absolutely necessary. If you're unsure or hesitant about deleting, put brackets around words which might be redundant or unnecessary.

Hold your scalpel over the heart of your story and don't hesitate—not even for a moment—to slice into the bloody organ and hack away until you are left with a body of work you can be proud of.

I think I will put down my pen momentarily. I am not sure that my handwriting is even recognizable and I am running out of napkins.

The neon light in the window flickers and it bothers my eyes, even though I can barely see at this point. The air moving in and out of my lungs is taking longer and longer to run its course. Damned zombie bite. I should have been paying attention instead of thinking about my next horror novel. I should have known better being the expert I am on all things horror. Yes, bitter irony raises her head and takes another giant chomp, just like my zombie compadre.

I should have watched where his rotting chompers were aimed. I should have seen the hunger in his eyes and the slobber running down his decaying chin.

But I didn't.

At least I got this little ditty penned for you before unconsciousness drags me into the darkness. Will I awaken as a starved, mindless drone intent on eating everyone around me without discrimination? My mother? Your mother? Bub's mother? It won't matter. I'll be driven on by the sheer force of my bottomless gullet.

Now that I think about it, that driving hunger that never ends is not unlike my urge to write. I have to write. I must write. Writing fills the emptiness in my abdomen. Soon.

I'll fill that emptiness with you.

Writing Prompts for Chapter 1

1. You (or your character) have just lost a battle against a zombie and its teeth have penetrated flesh. You (or your character) know it is only a matter of time before turning into a zombie. Write about what the character does in those final moments of consciousness, and maybe even what happens after the transition.

2. You are on your deathbed. You know will die soon and there is something you need to share, some jewel of knowledge that simply cannot die with you. This jewel is something you know so much about, you are an expert on the subject (much the way Spittoon is an expert on writing). The clock is ticking and your timer is almost up. Set a timer for one hour (or less) and write out your expertise—what do you want to teach the world? What legacy must you leave behind?

3. Write your own "writer autobiography." Who are you as a writer? Who or what has influenced your writing? What are your feelings about writing—good or bad? What is your writing process? Have you ever suffered from writer's block? What was it like and what did you do?

Writing Exercises for Chapter 1

1. **Writing Space:** Dedicate a time and space to writing for one week. Begin by drawing a basic design of what you want your writing space to look like. Is it a closet with cushy pillows piled on the floor and a star-shaped touch lamp? Is it an office crammed full of books? After you've drawn the space, make the space a reality. Carve the space out for yourself and commit for one week to write anything you want for ten minutes a day every day.

2. **Writer's Block:** Create a writer's block tool kit! Take a sheet of paper and cut it into little strips about the size of a slip of paper from a fortune cookie. Separate the strips into three piles. On one set of strips, write types of characters (for example: "a blind samurai warrior," "an accountant who wants to be a lion tamer," and "a vampire with a soul"), on another set of strips write types of settings (for example: "Death Valley," "high school gym class," or "the Carpathian Mountains"), and on the last set of strips write types of conflicts (for example, "in love with brother's wife," "orphaned and raised by a travelling tribe," or "doesn't know that s/he is a vampire"). Then, place the strips into labeled paper bags ("Characters," "Settings," and "Conflicts" respectively). Draw out one of each and use it to start writing!

3. **Prewriting**: Take an idea you have for a piece of fiction or a school assignment and try a new prewriting strategy. If you usually write outlines, try freewriting. If you don't usually do any prewriting, pick and try one. Then write a 5-minute reflection: did this strategy work for you? Why or why not? What will you try next time?

4. **Understanding Audience:** Take a piece of writing you are currently working on—it can be anything from a novel to a letter to a business plan—and try to imagine who might be reading it. Try to picture a room full of characters who would likely pick up your writing and read through it. Who are they? Write down as many details as you can about each member of your audience. Now, look at your document carefully—have you explained everything in a way that the people in this audience will clearly understand? What questions might these characters have about what you've written? What do you need to address?

5. **Introductory Paragraphs:** Imagine you are writing an essay that will appear in your favorite horror magazine. It is an essay comparing similar themes between your favorite horror films. Write three different introductory paragraphs, each using a different style of hook: begin one with a question, another with a challenge, and the last with a narrative or anecdote. After you are finished, decide which one works the best and then write the article.

6. **Cohesiveness in Paragraphs:** Take this sample paragraph and cover up all the sentences but the first (a piece of paper works best). Read that first sentence. What do you expect the next sentence to be about? Write down your expectation. Uncover only the next sentence and read it. Did it meet you expectations? Why or why not? Continue through the rest of the paragraph, writing down your expectations along the way. What would you do to improve cohesiveness? Use transitions or delete, move, or add sentences.

My eyelids fluttered open.

The guy lay yelping in a pool of blood trying helplessly to hold his guts in as they spilled through his fingers.

I looked around the room.

He screamed at me as I bit into the soft flesh behind his elbow.

My vision was blurry and bloodshot. I rose clunkily from the bar stool and walked toward a man leaning over a pool table.

It appeared I was sitting in a bar, a pile of scribbled napkins cluttered around me.

I reached into the man's stomach and ripped out his small intestine with one quick punch.

Try this same exercise with a paragraph from a published work. What are the differences?

7. **Transitions Between Paragraphs:** Set a timer and create a list of as many nouns as you can in five minutes. These can be anything you like. In fact, the less related they are to one another, the better. Once finished, choose two nouns from the page and imagine that each noun is the topic of two separate body paragraphs in your essay. Create a transition between the two imaginary paragraphs.

> *For example: I picked "leprechauns" and "ninjas." I will use the term "while" to demonstrate the relationship between the two ideas while transitioning from one to the other: While leprechauns are imaginary creatures that horde gold, ninjas are very real people who can throw bladed stars with deadly accuracy.*

Continue making transitions between topics until you've exhausted your list.

8. **Voice and Tone:** Write a paragraph describing a scene from one of your character's perspectives. Now, write a new paragraph describing the same scene from the perspective of a teenaged emo girl, a caustic retired war veteran, a cougar single mother, and a career cowboy/girl. How is the scene different? How does voice change? What tonality changes do you detect between the different attitudes of the different characters?

9. **Voice and Tone:** Choose a paragraph from this book (or another piece of non-fiction) and write two versions: one in a formal tone and one informal. Try doing this with your own writing and experiment with blending formal and informal tones.

10. **Revision:** Take one of the writing prompts you've completed and prepare it for revision by printing it double-spaced so there is ample white space within each line. Take a pair of scissors and carefully cut out each individual paragraph. Spread them out before you and start rearranging the paragraphs until you find a sequence that you think works well. Finally, craft a transition and edit any connections in the new structure of paragraphs before changing your original document.

11. **Revision:** Read your writing out loud (either to yourself or others). Read slowly and carefully, listening to the rhythm of your language. As you read, mark places that sound choppy or repetitive or anything that sounds awkward, such as where you stumble or run out of breath. Revise those sections with a focus on sentence length and variety, word choice, transitions, and eliminating redundancy.

—2—

FICTION WRITING

or

Creating Dead-Time Stories

Sybil is a wisp of a woman. Born in ancient Cumae, she wished for eternal life and, failing to also wish for eternal youth, became a zombie instead. (Let this be a lesson to writers everywhere on the value of precise language.) Zombified at the tender age of twenty—long before Emperor Nero's reign—there's very little left to her now. She's nothing to look at, and the years have not been kind. To say she's skin and bones wouldn't be an accurate cliché; in fact, she's barely a whisper trapped inside a hanging basket now. Decay will do that to a person. If only she'd realized sooner that eating the flesh of the living could have eased that terrible ache inside her. Still, she's a heck of a writer. With practically nothing but a mind left, she's fortunate that's the case. We helped a bit with the translation and transcription, since she speaks an ancient Greek dialect and her fingers are literally worn down to nubs, but this chapter comes from her.

YOU MAY BE asking yourself why the legion of the undead would bother showing an interest in fiction. Being the base creatures that we are (reduced to our seemingly unending desire to tear the meaty flesh of the living from their bones), we can be nothing more than what the common observer assumes: mindless drones resurrected from our brittle deaths by some irresistible force. Parasites. Meteorites. Viruses. Germ warfare. Serums. Nanotechnology. Mixed blessings from our Gods granting our wishes. Whatever it is that animates us, one thing seems to be consistent across the spectrum: zombies stumble, run, chase, and eat, but nothing more.

Perhaps that's why you find us so frightening. After all, such a creature as this can't be reasoned with. We'll keep coming and coming until we've eaten you all and there's nothing left for us to do but to wither or freeze or rot into the earth—at least, those of us that still have limbs.

But there's so much more to us than that. In spite of mother's warnings, many of us like to play with our food, batting it around like a cat with a spider before we gobble it up. Some of us build rudimentary structures, or take up residence in empty dwellings and caves. Others enjoy the thrill of body piercing, or conversations with the living. And still more of us just get thoroughly angry because you, the supposed "sole survivor," keep stealing our girlfriends for your genetic experiments. And you call *us* the monsters.

The point is that even the undead are in need of a little light entertainment now and again. As Stephen King, the master of horror, once said in his book, *It,* "fiction is the truth inside the lie." Or if King doesn't do it for you, how about Oscar Wilde (yes, I've eaten, ur, read him), who said in an 1886 edition of the *Pall Mall Gazette,* "one should not be too severe on English novels; they are the only relaxation of the intellectually unemployed." And what are we zombies but the intellectually unemployed?

So, yes, we enjoy our fiction just as much as the next person, whether living or undead. We also enjoy writing about our experiences. The ironic thing is that when we write horror, we are usually writing from experience, but it is still fiction (most of the time), and some of it highly intellectual fiction, at that. We laugh at the fools who tell us horror can't be literary. After all, aren't these the same people who study Mary Shelley's *Frankenstein,* Bram Stoker's *Dracula,* and Shirley Jackson's "The Lottery" in their English criticism classes? Yet somehow horror is classified as genre fiction, and genre can't be intellectual. Well, okay. Maybe sometimes it is a little low-brow, but that doesn't mean it's shallow or empty.

I pride my undead self on my intellect—for what else do I have left after all these years? Sure, cerebrospinal fluid no longer flows to my nonexistent brain, I don't inhale oxygen to feed those missing brain cells, and I don't drink water to enhance the electrical firing across absent neural pathways that create thought, and—are you not noticing that I'm fairly prolific for a woman whose brain was once exposed like a pop-top can of tuna and now has shriveled to wisps of

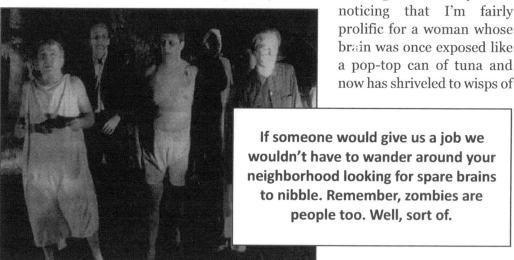

If someone would give us a job we wouldn't have to wander around your neighborhood looking for spare brains to nibble. Remember, zombies are people too. Well, sort of.

dust in a basket? I'm not saying your neuroscience is wrong, per se. I'm just suggesting that maybe you undersell us a bit. Not all of us are reading Doctor Seuss, though you may be surprised to learn that many of us prefer reading Doctor Herbert West instead. (Not saying we don't enjoy the writings of Mr. Geisel, especially new versions such as *Bat in the Hat, Green Eggs and Brain,* and *Horton Eats a Who*.)

Bottom line? Even the dead need stories. What else would we do with our time? Stumble, run, chase, and eat? That gets pretty old after a while, trust me. You end up holed up in your high schools and shopping malls. We end up milling around outside. We

> *Bat in the Hat*
> *Green Eggs and Brain*
> *Horton Eats a Who*
> **Who can ever forget the classics?**

mill. You hole. It's just the way it works. Of course, we eventually find you anyway, and then we start the process all over again. There is a reason we eat brains, you know. Intellectual stimulation. And, boy, do zombies need a little more of that.

But even brain-eating zombies need some guidance when it comes to writing fiction. It seems everyone "has a novel they're working on," and yet somehow, the world is not flooded with unedited tripe. My point is that every zombie has a novel within them, too, but few of us use computers and even fewer are taking classes. And you don't want to be the first zombie literary critic if you're a breather. Let's just say you might have an unexpected guest for dinner.

Still, we have to *learn how to write*. That's why we read books about our people or take classes from creative writers with terminal degrees in the field, like Araminta Matthews, or enroll in academic writing classes from instructors like Rachel Lee, or read the works of fellow zombie enthusiast authors and publishers, like Stan Swanson. Swanson's *Forever Zombie* was some funny stuff, and Matthews' *Blind Hunger* really captured the essence of our insufferable starvation.

It is through reading and interaction that we become better writers—even those of us whose fingers are rotting off, leaving bloodstains and little fleshy bits all over our keyboards. We're no different than you are. Those of us with the drive know: if we don't write, we die—again. So indulge this brainy beast as I recount for you the lessons I have learned from eating a few English professors while I still had teeth, devouring a few good books, and sharing my work with other zombies.

Like other types of writing, most of what we know about telling good story comes from Aristotle—whose favorite food, by the way, turned out to be followers of Plato— in the elements of good fiction. In addition to a preset list of elements, good stories require a few tricks of the trade: tension, sensory details, showing language, and a strong edit. After all, writing is a conversation between a writer and a reader—even if that writer happens to only speak in grunts and moans and the reader is trying to staunch the blood flow from a leg wound using the pulpy pages of a novel. Either way, it's dialogue.

Elements of a Story

Aristotle once came to my house for a dinner party, and while everyone shared some finger sandwiches dipped in viscera, he told us all about his days as a writer. It was a compelling story. My jaw literally dropped in the middle, but luckily women of my time were very good at needlepoint. Here's what I learned:

Every good writer uses story structure even if they do not realize it. (And, if they do not realize it, then they are either very good or they are just plain lucky. And even though luck plays a huge role in whether a zombie finds a decent brain to munch on, luck doesn't play much of a part in writing.)

The structure of all stories includes a beginning, a middle, and an end. Even stories that experiment with those features—for example, starting in the middle and telling a nonlinear narrative, or using open-ended finales to keep the reader engaged—need to follow some kind of directional flow in order to keep a reader's interest. In addition, good stories have characterization, setting, climax, and resolution. Even when the characters aren't people, and even when the setting is a void, stories engage readers when they have these elements.

BEGINNINGS

Now, before a story is attempted, the writer has some serious choices to make about whose perspective to use in order to tell the story. Will it be an unreliable narrator, like the townsperson in William Faulkner's bleak tale of murder (and possibly necrophilia), "A Rose for Emily"? Will it be a character in the story itself like the depressed (or possibly demonically-possessed narrator) of Charlotte Perkins Gilman's "The Yellow Wallpaper"? Or will it be a third party, like a fly on the wall watching everything the characters do from an objective vantage point, such as the cold account of Tessie's stoning in Shirley Jackson's "The Lottery"?

Point of View

Now that you know "who" is telling the story, which point of view will the character use?

Should it be first person ("I"/"we") or third ("he"/"she"/"it")? You could even try second person ("you") although that is not common and difficult to do with any effectiveness, unless of course you are *Half Asleep in Frog Pajamas* or writing *Choose Your Own Adventure* novels. You should give your viewpoint some serious thought. How will your story come across best and how effective will your characters be in one point of view versus others? Some plotlines almost demand one or the other. Others can use either, but the story will not be quite the same, so consider your choice carefully. Imagine how the story you want to tell will change when viewed through the lens of different perspectives. How different, for example, would Faulkner's "A Rose for Emily" have been if it was told from the perspective of Toby, her former slave? Or even Emily herself? And further still, what if the entire tale was told in second person, making the readers—whoever they may be—insert their own personality into the arc of the story? You'd have three very different tales on your hands as compared to the one told by Faulkner, that's for sure. As you can see, this decision should be weighed carefully.

After giving some thought to the point of view, you are now ready to begin your story. You can begin a story right in the middle of the action, but readers need to feel invested in your concept before they'll willingly immerse themselves in the blood and guts of your tale. To demand the attention of a reader, you usually have to set them up.

The beginning of fiction is like the beginning of a good play or movie: we meet the cast, we meet the protagonist (hero or anti-hero), and we find out what's happening—that is, what's the central conflict that is going to make engaging with these characters interesting?

Please believe me. I thought I <u>was</u> using an engaging point of view!

Characterization

We learn about characters through characterization, which requires some level of psychological, sociological, and zombological understanding of the character's way of life. What choices would your characters make? How do they live, or unlive, as the case may be? We learn about setting, like characters, through snippets of scenery that surround the characters in a story. What is important for the reader to see?

Your characters are more important than you might imagine. If you have developed characters that are vague, your reader will not identify with them. If your character does not seem real, then even the excitement that ensues will not be as valid. And while we do not need to know as much about the people in your writing if you are creating a short story as we would in a novel, we still need enough information to bring them to life. Ask yourself where they live, where they come from, what do they like and dislike, what do they look like and, maybe most importantly, how do they deal with conflict and change. Bring your vampire to life. Make him scary or make him wimpy, but don't ignore who he is. Even if you don't weave every fact about your character into the story, at least you know how he will react to any given circumstance.

Dialogue

One way we characterize the players in our tales is through dialogue. Dialogue can betray some intimate details about a person's (or creature's) inner machinations. Imagine, for instance, the voice of the seventy-year-old, short-tempered lifelong smoker who is your waitress at the all-night blood bank. She uses very different words when she speaks than, say, the Romanian count who studied overseas at Harvard before starting his own law firm in Romania.

Remember, then, that it is nearly impossible to write a well-formed story that shows but doesn't tell without good dialogue, and it is easy to get it wrong. Make your characters talk as they would in real life. With solid dialogue you can bring life to characters, describe your setting without writing two paragraphs about what the bar looks like, and move your plot forward organically.

Dialogue can sometimes be impacted by the setting of the story, too, drawing upon the dialect and language used by characters from different regions, time periods, or even species in various tales. For that reason, don't ignore the setting of your story. You don't have to go into great detail to set your scenes, but they are integral to the ambiance your tale conveys. Use your five senses to create your setting. What does that dark bar look like? Is it a dump? Is it an upscale restaurant? Does your vampire smell steak (very rare, of course) or the scent of an unclean restroom? Is there the clanking of knives? The murmur of a rough crowd who are not fond of vampires? Run through all five senses until the scene feels right.

Chekhov's Gun

In addition to having your characters firmly in your head (not entirely unlike another famous Sybil), you need to set the reader up for conflict and also use your images sparingly in the beginning. Russian playwright Anton Chekhov—one of my most dramatic meals—once said something very important about beginnings. Of course, it was in Russian, so I'll have to translate (yes, I can do that—stop underestimating the undead!): One must not put a loaded rifle on the stage if one is not thinking of firing it.

What this means is that readers want to know what is coming. When the climax happens and all the excitement begins to pour out in waves, readers will know that the moment was inevitable, but still expect to be surprised. That means that you need to *foreshadow* the future for the reader—that was my area of expertise in life. Show the loaded gun so that 200 pages later when Zach the Zombie gets his brain splattered over the side of the ice cream truck by its blast, the reader remembers the gun and feels the tension it caused all over again.

Chekhov's gun also means that good stories introduce all the major points early in the tale. If there is a zombie slayer and a zombie in the mystery of the story (for all stories have some level of mystery until the end), then we meet them all in the first few chapters (or pages if this is a shorter work). Maybe the zombie slayer is just a bit character at first—the girl who delivers the water for the water cooler, or the secretary at the law firm who verifies you have an appointment—but seeing the slayer early on will make the "big reveal" of who the slayer actually is that much more enjoyable for the reader. Your goal is to get your readers to slap a bloody palm to their head and say, "I knew it!" or "I didn't see that coming!"

Thus, beginnings perform many actions all at once. They hook the reader in, establish base characterization, and offer up Chekhov's gun at the same time as the central conflict—all within the first few paragraphs, pages, or chapters depending on the length of your work. Regardless of the length, it is essential that you introduce these elements to the reader early on.

If you are writing a short story, you can present these details sparingly, but never leave them out entirely. In fact, in a short story you might only have one or two characters and only one conflict. A novel might have a dozen or more characters (each possibly with a different goal) and more than one conflict (although the story should still only have one major conflict even if it is a novel).

Here is the *beginning* of a short fiction piece:

> *Hannah groaned.*
>
> *Fingers tingling, she tentatively touched the side of her neck. Sticky wetness . . . She turned her hand and, with sleep-weary eyes, struggled to focus on the crimson blobs of blood.*
>
> *She grinned. "You did it?" The words were a blend of wonder and excitement.*
>
> *"What choice did I have?" Lonnie muttered. "You've been begging me every day for months. I was getting tired of hearing it."*
>
> *She leaned forward, wincing at the sting of the wound. "Jeez! That hurts!"*
>
> *Lonnie laughed. "What did you think? I didn't exactly give you a tender love bite."*
>
> *Despite the pain, she threw her arms around Lonnie and planted a slobbery kiss on his lips. Her body tingled although she wasn't sure whether it was from the kiss or just a side-effect of the bite.*
>
> *Lonnie stood, his taut muscles flexing as he stretched. Hannah was unsure what thrilled her more, having such an exotic guy for a boyfriend or the eagerness of what was to come.*
>
> *"And I'll change soon?" she asked.*
>
> *"That's why we did it tonight, babe. Remember? There's a full moon." He wiped a dab of blood from his cheek.*

In a longer piece (this one is just a little over 500 words, which is your standard starting length for "flash fiction"), you would introduce a little more of the scene, but as you can see, we've introduced our characters (albeit very briefly) and told you what the situation is. The introduction of the story leads us into the "body" or "middle" of the tale we are telling.

MIDDLES

The middle is where we get to the guts—those slimy, steaming slithers of sausage fresh from the abdominal cavity of a living person.

It melts in the mouth.

After the beginning, the middle tells the story. It follows the main character or characters around, giving us snippets of the future (foreshadowing), and drawing us in so that by the time we reach the ending, we are ready for the thrill of the climax. Good middles move up and down like a rollercoaster at Zombieland, slowly building tension, climaxing, then leveling off over and over until we reach the crescendo, the true climax, the moment when the reader's knuckles whiten against the page, their eyes growing wide and round.

Plot

The middle is also where the bulk of the story known as the "plot," takes place— and, no, we are not talking about burial plots here. The plot will continually drive us towards the climax of the story.

In a longer piece, you may have several subplots and minor conflicts which are dealt with along the way, but you are always working toward solving the story's major conflict. If the town is being invaded by alien zombies, the author must take us on the wild ride so that we feel we are right there alongside the characters. You put your reader on that giant scary roller coaster with all of its ups and downs and never let them go until the ride is finished.

The plot is what separates stream-of-consciousness writing (for example, your journal entries) from an actual story.

You might have great characters, a perfectly scary setting, and lots of bells and whistles (or chainsaws and machetes), but until you develop a plot, you have nothing. The elements of the plot are typically wrapped up in the exposition and the conflict that drives the story.

The *exposition* is the background information that your reader needs to understand what is going on. Sure, you're sitting in a bar having a cocktail with a vampire, the grim reaper, and an orthodontist, and while that may be enough to pique a reader's interest, why are they there and why are they important to the story?

The *conflict* arises when your protagonist faces a problem and sees no immediate solution to that problem. (Don't let them resolve the problem too quickly either. If you give too much away too soon, your reader will be queuing up an Oxnard Montalvo movie faster than you can say stuffed jalapeños.)

Rising Action

Once you have set the stage by establishing your characters and conflicts, the next step is to introduce *rising action*. In a short story this rising action might only go on for a few pages. In a novel it could involve many chapters.

The middle usually only includes the exposition, conflict, and rising action as climax, falling action, and resolution usually take place at the end—and sometimes those last three elements of plot take place very quickly. So, looking at exposition, conflict, and rising action, let's consider the *middle* of the example flash fiction story we began earlier:

> Hannah could not contain her excitement. "What do I need to do?"
>
> Lonnie shrugged. "Nothing the first time. The change will come as midnight approaches. Just try to relax."
>
> Moments later, Hannah felt muscles tighten and twinge from head to toe.
>
> "You'd better get out of those clothes," Lonnie suggested.
>
> She smiled wickedly. "Do we have time?"
>
> Lonnie laughed. "Later, hon. The problem is . . . "
>
> Hannah flinched as spasms of pain jolted every nerve ending in her body.
>
> "Too late—" Lonnie whispered.
>
> Hannah's blouse ripped at the seams as the muscles in her arms bulged and stretched. She screamed with the intense pain. "You didn't tell me it would hurt this much," she gasped between shrieks. The seams of her jeans tore next and tears streamed down her cheeks.
>
> Between explosions of excruciating pain came blasts of pleasure. Sweet torture, then sudden release. The change was complete. With clothes torn to shreds at her paws, she turned to Lonnie and howled.
>
> She wanted to run and Lonnie knew he couldn't stop her. The urge to dash through dark woods and howl at the moon was ancient and powerful. Lonnie understood completely and quickly shed his clothes. A moment later, the silvery wolves howled in unison and bounded through the front door.

As you can see, we now basically know the story, and only need to resolve it. The middle starts to flesh out the body of the tale we are telling. In this example, we can see that the main characters are werewolves, and they are about to have a wonderful run in the moonlight. How romantic! Now, on to the ending.

ENDINGS

The end is where you weave together any loose threads so your story is wrapped up with a tight little bow. Even if zombies are taking over the earth in your tale, the goal of the protagonist must be achieved even if he gives up his life so that mankind might still have a chance at redemption.

The end usually has two parts: it starts with a climax, the moment in the story when all the elements come together in a collision of intensity, and it ends with a resolution, the moment when those elements settle down and a new path for the protagonist is revealed, whatever that might be. The climax is the moment of strong emotion and the resolution is the moment when the story feels done. The reader can now walk away from the story feeling a sense of completion, some understanding that things are over—at least for now.

Climax and Resolution

Things bubble to climax after the rising action from the middle is presented. This is where our protagonist resolves his predicament, even though things may not return to "normal."

Climax in a story is typified by tension rising to an almost unbearable pitch. It's when your fingers whiten and you dig your nails into the arm of the chair because you have to know what happens next, even though you can't bear to know at the same time. It's the moment of the story you've been waiting for—the very reason you picked it up in the first place. The moment when everything goes awry.

Think of the climax in the remake of *Dawn of the Dead* when all the zombies flood the mall and the characters run for their lives, forced to enact their plan of escape much sooner than they'd planned. (We got some good eatin' out of that day, I tell you.) The resolution comes next, when those who were meant to survive the onslaught find their way onto the boat and set sail toward a new horizon. No zombies are on the vessel with them; just open water and a new direction that may take them anywhere.

Which brings us to *falling action* and the *resolve*, or *denouement*. This simply means things go back to a state of non-action and life goes on, all loose ends are tied up and the reader is clear that everything has been resolved. Resolution is a very different thing to many people. Some writers might contend that the story is finished as written above. Others long for a twist or something unexpected. This is especially true in the horror genre. In a short story this might take a paragraph. In a novel, it might take a chapter, but you shouldn't linger long. The story is finished and you don't want to lose your reader now.

The same thing happens in our flash fiction story. It *ends* after a flash forward in the plot. Once you are finished you will see how the story structure comes together.

> ***
>
> *"Are you sure you haven't been drinking, sir?" the officer asked again.*
>
> *"No," the man gasped. "They . . . they just came out of nowhere . . . "*
>
> *"So, you're telling me you didn't notice two people, naked as jaybirds, run in front of your car?"*
>
> *"No!" the man insisted as he leaned against the fender of his limited edition Silver Bullet Mercedes for support. "And I told you already. They weren't people. They were . . . dogs . . . or wolves . . . "*
>
> *The cop looked at him with doubt, his gaze turning to the mangled bodies of a young man and woman lying in the glare of flashing red lights.*

Were you able to spot Chekhov's gun and the complication or conflict set up in the story at the beginning? Were you able to identify the rising energy and the tension it created in the middle section? Did the story "feel finished" to you following the resolution in which the starring characters, frenzied with the werewolf chase, died? Even modern literary devices still follow many of Aristotle's millennia-old methods. Maybe there is some truth in the idea that wisdom comes with age, after all.

Story Structure

Aristotle's story structure is known as the story arc. It is also referred to as the three-act structure. Whether it is a short story by Edgar Alan Poe or an epic novel like Stephen King's *The Stand*, the three-act structure is the foundation to the tale.

These three elements (beginning, middle, and end) can be played with, twisted up, and delivered in new and innovative ways, but essentially all fiction integrates these elements somehow. Some stories start at the end and work backward, like *Frankenstein* or *Dracula*. Other stories start in the middle and work both backward and forward at once, like *Dr. Jekyll and Mr. Hyde*. Either way, this format is common in works of fiction.

Now consider the following full-length short story. Pay attention to the pacing. Does it move too slowly, taking too long to build up to the climax? Or is it too fast, starting out right in the center of the action and jumping too quickly to the resolution? Is it tense—that is, do you feel your pulse increasing? Or is it flat and idle, kind of waning to a slow pace as you read? Does it begin well? Are you engaged and hooked, or did you have to dig deeper to get into the storyline—or perhaps you never got into it all. And what of the resolution? Did you get it? Was it believable? Do you care?

Being able to answer any of these questions (and, more importantly, explaining *why you answered the way you did)* means you are one step closer to writing a solid story.

The Boy in the Hollow

"Help."

The wind carried the word to the ears of Jeff Murphy as he sat resting against a tree to catch his breath. His head jerked as his brows knitted together. Had he really heard it, or was it just the faint echo of a frog croaking in the bog he'd just passed?

Plucking his telescoping hiking stick from where it leaned against the tree beside him, Jeff hoisted himself to his feet. The muscles in his calves pulled taut beneath the skin as he flexed his toes inside his boots. Sweat eased down the curve of his knee pit. Brushing a hand across his brow, he felt the dampness that had been sponged from his forehead by his once-white bandana.

"Please, help."

There it was again. There could be no doubt now. Jeff scanned the forest around him. Tree limbs bent and swooped over the mossy stones that lined the creek to his right. Impossibly large roots jutted up from the base of each tree to his left, and a cluster of jagged stones loomed in the path ahead twice as tall as the Jeep he'd parked miles back at the foot of the mountain.

If someone is stuck out here, they sure are far from home.

"Hello?" Jeff bellowed, squinting in the distance. He cupped his hands around his mouth to increase the volume. "Is someone there?"

Almost immediately, the wind carried back the faint reply. "Yes. Please, come quickly."

Instinctively, Jeff's head jerked toward the direction of the sound and his rugged legs began moving toward it almost immediately. The sound was coming from a little to the left, past the stones that loomed before him and a little further up the mountain.

"I'm coming," he shouted, placing a hand on a crag in one of the boulders. "Hold on!"

With his free hand, he hoisted the hiking stick onto the rock and tossed his backpack behind it before pulling himself over the rock. He'd been hiking for over five hours and the muscles in his legs were starting to buckle from exertion, but this was the first time he'd really needed to use his arms. Sweat beaded on his caramel-colored forearm as he pulled himself over the rock with gritted teeth.

After a moment of puffing, he slung the bag over his shoulders and picked up the hiking stick again.

"You still there?" he shouted between breaths.

"Yes! I'm trapped." The voice came from directly ahead. It sounded muffled.

A quick glance above at the dusty rose horizon told Jeff it would soon be dark. He'd have to find the lost hiker quickly before the night descended on them with all the darkness of a death shroud.

"Good. What's your name?" Jeff shouted back, trying to keep the voice talking so he could better track its source as he plunged forward up the mountain. He moved toward a cluster of oaks that intertwined near their bases as they'd grown together. They seemed to block the path about twenty yards ahead, and he was almost certain the sound came from behind them.

"Peter," came the voice, echoing off the trees around him stronger than before.

Funny. I thought it was a woman lost up here. Could it be—

"Peter," Jeff bellowed, straining closer to the source of the sound. "How old are you?"

There was a pause. Jeff listened to the wind as it rattled through the leaves all around him.

Then the voice shouted again.

"Nine."

A child? How?

Jeff whipped out his cellphone and checked for a signal, though he knew it was pointless. He'd hiked New England mountains before and well knew how spotty the reception was even in the most industrial areas of the Northeast. The phone blinked dumbly at him.

No signal.

"Where are your parents?" Jeff's heart thumped against his ribcage as his breaths came in hot, steamy bursts. He pulled against the rooted hiking stick with both hands as he came up to the cluster of oaks.

"I –I don't know. I'm lost."

Worry wrinkled Jeff's gritty, sun-kissed face. "Okay, Peter. Tell me where you are trapped."

"I can't tell. It's so dark down here."

Fear knotted inside Jeff's throat as he swung his pack through a gap in the tree cluster and dropped it on the leaf-covered ground below.

"I'm scared." The voice was louder now. Closer.

Just on the other side of those trees.

"I'm coming," Jeff shouted again, pulling himself through the thin opening between the intertwined oak tree trunks. His bare forearm scraped against the bark and tiny balls of blood freckled his arm.

"I think I'm in a cave," Peter said, a slight tremble in his voice. "The ground feels hard."

Jeff left the pack where it was on the ground and pressed his walking stick into earth beside him for balance. Beyond the cluster of trees, the ground sloped dramatically downward before rising in a sharp ridge straight ahead.

He scanned the valley between him and the ridge.

Squinting in the dimming dusk-lit forest, Jeff spotted a sharply angled tree root with a dark hollow just beneath it. His heart thumped hard.

"Peter, can you see a light where you are?"

"Sort of. There's a little light coming in from over my head."

Without another thought, Jeff leapt from the top of the tree-clustered hill to the sloping valley below. His feet landed softly against the forest floor as he settled his balance with the hiking stick. In three quick strides, he was at the hollow and stooping to peer inside.

"Peter?" he asked.

"I'm here," came the shrill reply, excitement emanating from the voice loud as a lighthouse beacon.

Jeff squinted into the darkness of the hollow, angling his head away from the dipping sun behind him to let a little light through. In a moment, a pale, freckled face appeared in the light, blue eyes glinting in the setting sunshine.

Peter.

"Give me your hand!" Jeff shouted, bracing one hand against the tree root above him for support while reaching the other deep into the hollow toward Peter's face.

Peter opened his mouth. "I can't. I can't reach it."

Jeff adjusted his position, bracing a foot against the base of the hollow to allow him to reach his arm deeper inside. Dirt tumbled into the hollow beneath his boot.

"Almost," the boy said. "A little closer."

Straining to reach the boy, Jeff didn't notice as the soft, forest ground beneath his boot shifted and began to give way beneath his weight. With a shocked scream, the man tumbled into the hole face first. The wind banged out of him as his chest collided with the earth below, and a few crumbles of soil found their way into his open mouth.

After a moment, he sat up quickly and looked around, allowing his eyes to adjust in the dark. He brushed the dirt from his mouth and searched for the silhouette of the boy in the shadows of the hollow beneath the tree.

"Peter?" he asked. "Are you okay? Listen, don't worry, okay? We'll get out of this."

The boy was silent.

"Peter?" Jeff began patting his body and the ground near him, suddenly paranoid he'd landed on the child and crushed the poor boy to death.

Something shifted in the darkness. Jeff squinted, straining to see what was moving in the thin trickle of light that filtered through the root-covered hole above him. In the shadows, he could just make out a pair of arms swaying toward him. A child-sized torso. A head with a bowl-shaped haircut and a Little

Rascals cowlick protruding from the back. A pair of legs swaying just above the ground.

Is he floating?

As soon as the thought occurred to him, he was laughing at how preposterous the idea was.

Must be a trick of the light.

But as the boy's silhouette drew nearer, he noticed the distinct lack of sound. No shoes scuffling along the dirt-covered cave floor. No childish whimpering or rustling of clothing. No breathing.

"Peter?" he asked, hesitating.

The boy's body swayed into the fading sunlight that spilled onto the cave floor. At the sight of him, Jeff's face twisted into a gruesome grimace. Indeed, the dummy-like boy with his waxy skin was hovering above the ground, his hands and feet webbed together with all the detail of a ragdoll's, not unlike the rest of his undetailed body.

Only the boy's face bore any resemblance to a human, with its belt of freckles across the nose and its glimmering eyes and smile. As Jeff looked at the creature hovering before him, the boy's mouth opened and Jeff soon realized the sound wasn't coming from the boy-puppet at all, but behind it.

"I'm so hungry," the voice intoned.

Jeff's eyes followed the tube that protruded from the boy's back in an arc above his head until it reached the source of the sound. There, like some horrible, land-bound angler fish, the tube rooted from the forehead of a black-skinned creature with glistening yellow eyes and a mouth—a wide open mouth with rows of jagged, blackened teeth—that stretched into a Cheshire Cat grin wide enough to swallow Jeff whole.

The boy's body bobbed like a marionette on the angler's tube—bait on hook—as the creature's mouth closed around Jeff's screaming face, chomping at the neck. Jeff's body went slack and slumped to the ground. Blood spurted over the sharkskin of the creature's face as it gnawed on the skull, tonguing the bandana from Jeff's head and spitting it out.

In the distance, the sun slipped behind the mountainside, casting the forest in the dull gray cobwebs of nightfall.

This story employs several techniques I have previously discussed. First, it attempts to create tension by opening the story in the heart of the action with the word "help," and then continues to build tension by slowing the process down so that the reader sees certain things more clearly than others. (This is also a flash fiction piece, by the way. It is at the upper range of what is considered flash fiction at 1500 words, whereas the earlier piece was only 500 words.)

Next, the story employs sensory details, inserting images and sensations into the tale that explain the smells, sights, and feelings that the main character experiences to draw the reader in. The goal is to use clear and specific language to show the reader an image that he or she cannot physically see. The goal is to create that picture distinctly with just a few sentences. In doing so, you've actually "written" a thousand words if you agree with the age-old adage.

Lastly, if this story were longer, it might employ cliffhangers to keep the reader held firmly in its iron-clad grip by flashing between a moment of high stress and a moment of low stress. In this short story version, you can see this shift when the story alternates between the reason the hiker is in the mountainous wood versus the tension created by the stranded child, augmented by the setting sun.

These tricks of the trade can be yours, too, for the price of two spleens, a brain, and one fully-drenched, pumping heart. Perhaps some fava beans on the side—nothing complements a brain like fava beans, don't you think? Creates just the right mood. Ambience. Tension.

Tension

One of the most important aspects of your fictitious works will be the tension—the physical response—you are able to create in your readers. Tension works best when things slow down. Consider this classic movie cliché: enter a bad guy—whether it's a flesh-eating zombie, a vampire, or just some everyday serial killer. The bad guy decides to hide in the basement. Usually, we see his boot pressing into the floor. The floor creaks. A sound alerts him, and he moves into the basement. Then, through a thin crack in the door (perhaps hearing our bad guy's slow breathing or the slobbering of

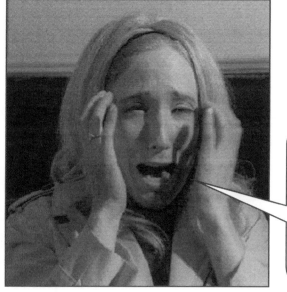

blood down his chin) we see a glossy-haired soccer mom enter, careless and fancy-free, perhaps chatting on a cellphone or bringing in groceries.

We watch this scene unfold as if it were a typical day, knowing the situational irony of the killer in the

Either there's a serial killer behind that door or the kids are home from school!

basement. The innocent woman, of course, goes about her business unaware that she is being watched by the bad guy in the basement. But, *we* are aware. And because we are aware, we begin to breathe more quickly (or chew more slowly, take your pick), and our eyes widen because we know, any moment now, our heroine's day is going to get much worse. And the longer it takes for her to progress from point A to point B, the more tense the scene becomes until, slowly, the protagonist turns toward the basement. Oh no! She knows. She senses that something is out of the ordinary. Something is there. She inches toward the door, places a trembling palm on the knob, begins to pull to open, and then—

So how do we slow things down? In Stephen King's book, *On Writing*, the "king" of horror suggests that fragmented sentences—phrases which do not possess all the elements necessary to form a complete thought—can be used to slow or speed up a scene. While fragments are grammatically incorrect, they are stylistically powerful when used carefully and with precision. Like ninja throwing stars. Or scream queens.

In addition, tension can be achieved by slowing things down with a particular type of description known as *sensory details* or *showing language*. Sensory details are moments in a story described through the senses of sight, sound, taste, touch, or scent. This creates a connection for the reader and engages his yummy brain while at the same time slowing down the pace. Showing language engages sensory details (and *not* interpretative details) to describe a scene, essentially slowing the pace down by explicitly pointing the reader's attention to certain amplified cues. Examples of sensory details include:

Sight	color, shape, size (crimson blood, long fangs)
Sound	onomatopoeia (when a word sounds like what it refers to, like "splash" or "zip")
Smell	evocative of memory, scents (vanilla, cookies, rotting corpses)
Taste	evocative of memory; similar to scents (lemonade, chocolate, burning skin)
Touch	textures (coarse, striated, gushy, wet)

You can pair sensory details with showing language by using specific, accurate, or precise language to evoke sensory experiences. The key is to only write what you see (or hear, or taste), not what you *think you see*. In other words, describe the face and not your interpretations of the face.

One of the hardest turns to this trick is that you probably think you see what you are interpreting. For instance, if your survivalist pal walks in with his brow furrowed, a bead of sweat dripping down his chin, and his finger clenched around the handle of a black machete, you probably think you see concentration. You might say, "Billy was concentrating." Unfortunately, that doesn't work. "Concentrating" is a concept—it is your *interpretation of what's going on with Billy.* To really show the reader what is going on with him, you can only describe what is on his surface—just as I did when I described his brow, his chin, and his hands at the beginning of this paragraph.

This technique can be more difficult than it seems and takes practice to master. One way to improve your aptitude is to take an object near you—something simple and common, like a water bottle, or the still-beating heart of your next door neighbor (extracted from his chest, of course), and lay it down in front of you. Now, try to describe the object non-visually, using only your other senses. What does the heart feel like? Wet, sticky. When my fingertip touches its surface and tries to pull away, the stretchy membrane goes with it. What does it smell like? Gamey, and a bit like iron or celery. What does it sound like? It thumps and thuds in my palm like that scene from *Indiana Jones and the Temple of Doom.* What does it taste like? Red globs of rich meat rolling over my tongue.

Another trick is to take a series of the same object, like a bunch of severed hands. Or a bag full of pears. Then, line them up and choose one of them to describe. Your goal is to describe the item in a way that a friend could walk in and choose the one you described from a line-up based on the words you chose. If your friend can spot it, then you did a good job describing what you saw.

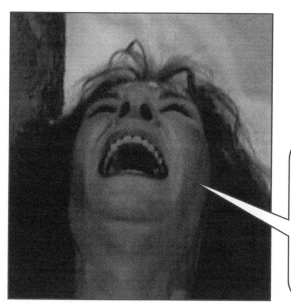

Cliffhangers

Cliffhangers are another great trick of the trade, especially for genre fiction—that is, stories that are written to entertain readers rather than to make them think or to explore some

I know it's after midnight, but I can't believe you aren't going to read the next chapter to see what happens to me next.

great topic. Stories are genre when they are action- or plot-driven, rather than character-driven. A cliffhanger is when you see an important character in a scene facing some imminent danger, and then you cut to a new scene, leaving the reader to wonder what is happening with that cliffhanging character from the previous scene. The key to this trick is to always leave the reader wanting more. If you have a few main characters, leave one to be eaten by yours truly and break the scene just as my teeth are about to penetrate his cheek—then, cut to a new scene with another character doing something else.

Cliffhangers are most effective at the ends of chapters or sections. For those who are more familiar with the classics, many writers in the 19th century employed cliffhangers extensively as their works were often printed in serial installments, such as H.P. Lovecraft's Re-Animator series, which featured my own doctor, Herbert West. Charles Dickens helped popularize this format in *The Pickwick Papers, Oliver Twist,* and *Nicholas Nickleby.*

Feedback and Revision

You should also embrace the opportunity to enlist feedback in your writing process. A solid edit is a vital component to anything you write—not just fiction. Anne Lamott, a famous non-horror writer, wrote an informative essay entitled "Shitty First Drafts" in which she explains that master writers—even writers like Stephen King and Jack Ketchum—don't always get it perfect and right the first try. Writers' first drafts are rarely golden (a notable exception being Shirley Jackson's immortal story, "The Lottery," wherein a town stones a woman to death, which Jackson claimed needed very little editing), and that means that we need to rewrite and revise our work, often extensively. At the same time, we can't rely on our own judgment to accomplish that task because we are too close to the material and miss our blind spots. It would be like asking a zombie to lick your wounds. It will backfire like a shotgun from S-Mart.

Instead, enlist the help of an objective bystander. Solicit another opinion. Take the feedback you get and find a way to incorporate it into your manuscript. Even if the person giving the feedback says something you disagree with, don't just stand there and argue—examine their point of view. Was he right about the climax falling flat on the reader and being a little boring? Does it make sense that your character— a quiet and reclusive librarian—would be the leader of your band of necrocalypse survivors given that she doesn't normally organize anything more than a stack of books? Remember, writing is a dialogue with your reader—that means, while you get to be the one who ultimately decides what your book says, you still need to listen to how your book is received to some extent. It is, after all, how we grow. We all need to learn. Zombies fresh from the grave wander aimlessly hoping that food (that's you, of course) stumbles into their path through sheer luck. Zombies that have survived several days know that you will eventually hole up in the nearest shopping mall, school, or grocery store.

But when all is said and done, the most important thing to remember is to just write. It is a formula that will ultimately lead you to success whether you are smashing in the heads of zombies or winning the heart of the cute vampire you met in homeroom.

Write, write, write, then write some more. And then rewrite. The journey through this apocalyptic world of writing isn't easy, which is precisely why not everyone can do it. Now, go slay that zombie before he feasts on your brains. After all, everything is fair in love, war, and creative writing—perhaps even flesh-eating.

Writing Prompts for Chapter 2

1. Write a flash fiction story with no more than 500 words. Include the words "dark," "moon," "undead," and "graveyard."

2. Write a short story featuring a new kind of vampire. How will your vampire be different from all the others we've read about or seen in the movies? What does it feed on? How is it turned? Can sunlight or wooden stakes harm it, or does it need something else? Try this same prompt with zombies and witches, as well. Can you think outside the coffin?

3. "Rewrite" the story of a favorite character from a play, book, movie, etc. with a completely different time period and setting. What would happen? What scenes would take place? How would the character interact with the people of the new time and place? Write a series of scenes or an entire short story.

Writing Exercises for Chapter 2

1. **Inspiration and Ideas:** Keep a writing journal. Use this space for: recording ideas for stories, snippets of conversation that catch your attention, details from your day-to-day life that stick in your mind, new words that you encounter, or even interesting or unusual facts from history or science. Did the TV announcer just say something about cannibalistic humanoid underground dwellers?

2. **Showing and Telling:** Look around your writing space and grab the first thing you see that you can fit into your hand. Pick it up and describe it in one page using only descriptive language (shape, size, color, texture, smell, taste, and any sounds it might evoke). Be as detailed as possible and avoid any telling words (explanatory adjectives, concepts, and emotions).

3. **Characterization:** Imagine yourself as a character. What do readers need to "know" about you? Use direct characterization to tell readers two important details about yourself; then, use indirect characterization to show readers who you are by describing your clothes, how you look, or what your environment is like.

4. **Dialogue:** You have two characters—one is a precocious eight-year-old child and the other is a senile 98-year-old adult. They are sitting beside one another on a

park bench awaiting the end of the world. What do they say to one another? Tell this story using only dialogue. That is, you may only use the words they say to one another to show the plot.

5. **Plot:** Use what you know about climax, tension, rising action, and endings to create a plot centered on revenge. Use a pre-writing technique (such as freewriting, webbing, outlining, etc.) to develop the details about what happened. How can you create cliffhangers or tension for your reader?

6. **Tension:** Watch your favorite horror movie or thriller again from the beginning. Watch intently without distractions. Pay attention to your body as you watch the film, looking for moments when your pulse quickens or your muscles tense up. When you find that moment, stop the film and start it again from the exact point you started to tense. Grab a pen and paper or a laptop or tablet and write everything you see in that moment. Go back and look at what you transcribed. How did the film demonstrate tension? Was it the music? Did things slow down? What did the film focus on? How long did it take? What details popped out at you?

—3—

WRITING POETRY
or
Do Poets (De)Compose Like the Thorn, or the Rose?

The Big, Bad Werewolf, featured in such classics as "Little Red Riding Hood," "Bisclavret," and everyone's favorite, "The Wolf Man," agreed to write this chapter on poetry for us as testament to his softer side—and we're not talking about his undercoat, friends. While we know, strictly speaking, Big Bad is not a member of the undead, we simply couldn't refuse him. And not because he threatened to tear out our throats if we didn't let him, either. His poetry is actually rather good. So, without further ado, we bring you the very best of Big Bad.

MOST PEOPLE THINK I only spend my time huffing and puffing and blowing down houses because I have a constant yearning for ham. (Much the same as zombies love brains, I guess.) The truth is that I just can't help myself. I was human once, just like you. Still am except on a full moon, when life changes for a few hours. But the rest of the month I teach poetry at the local community college.

Poetry may be simultaneously the simplest yet most complex topic discussed in this book. Now, I know that as a werewolf, I'm not technically undead, so you should really take it seriously when I stake my life on something. In fact, I'd be willing to bet a silver bullet or two that more people have likely written a poem in their lifetime than any other creative genre. Of course, whether the poem was good or not is something else which would need to be considered. But a poem is still a poem regardless of the perceived quality.

A poorly written poem created during a Mother's Day school project will be treasured by said mother regardless of the quality. Heck, even a zombie can write a poem. I have a few zombie friends who gnaw on more than just brains, you know. Some of them grapple with the complexities of meaning, existentialism, and even politics. All that emotion and angst has to be channeled somewhere, and, well, much of it ends up in the land of poetry. So maybe someone else had to transcribe their guttural, monosyllabic sounds into coherent verse and words, but you get my point. And it is definitely to your advantage that they do something more than seek the sweetness of your medulla oblongata.

Since quality isn't a factor in the definition of poetry, how do we define the genre? Some suggest that the "if it looks like a vampire, and it bites like a vampire, it's probably a vampire" argument holds weight in determining whether a poem is a poem. That is, if it looks like a poem, all broken up with half-sentences and red-wheel-barrowian line breaks (so much does depend upon the red wheelbarrow, as William Carlos

> **If it looks like a vampire, and bites like a vampire, then it probably isn't a zombie.**

Williams suggested), it's probably a poem. Well, that's true for some verses, but what about lyric essays, such as those penned by Anne Carson, Carolyn Forché, or Sherman Alexie, in which poetic devices such as metaphor, imagery, and rhythm are used either in an essay or traditional prose (any writing that has no rhythm, like stories and articles)? What about block poems, free verse, or stream-of-consciousness work like that of Neal Cassady, Jack Kerouac, and Allen Ginsberg? (All, I might add, werewolves in their own right, battling their inner beasts as they "howled on their knees in the subway" (Ginsberg "Howl"), trying to break free of the conformity of their predecessors and establish a new type of poetry.)

Surely poetry has no rules, then. I mean, if an essay written with poetic devices, or a stream-of-consciousness manuscript can all fall under the umbrella term of "poetry," then poems themselves can be anything you want. Right?

Does that mean poems can be anything you want them to be? Well, sometimes. Even the world of ghoulies and ghastlies, such as ours, revolves around rules. Rules of etiquette—why else would vampires need to be invited into your home? Rules of social order—zombies don't eat other zombies, do they? Rules of human self-preservation in the proper methods of eliminating werewolves, vampires, and zombies (oh, my!)—silver bullets, wooden stakes, fire, and decapitation, right? The world of poetry is no exception. At least, most of the time. There are rules that apply to some types of poems, and other types of poems that have no rules at all.

Many think that we werewolves are morally opposed to rules. We just want to run wild with our packs under the light of a silvery full moon while we eat rabbits and foxes, nibble the hands of children to bring them into our pack, or wage the never-ending battle of Capulet and Montague proportions against the vampires who seem to detest us for whatever reason.

But werewolves do have a few rules, you know. For one, we have to abide by the social order of our pack, starting with whatever the alpha dictates. We have to be careful whom we bite without permission. We have to pay attention to the phases of the moon, and, naturally, we have to keep our condition a secret to you mortals who would push us away, make us close down our bars or move out of town, if you knew.

Remember one thing, though—you mortals and we supernatural creatures come from the same stock. We bite you, you become vampire, werewolf, zombie, or just plain rabid. You bite us and will likely have regrets in so doing, but my point is that we are all people on the inside.

And people need poetry—with or without rules.

Sometimes, howling at the moon is enough. It's the perfect way to express all the existential angst of being part human, part wolf. To call out to my fellow canid brethren. To growl at the world.

But sometimes, it's not enough. Sometimes life is bigger than a howl: the joy of the chase, or the thrilling pain of transforming from clunky human flesh to a sleek wolf pelt—that horrible shifting of bones under the skin as my joints dislocate and relocate into the form of a wolf—or the inability to stargaze with my sweetheart during a splendid full moon. And it's because of moments like these that I turn to poetry.

I consider myself to be a poet. Sure. Why not? You know Edgar Allen Poe was actually a vampire, right? So were Lord Byron and John Keats. Walt Whitman and Emily Dickinson, the supposed mother and father of free verse—or poetry without rules—were actually werewolves like me. So's Allen Ginsburg, but I'm sure you guessed that one already. And Sylvia Plath is a sentient zombie. I mean, have you read *Lady Lazarus*?

In poetry, language itself is the artist's tool. Its rhythms, its rhymes, and its double meanings allow the poet to express his or her ideas, but the rules of poetry also force limits to that expression. Poetry forces creativity through confinement. It's the wolf in the skin of a human. I am free to wield my words like weapons or caresses.

Poetry has a long history and comes in many forms. Sometimes poems are never written down and take days to recite. Sometimes poems

When Fido does it it's funny. But when I do it, I get chased by torch-bearing villagers.

are scrawled on glass, trees, or stones. Sometimes poems need to be *seen* to be understood—the shape of the text on the page helps create the poem's meaning. Sometimes poems act like secret messages, saying one thing while they mean another. Poems can be old-fashioned and traditional, or mad experiments that break all the rules. But always, poetry is a powerful tool of expression.

And, as a powerful tool of expression, it is no wonder that the most passionate creatures of this twisted, supernatural world would reach for it. Someone famous supposedly said that the only things worth writing about are sex and death, right?

So who better to write them than the masters of both? Vampires are eternally both. Werewolves are passionate, natural, sexual beasts. Zombies devour us into death. It makes sense that I'd like to write poetry. I mean, what's your problem with that idea, anyway? I can follow rules. Some of my favorite poetry consists of words and sounds stuffed into the rigid structure of poetic rules. Sonnets, haiku, and limericks, to name a few.

**A zombie named Zed
from Nantucket . . .**

Most of the rules surrounding different types of poetry revolve around the number of syllables you use. So what's a syllable? Syllables are units in a word. Here's a good way to remember it. When I was in grade school (yeah, werewolves go to school. Jeez, haven't you ever seen *Teen Wolf*? We're *people* most of the time, guys. Come on.) I had a teacher that said a syllable was every time a word had a beat. Like, if you put your hand under your chin and say a word like "viscera," you have a syllable for every time your chin hits your hand.

Now, I don't want any of you zombies complaining about your jaws falling off during this exercise, so here's another way of looking at it. Count the vowels in a word, but be sure to ignore any silent vowels or vowels that are stuck together like two kidneys in an abdomen (or like the "e" and the "a" in the "weakling" you are), and that should give you the vowels. So, "viscera," right? (Yummy, yummy viscera—so soft between our canine incisors.) We have an "i," an "e," and an "a." That's three vowels, right? And voila, three syllables in "viscera."

Did your jaw just drop?

Some of the poems that revolve around syllables are the haikus, limericks, and sonnets I mentioned earlier.

The latter two (fancy word for a dog, huh?—I meant the word "latter," which means the last in that list. Not the word "two." Just saying.) also have rules about rhyming. Rhyming happens when words sound alike.

Wait. What? Did I just read that right? Aren't we dealing with writing, here? Not talking. How can writing have sound? Well, if you've been paying attention, you have caught on by now that all writing has a "voice" and a "tone," right? Let me see if I can put my subtle twist on this tale.

I know that language came before my ancestors, Romulus and Remus, set to ironing out Latin, the father tongue, but it was those little wolfy dudes that spread the word down the werewolf line that all letters are designed to represent sound. That means that writing is really just talking without a voicebox—which can be arranged if you make me angry enough to tear out your larynx, so just run with this, okay? Theoretically, of course; not through the dark woods near the cemetery.

This means that words *can sound similar to one another*. Rhyming usually requires the syllables in two words to line up with similar sounds, too. That doesn't mean that a single syllable word can't rhyme with a double-syllable word, like, say, "moon" and "lagoon"; but, it does mean that "sister" and "saucer" don't really rhyme, even though the last syllable of each word lines up. In this example, the first syllable of each word does not sound alike. But, say, "sister" and "resister" or "sister" and "blister," or even "sister" and "kissed her" and you got yourself a deal. (A sisterly kiss, of course. We are not inbred, chainsaw-carrying Texans for goodness sakes.)

Rhyming is a whole other complication when it comes to the rules of poetry, so we'll start by talking about syllables. Haikus are my favorite. A traditional Japanese verse, these complex creatures have a series of rules which are specific to the Japanese language. As a result, the haikus you read in English are less likely haikus than Americanized, syllabic-stylized poetry. In fact, most often when we hear the word "haiku" in the West, we are referring to senryu, as haiku are traditionally about nature, whereas senryu covers the gambit of other topics. When I refer to haiku, however, I'm referring to the Americanized version of the poem (because, frankly, I don't speak a lick of Japanese, but howling at the moon works in any language, does it not?). In the Americanized version, the entire poem is comprised of seventeen syllables over three lines: the first is five syllables, the second seven, and the last five. Here's an example:

> The silvery moon
> Calls out my beastly fangs and
> Talons. You should hide.
>
> Let's look at that same poem with breaks to indicate the syllables:
>
> The / sil / ver / y / moon
> Calls / out / my / beast / ly / fangs / and
> Tal / ons. / You / should / hide.

Fairly simple, right? You'd be surprised how many hours go into making one of these puppies. My buddy, zombie poet Blue Tongue Basho, wrote this haiku while roaming the Asian countryside looking for people to eat. We'll use this as another example of simple syllables in poetic action:

I am open-mouthed,
Waiting to devour your heart,
So please stop running.

Ha, ha. You gotta love that guy. Simple man, old Blue Tongue. Always thinking with his stomach, even if it is ripped open and hanging from his abdominal cavity by a single cord of intestine like a pendulum. Snappy dresser, too.

While Blue Tongue was wandering about looking for stragglers whose brains he could munch on, he also began to notice that there were zombies in the world who were never bitten by another member of the undead. He wrote this haiku, too, to illustrate the idea:

There are real zombies.
They cannot put down the phone
so to read a book.

We've already covered that the direct translation of syllables and words from Japanese to American English is inaccurate; traditional Japanese haiku are actually composed of "on" (which are similar to syllables). And if we really want to look at traditional Japanese haiku, remember that they are about nature (so, technically, the "American haikus" you see in this chapter are senryu poems). Not to mention the fact that the line break at the end of the second line is usually a "kiru," or the word which "cuts" the poem from one subject matter to another. These simple syllabic poems

actually are a bit more complex than you may have originally imagined. But don't worry. You are free to embrace and change the rules as you see fit. After all, this is creative writing.

Now that haiku expression has been explained, I guess this brings me to limericks. Limericks are similar to nursery rhymes: they are simple little ditties with simple rhyme schemes and are typically kept short so they can easily be remembered. Who's afraid of the big bad wolf? That's one of my favorite nursery rhymes, in case you haven't already guessed.

Limericks tend to have a stricter rule, though, about the way syllables and rhymes line up. They are five lines long with an A/A/B/B/A rhyme scheme. No, not some groovy ABBA song—I'm talking about rhyme scheme. Here's how it works. At the end of each line of poetry, assign the rhyme sound a letter. If the next line has the same rhyme sound, you give it the same letter. If it doesn't, you assign it a new one. Here's an example of one of my limericks demonstrating rhyme scheme.

> There once was a wolf man who howled,
> He gnashed his teeth when he growled.
> > When he went to bed
> > Dreams swelled in his head
> Of a red-caped girl who scowled.

Here's the same limerick with an explanation of how I assigned rhyme scheme:

There once was a wolf man who howled,
> *(First line gets assigned an **A**)*

He gnashed his teeth when he growled.
> *(Since "growled" rhymes with "howled," it also gets **A**)*

> When he went to bed
> > *(This doesn't rhyme with any line that has come before it, so it gets **B**)*

> Dreams swelled in his head
> > *("Head" rhymes with "bed," so it gets **B**)*

Of a red-caped girl who scowled.
> *(And, as this rhymes with "howled" and "growled," it is also an **A**)*

There are some syllable rules that apply to limericks, too, but they are not as strict as haiku. Typically, the first A-rhyming lines are 8-9 syllables and the B-rhyming lines are 5-7 syllables.

I've got another zombie buddy, Jake Spearo, who writes poetry. Why do all of my friends seem to be zombies? Well, that's a long story involving a particularly frisky evening with a werewoman in heat, a bottle of malt scotch, and a hundred or so of those solar-powered bobbleheads—but ultimately, that's beside the point. Here are some examples of limericks written by Jake Spearo. Check them out:

> There once was a man who was bitten
> by a woman with whom he was smitten.
>> Her chomp drew his blood
>> as he writhed in the mud,
> now he gnaws on the head of a kitten.

> There once was a man with an axe
> who dreamed about zombie attacks.
>> Until his sleep-walking wife
>> met the end of his knife,
> and now he lives with whackos and quacks.

Dark Poets of the Ages

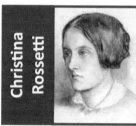
Christina Rossetti

> We must not look at goblin men,
> We must not buy their fruits:
> We knows upon what soil they fed
> Their hungry thirsty roots?

"The Goblin Market" (1859)

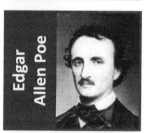
Edgar Allen Poe

> It writhes! - it writhes! - with mortal pangs
> The mimes become its food,
> And seraphs sob at vermin fangs
> In human gore inbued.

"The Conqueror Worm" (1843)

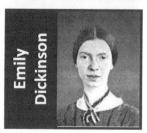
Emily Dickinson

> I felt a Funeral in my Brain,
> And Mourners to and fro
> Kept treading, treading till it seemed
> That sense was breaking through.

"I Felt a Funeral in my Brain" (1896)

There once was a zombie named Fred
who did not understand he was dead.
  But brains he desired,
   soft entrails required.
Best defense? Just lop off his head!

Jake Spearo also tried his hand a few sonnets, another set of poems that have a few rules—probably the "ruliest" poems of the bunch. Yeah. I'm making up a word. Deal with it or I'll bite you.

There are different types of sonnets, but the ones you are most likely to encounter in the world of literature are Shakespearean or English sonnets. They have 14 lines with 10 syllables on each line broken into sets of "iambic feet," or pairs of syllables where one syllable is stressed and the other isn't—see? I told you they were hard. They have an A/B/A/B/C/D/C/D/E/F/E/F/G/G rhyme scheme. See that G/G at the end? That's what we call a "couplet." In love sonnets, it's usually where love is declared or the lovers, uh, couple.

To master the form, consider the way it sounds in terms of beats or rhythms. Imagine, for instance, thumping a drum to the rhythm of a human heart: "*dee dah dee dah dee dah dee dah dee dah.*" That represents the iambic feet. Hear how one syllable is more resonant or sounds more "final" than the other, which feels more like a lead-in to that resonant syllable? That's an iambic foot. The pentameter of English sonnets (there are also a bunch of different types of sonnets which have all their own rules, too—crazy) refers to the fact that there are five sets of iambic feet per line ("penta" means five), for a total of ten syllables.

I have never tried my paw at sonnets. Too tough for these claws. But, Jake is something of a master, so I'm leaving this one to him. Here's one of his traditional English sonnets:

My eyes and limbs have turned gray and blood-black;
My clothes, dirt-stained and dank, hang in tatters.
Though you may think my thoughts I surely lack,
You will soon see how that hardly matters.
For if a creature of darkness gives chase,
Doubtless you simply run and run some more,
Giving little thought to the time and place,
Let alone the existential what for
Of a zombie's inner machinations.
Rather, you'll think of viscera and veins,
And sharp teeth and undead vaccinations,
And gore and ghastlies and gut-wrenching pains.
For zombies walk to gnash your living flesh,
And we so much prefer it to be fresh.

Let's look at that one again with the rhythm of each line so you can more readily hear how the syllables thump out on that imaginary drum. Now, writing in perfect iambic feet is not so easy, so you'll also notice some improper iambic feet below. That's okay. Remember, poetry can break the rules every now and again. The point is to know what they are so you can spot them. I've also included the rhyme scheme to the right so you that can see it in action, too:

Dee   dah   dee   dah   dee   dah   dee   dah   deedah
My   eyes   and   limbs   have   turned   gray   and   blood-black;   A

Dee   dah   dee dah   dee   dah   dee   dah   dahdee
My   clothes,   dirt-stained   and   dank,   hang   in   tatters.   B

Dee   dah   dee   dah   dee   dah   dee   dahdee   dah
Though   you   may   think   my   thoughts   I   surely   lack,   A

Dee   dah   dee   dah   dee   dah   deedah   dahdee
You   will   soon   see   how   that   hardly   matters.   B

Dee   dah   dee   dahdee   dah   dahdee   dee   dah
For   if   a   creature   of   darkness   gives   chase,   C

Dee   dah   dee   dahdee   dah   dee   dah   dee   dah
Doubtless   you   simply   run   and   run   some   more,   D

Dahdee   deedah   dah   dee   dee   dah   dee   dah
Giving   little   thought   to   the   time   and   place,   C

Dee   deedah   dee   dahdeedahdee   dee   dah
Let   alone   the   existential   what for   D

Dee   dee   dahdee   dahdee dahdeedahdee
Of   a   zombie's   inner   machinations.   E

Dahdee   dee   dah   dee   dahdeedah   dee   dah
Rather,   you'll   think   of   viscera   and   veins,   F

Dee   dee   dah   dee   deedah   dahdeedahdee
and   sharp   teeth   and   undead   vaccinations,   E

Dee   dah   dee   dahdee   dee   dah dahdee   dah
and   gore   and   ghastlies   and   gut-wrenching   pains.   F

Dee	*dahdee*	*dah*	*dee*	*dah*	*dee*	*dahdee*	*dah*	
For	zombies	walk	to	gnash	your	living	flesh,	G

Dee	*dah*	*dee*	*dah*	*deedah*	*dee*	*dah*	*dee*	*dah*	
And	we	so	much	prefer	it	to	be	fresh.	G

Phew. Look at that. Even a master like Jake Spearo really struggled to make those syllabic pairs work together the way they're supposed to. Can you imagine how hard it would be for a wolf like me? As I'm sure you can imagine, all these rules tend to turn a few stomachs after a while. I mean, some of us are rebels. Some of us really do like to run wild under the light of a full moon, and that's why free verse was born. Simply put, free verse ain't got no rules. It's poetry that does what it wants, when it wants. Lines can rhyme or not. They can be long or short. They can have as many syllables and as many lines as needed. It is open to different syllable structures, line breaks, images, and rhyming patterns. In short, it can be structured however the writer wants.

Now, I know you are probably wondering, "how is free verse different than an essay, article, or story?" You might remember someone calling that type of writing "prose," right? Prose is writing, exposition, or composition that has no rhythm, no meter, and limited imagery. The point is to get something across—something, perhaps, that is a little less emotional and a little more lengthy. On the other paw, poetry is different from other types of writing in that it allows us to be very descriptive and say meaningful things in few words. (Not that poetry has to be short. *Paradise Lost* by John Milton contains more than 10,000 individual lines of verse. At the other end of the spectrum is what is considered the shortest poem ever written and contains just a title and one word. Titled "I" with the single word "Why?" as the poem, it was written by Charles Ghigna, also known to his followers as Father Goose.)

Free verse was perhaps started by writers who translated poetry that rhymed in one language into poetry or music which no longer rhymed when

Poetry certainly brings out romance, but it does nothing for halitosis. It smells like something died in your mouth.

configured into the new language; but it didn't become popular until Walt Whitman and Emily Dickinson, the supposed "mother and father" of rules-free poetic verse, came along a couple hundred years ago. Then it caught on like a zombie-virus epidemic.

As writers of fiction and non-fiction, we are told not to be overly verbose or descriptive in our writing (even if it worked for our wolf-like brethren, Mr. Kerouac and his ilk). But free verse poetry gives us the freedom to do exactly that. In fact, it not only gives us the freedom, but expects it. It forces us to give it all as quickly and as powerfully as possible. Take a look at the following prose example:

The feet of the woman, porcelain white like some ancient statue of a gargoyle, whispered like a winter wind wrapping its arms around the stately mansion in a cold embrace. She moved sleepily across the cerulean blue carpet, her ruby red lips parting like the gates of Heaven (or possibly Hell), to reveal razor-sharp fangs and I shuddered as if the angry storm that raged outside had found my weeping soul.

Not exactly the words one would want to use to begin the next great horror novel. It's beautiful language, but a bit slow for the high-tension, action-packed genre of horror. This might be embedded in a chapter, but it could be so much stronger as a poem. If we rearrange them and change them a little, the words and images become poetic:

Porcelain white,
Like the stone
of some ancient
gargoyle statue,
Her feet
appear from the mist.
They dance (with nearly
imperceptible
movement) Across
the cerulean blue
carpet.
I hold
my breath and
arch my neck in
supplication,
Welcoming
her fangs without
regret.

See? No rules about the overuse of adverbs or adjectives. Fewer rules about sentence structure or punctuation. Poetry is about creating a mood or a feeling first—grammar, mechanics, and function all come second in that dance.

Look at the new power given to the words at the line breaks. Now, it is important that you understand how to read a poem before you can fully grasp the new power those words convey. When reading a poem, it's not cool to pause—even to take a breath—simply because there is a line break. Instead, you pause as you normally would when reading these lines as sentences, at all the stops created by punctuation, such as the commas after "white" or "statue," or the period after "mist." But you would not pause after "stone" because there is no reason to. That is, the break does not indicate a pause in recitation—only in the movement of the eye across the page.

Having said that, look at the new line breaks. It almost creates a poem in itself to look at only the words that end the lines. William Shakespeare was a master at this phenomenon and I learned this trick from reading his plays and sonnets. If you simply take the last word from each line and stack it up in a column, you can see the meaning the poem or verses are meant to convey.

> white
> stone
> ancient
> statue
> feet
> mist
> nearly
> imperceptible
> across
> blue
> carpet
> hold
> and
> in
> supplication
> welcoming
> without
> regret

Do you hear this more clearly now?

"White stone ancient statue" now becomes a living being whose "feet mist"—or, who treads lightly on the ground like a fog, or perhaps she has the vampire ability to turn into mist as Dracula did? She is "nearly imperceptible." (A ghost? An apparition?) "Across blue carpet"—she's moving quietly. Calmly, as "blue" invokes a sensation (mood or feeling) of calm. "Hold and in supplication"—you pause and then move as if you are in prayer and making an offering. "Welcoming without regret"—offering yourself to this ancient statue without remorse. No looking back. The line breaks create this power—a power prose cannot fathom.

Poetry works much the same way as music, which any werewolf can tell you is the inner language of the soul. After all, music soothes the savage beast, does it not? It moves us. It makes us happy or sad. It makes us think or reminisce. It tugs at our shirts (or possibly our tails) and pulls us along for the ride. It is not only the meaning of the words, but their placement and sound as well.

The structure of each line and each individual word make all the difference in the world. A bullet lodging itself in the stomach or chest of a zombie has little impact. A well-placed shot to the brain is another story. Not that I would want to off any of my zombie friends, even if they do go around eating some of my neighbors. Hey, at least they leave us dogs alone. Now, we split-dogs at Uneeda Medical Supply; well, that's a different story. Same goes for the poor pups at Umbrella Corporation, but I digress.

Back to poetry. Look carefully at the next example. Read each one the way you would read a poem or a paragraph in a book and consider which works better. Think about the line breaks and the power or emphasis the line breaks put on certain words or images. Think about the movement or flow (or musical rhythm of each piece):

A wooden cross, bleached skeleton white by the desert sun,
stretches toward the sky as if seeking a life of its own.
It is only the weight of a feather from a soaring hawk,
conquering a hundred years of existence that causes the marker to topple
without complaint as it too finds its final resting place in the dust and dirt.

Now the same poem structured differently:

A wooden cross,
bleached
skeleton white
by the desert
sun, stretches
toward the sky
as if seeking
a life of its own.
It is only the weight

of a feather
from a soaring
hawk, (conquering a hundred
years of existence)
that causes the marker
to topple
without complaint
as it too
finds its final resting
place in the dust,
dirt
and sand.

If you consider the way the former example works, with its longer lines and short line breaks ("sun," "own," "hawk," "topple," "dirt"), it almost reads more as a ballad, a rock opera from the 1970s. It's longer and clunkier, and it puts emphasis on the storytelling aspect more than the individual images. Also, because of the lengthier lines, less energy is given to movement. The poem stagnates a bit, almost like the skeleton stagnates and bleaches in the hot desert sun year after year, dust storm after dust storm.

The latter poem moves more quickly. It breaks differently ("cross," "bleached," "white," "desert," "stretches," and so on). It puts more energy into movement and thus the scene flickers by more quickly in the mind's eye. You can see the skeleton as if sped up on a high-speed camera, as dust collects on it and it sinks deeper into the golden sand.

In truth, both poetic structures work. The question is really, what are you trying to accomplish? What is more important—movement or

Poetry feeds the soul, but trick-or-treaters still expect candy. (The exception, of course, might be Michael Meyers.)

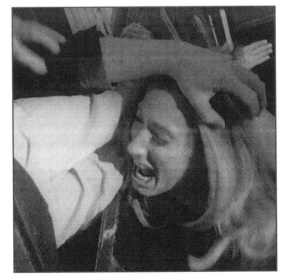

stagnation? What mood are you trying to convey? What feeling do you want to leave the reader with?

Two of the most important things to consider when writing mood or feeling are lines and stanzas. You can think of a line as part of a sentence. It is the point at which you feel (in your gut or soul or whatever you have left after the zombie invasion) a line must end. It might simply be one word. It might be a complete sentence. Or anything in between.

Each line break gives readers time to digest what they have just read. It means that "the line you have just read deserves its own thought and reflection" before you move on to the next line. It affects the sound of the poem whether you read aloud or in your head. It also affects the "speed" of a poem as our eyes automatically pause at the end of a line. The "speed" of a poem is also, of course, affected by

The length of the lines in your poem affects the white space and how your creation looks on the page. These shapes can say as much as the words themselves. Poems written with specific shapes are called (you guessed it) shape poems.

the length of each line. Short lines, for example, may seem to make a poem read faster when the opposite can sometimes be true simply because of the inclination to pause after each line regardless of its length.

The length of the lines of your poem also affects the white space and how your creation looks on a page. Is it inviting? Is it like the sight of blood to a thirsty vampire? And, don't forget, words placed at the ends of your lines are very important—the line break gives those words special emphasis. Take care where you end lines and pause thoughts.

Stanzas group lines together, and how many stanzas you have depends on the style of poetry you're writing. A stanza is kind of like a paragraph in poetic form. It isn't quite the same—that is, it may not expound an entirely new or unique topic in one chunked section—but it will serve to remind you that line breaks are the ends of each line and then the white space that sometimes appears between lines are stanzas. The number or length of the stanzas you have is not important unless you are constructing a particular style of poetry.

Another thing that separates poetry from prose is not only the amount of words you use, but the impact and importance of those words as well. Be stingy with your words when writing poetry. Do not only take into consideration whether a word is needed, but the impact of that word. Don't water it down with words until it is weak and boring. Use words that touch the soul. Use words that make use of the five senses.

By the same token, some of the best poems go far beyond the five senses, uniting all into metaphor or figurative language. A metaphor is a comparison made between two seemingly unlike things using a form of the verb "to be." A simile, another form of figurative language, is the same type of comparison using the construct of "like" or "as." In the book *The Curious Incident of the Dog in the Night-Time* by Mark Haddon (yes, I read about other dogs. I'm not completely self-absorbed, you know. I can even play "My Dog Has Fleas" on the piano and recite "This Old Man" from memory—probably because I like the part where he gives a dog a bone. Although, we werewolves prefer a little meat on the bone. Anyway . . .), Christopher, the main character, suggests that similes are the truth, whereas metaphors are lies. Take the following example:

The blood that streamed down her neck was the River Lethe. Her life flowed out of her in a steady stream of forgetting.

This is metaphorical language. The word "was" in the first sentence is a form of the verb "to be" (past tense). Her blood *was* the Lethe. To use Christopher's example, this is not, strictly speaking, the "truth." That is, her blood is not a river, nor is it specifically the Lethe River of Greek mythology that causes dead souls to forget their mortal lives as they cross into the netherworld. The use of the metaphorical form, however, is powerful. It plunges the reader directly into the fray, forcing him or her to face the image head on. It doesn't come at it sideways, as with a simile. Let's look at the same example in simile form:

The blood that streamed down her neck was like the River Lethe. Her life flowed out of her as a steady stream of forgetting.

In this example, the blood is now "like" the River Lethe (rather than actually *being* the river). In this way, it is the "truth" that Christopher suggests. Anything can be *like* something else—it can be *similar to it* (hence the root of that word, "simile")—without making the object into an entirely new thing. In this example, the blood is only similar to a river, and the life flows out of her *like* a stream of forgetting.

In poetry, figurative language allows the reader to experience the image or feeling from a different vantage point. The comparison allows the reader to be transported into the moment through another lens, causing a different (and sometimes more authentic) set of feelings or mood to transpire. Unfortunately, unclear or even mixed metaphors can have the opposite effect on your reader than you intend. For example, if I create a comparison between the blood on the victim's neck and, say, the image of ice cream melting over a child's chin in the summer, the result is a completely different mood than I intended.

The blood streamed down her neck like ice cream drooling over a child's chin. Her life flowed out of her like melting threads of chunky chocolate cream.

In this example, the reader now thinks of the woman's bloody neck as a child's ice cream treat. This might be fine if I want the reader to feel like the blood is a dessert food or if I am attempting some humor here. But if I intended for the reader to feel sorrowful for this woman whose life is being drained by a vampire, the metaphor of ice cream makes it comical, changing the mood entirely.

And mood naturally brings us to emotion and its place in poetry. If a poem doesn't bring us to some kind of emotional response, whether in the form of a laugh or a tear, it has not done its job. You might be able to run the hundred-yard dash in ten seconds, but if you can't reach that abandoned grocery store half a mile away, well, the zombies are going to have you for dinner. It is not the race that counts, but the "getting there" part.

If you don't bring emotion (and words that feed upon that emotion) to the table, the meal will be sparse and your reader empty. It is not easy in this day and age to be able to touch the soul of another human being, but that is the goal of every poet. So, as you can see, poetry is simple and complex at the same time. I suggest that you simply caress a lot of necks, taste a variety of blood types, and then go with the flow.

I'll leave you with a parting example of free verse from my axe-girlfriend, Sally Plot. We parted ways a few years back when her heart turned to another man, and all the skin on her face clean rotted off—not that that I had anything to do with it, of course. I've dated plenty of faceless weirdos. Even faceless ladies need love too. Right?

Do not think
I underestimate your
numbers.
Countless hours
tallying
each bite, each
gummy, gooey
grit of flesh.
For every one
I eat, one
rises up to eat
another.
And so, into
the corner
we paint ourselves
with blood.
For if I eat
you, and you,
so infected,
rise to eat

others—how many
hours before
we have no
more people
to eat?
It is a question
of population control
governed by
appetite.
Turn a blind
eye, lifeless,
and keep gnawing
on the bones.
Numbers.
Do not bother
me with numbers.
We zombies
are not so unfamiliar, then
to your way
of life.

Writing Prompts for Chapter 3

1. Write a free verse poem (in which there are no rules) about a cannibal.

2. Write your best undead haiku featuring either a vampire, mummy, or werewolf.

3. Write a limerick about a necromancer. Aim for thirteen stanzas.

4. Write a love sonnet from a vampire to zombie (or any other unlikely romantic couple).

Writing Exercises for Chapter 3

1. **Syllables:** Take a paragraph from a piece of prose you have written (prose is basically anything that doesn't have a clear rhythm or rhyme—such as most essays, short stories, or novels). Look at the syllables of each word in the paragraph and write either a "dah" or "dee" above it to determine which syllables are stressed and unstressed. You may use a dictionary if you need help. After you've assigned sounds to each word, try to rearrange the words by the flow of sound. For now, don't pay attention to what the words mean—just the flow of syllables in the words. Read what you have out loud.

2. **Syllables:** Try dropping all of the "small words" from your new piece (prepositions, articles, and conjunctions, for instance) and see if you have a readable poem.

3. **Line Breaks:** Take a paragraph of prose and randomly break the lines to form a poem. Rearrange the lines to form new poems. Pay careful attention to how breaking lines in different places changes meaning.

4. **Mood:** Take a lesson from Edgar Allen Poe and develop your next poem in reverse order. That is, rather than write out the poem, start with a mood and write a poem around that. Generate a list of words that you relate to a certain mood ("terror," "joy," "loathing," or "depression," to name a few possible "moods"). Treat this exercise like a game of word association and only list words that genuinely spark that mood inside you, whether by the sounds within the word (like the famous "cellar door") or the word definitions themselves. Then, craft a poem using only these words.

5. **Emotion**: Find a piece of writing that has a strong impact on you, such as a favorite passage or poem. Freewrite about the emotional impact of this piece of writing. Try to pay attention to word choice, rhythm, the sound of language, and the mood created by the piece.

6. **Rhyming:** "Alliteration" is when the beginning sounds of words are repeated, such as in "vapid vampire vixens." Write a poem that uses alliteration. For example, you might write a line for each letter of the alphabet—do your best to *only* use words beginning with that letter for each line.

—4—

NARRATIVE WRITING

or

Are You My Mummy?

This chapter was penned posthumously by none other than the late, great Tutankhamen, pharaoh of Egypt during the 18th dynasty, awakened from his supernatural slumber by Howard Carter. The opening of this ancient king's tomb unleashed a terrible curse that swept through the media like a monsoon. A confirmed victim included one financial backer for the archaeological dig: Lord Carnarvon. Unconfirmed victims of the curse included Carter's pet canary and Carnarvon's dog. With odds like that, there can be no doubt that Tutankhamen was a zombie bent on the destruction and digestion of the living. We knew about the curse of Tut's tomb, right enough. What horror writer hasn't heard of the dreaded canary killing?! What we did not know was that Tutankhamen was a prolific posthumous writer. We suppose the pharoah's penchant for wordsmithery is only natural, though, considering Egyptians (and their neighboring Sumerians) were the first to establish systems of written language. That gave Ol' Tut a few extra millennia to practice (we are positively green with envy). We include his preserved words on best practices of narrative writing here, for your learning pleasure. Just beware: all ye who read these words best sell your canaries now, before it is too late.

I'D LIKE TO tell you a story. Now, you probably don't want to hear it, but I'm going to tell it anyway. That's what I do. Some call them tall tales. Some call them fiction. And although fiction certainly falls into the category of narrative writing, I'm telling you nothing but the facts today. Call these tales what you want—whether you think they are a yarn, an anecdote, or myth, so be it. For my story should have you all wrapped up in a matter of mere moments.

I shall never forget the moment Howard Carter awakened me from my immortal slumber—when he pierced the stony confines of my tomb and found me bound in flax fibers embedded in the gold and lapis sarcophagus created by my devoted servants. The year was 1922 and an eon's tide of sand had lapped against my tomb, hiding it from mortal view for more than three thousand years. But it did not matter; magic does not dissipate with age like the sandy banks of the Nile erode into the sparkling waters. Oh, no. Three thousand years were not enough to push aside my curse.

I was awake.

Fortunately for Carter, my master plan did not actually involve the brutal torture and mummification of him or the members of his excavation crew. The curse that reanimated my brittle bones and dry, husky flesh also reawakened my brain. Granted, my brain had been removed with a hook and discarded like a sack of asps in a lady pharaoh's bedroom, but I still could think for myself, dang it. If your scarecrow could do it, why not a great and powerful mummy? Pay no attention to the man behind the bandages. Ha!

Anyway, I still had my heart, and that's all one needs to become a prolific writer in the twenty-first century. Well, that, a stable Internet connection, and maneuverable digits. That can occasionally be a problem for a mummy, what with the dried finger joints and mitten-like bandage wraps. But any real writer will tell you that it

> **If a mummy with dried fingers joints and bandaged hands can find the will to write, then what is your excuse?**

takes a lot more than a few thousand years of decay and a desiccated brain to deter you from the desire—no, the *compulsion*—to write. I wasn't going to let a few semantics stop me from pursuing my passion. Duat no! Those ideas can go straight to Duat and stay there. I'd given up my dreams of becoming a scribe when I was told I'd have to become a pharaoh (and probably die a tragic death as a result). Having found myself resurrected, there was no way I would let that dream slip through my bandage-wrapped clutches again.

And that's how I came to be here, writing this narrative of narratives for you. Consider me your own personal mummy, here to inform you about everything you'll need to know to weave a good narrative on the papyrus of your choosing.

Let's start by defining what a narrative is. In my time, we didn't have a lot of what you would call true narratives. The majority of our writing was ideographic, not alphabetic, meaning that we told our history and passed along our knowledge using pictures. There was no clear point of view in such instances.

One could never tell if Amenhotep, for instance, was telling his own history as he chiseled away at the stone wall, or if Amenhotep's servants were doing it. Language has come a long way since then—as has technology. After all, we didn't have computers—at least not like the ones you are enjoying today—and our writing was done on walls and scrolls, easily erased from history by the sands of time or a few well-placed fires. Ah, the library at Alexandria—what a loss that was! If we could have preserved some of that knowledge, you'd all be playing Senet on Mars right now. How's that for a point of view?

But I digress. Modern-day point of view most frequently refers to the perspective one uses when creating a text. First person (or first mummy) perspective would involve the use of "I" statements. Sometimes, such as when writing an academic or observational essay in which the writer seeks to explore a topic through passive observation (like, watching a crocodile fell a lion in the Nile), the perspective is an invisible "I." That is, the observer isn't part of the narrative—the reader just assumes the observer is watching the events even though the writing never says "me," "myself," or "I."

Second-person perspective refers to the use of "you" statements. While it may seem odd that a mummy might want to write a narrative using the term "you" (and not "I"), consider the many purposes of using "you." For one thing, it allows the reader to step inside your life for a moment. "You arose from your tomb and dusted off the yellow grains of sand that had settled on you over the course of the night, careful not to tear at the tender threads of your bandages." Now, the reader is transported inside your perspective, able to see things through your eyes and experience things your way.

The caveat—though I hate to use a *Roman* word . . . bastards—is that "you" can alienate a reader. If a reader feels or reads something in the second person perspective that is too far removed from his or her experience, it can make them feel disconnected or angry. Not a good thing if you are writing a narrative in the hopes of soliciting some sympathy from the mortal coil to, for example, discontinue the practice of unwrapping my mummy brethren at your speakeasy parties just so you can gather up the scarabs and trinkets that fall from his bandages. Mummies are people, too. Sort of.

Third-person perspective refers to the use of "he," "she," or "it" to narrate a passage. This is most often used by biographers and journalists describing subjects of

Perspective is very important for narrative writing, but don't get too wrapped up in just one viewpoint. Experimenting is a good thing as long as your heart and brain remain intact. If only the Egyptians had kept a canopic jar for the brains they hooked out of my nose. Sigh.

an interview or study, or observational essayists who are observing animate creatures or objects. I don't recommend you use third-person when narrating a personal event unless, like me, you are the immortalized undead son of the God Osiris and, as this esteemed god Horus, you are almighty. Because, if you are not almighty, there's a big chance your readers will think you are putting on airs.

> **The perspective you choose when writing a narrative is only part of "the story."**

The perspective you choose to use when writing a narrative is only part of the story. There are also different reasons why or when narratives are the logical genre in which to write. A personal narrative, or a story about your own life or memory, would most logically require you to write in an engaging voice using first-person perspective to narrate the events of your life or the memory of your life you choose to share.

A fictional account told from the perspective of a character or characters (whether first, second, or third) most likely will require narration to carry the reader through the story clearly. A biographical narrative, which tells the story of a real living (or undead) person other than yourself, uses third-person perspective and is somewhere between an informative essay and an observational one. And narrative essays, personal philosophies, experiential reflections, journal entries, or dramatic monologues all typically necessitate the narrative form.

Ah, I remember my youth: "My salad days, when I was green in judgment" (Shakespeare, *Antony and Cleopatra*, I:5) had me writing stories that were all over the place, mixing genres and metaphors. Now, I'm a much more mature writer, even if I had to die in order to develop that mature voice in my narrative form. Then again, what is there but quiet reflection when one is shut inside a vacuum-sealed tomb for three millennia?

Speaking of three millennia, the foundations of good narratives are roughly as old as that. I remember when the first narrative came out. I camped overnight outside the local sesh's house to get my papyrus-back copy. Of course, *The Tale of Sinuhe* had little on the original Cinderella story—"Rhodopis," which came out a few centuries later—but hey, I found it positively riveting. A real papyrus-turner.

So what are the foundations of good narratives like *The Tale of Sinuhe*? The same as the foundations of good fiction, of course: setting, characters, conflict, plot, climax, and resolution. Even if the story is true, your readers need to see the location and time in which the narrative is set.

Characters, whether they are the machinery you observe (inanimate or personified), animals you watch, or people that you and others interact with, need to show us what they are like, how they function, and who they are—and that includes *your own character*, especially if you are a central part of the narrative. Conflict is necessary to keep a narrative going, and if you really think about it—no brain jokes there, guys—you'll see that the reason you were inspired to write this particular narrative in the first place is because there was some kind of conflict—perhaps a problem you overcame or a significant moment that changed your life. Narratives have to follow a progression of plot from beginning to end. Plot is just the order in which a story is told and how causes and effects work together. The climax is the moment when the reader gets really excited and has to know what happens next, and the resolution is the point when the reader feels like the story is complete. Narratives are stories. Stories are usually narratives.

Writing narratives and stories, as with any other genre, certainly requires some level of formula to pass the test. I'm not talking about an alchemical formula like those used by my mystical physicians, but a formulaic style of writing used to address certain "expectations" that the different types of narratives will conjure in your reader's minds. Consider it similar to a trip to your local grease peddler—I mean, fast food drive-thru. You know, we had fast food in Egypt too. Yeah. I'm serious. Greece had it, too. You think you're so special, don't you? With all your "new ideas." Well, aren't we full of ourselves.

Ahem. As I was pontificating—formulas as they apply to writing refer to the rhetorical situations that readers will come to expect when they read what you have to say. For instance, if you are writing a personal narrative about one of your own experiences, a reader would be confused if you referred to yourself in the third person. If you are writing a biography about another person (not yourself), the reader would also be confused if you referred to the subject in the first person. This is a simplified

version of some of the narrative formulas. To get you more in the oasis of that subject, let's consider some basic rules for each sub-genre of narrative writing.

If I only had a brain . . . I'd be much better at narrative writing.

After Carter "rescued me" from my tomb, I happened to make the acquaintance of one of the best ghost story tellers of all time. He soon became one of my best friends, and I was always captivated by his thrilling tales, only able to offer up my bits of bandage in return. Hardly a suitable story-telling trade, but he was a man generous with his tales. He once told me a story about his wild rides through a place called Sleepy Hollow. Every time he tells me that tale I feel like I'm right there with him scaring the guts and gizzards right out of people's canopic jars. Yep, old Brom Bones could certainly tell a tale. I've used selections from his story about Sleepy Hollow to assist you in seeing the points of writing a *personal narrative*:

Make sure you use a first person point-of-view (I, me, my, we, our).

*I recollect that, when a stripling, **my** first exploit in squirrel-shooting was in a grove of tall walnut-trees that shades one side of the valley. **I** had wandered into it at noon time, when all nature is peculiarly quiet, and was startled by the roar of **my** own gun, as it broke the Sabbath stillness around, and was prolonged and reverberated by the angry echoes.*

Make sure you focus on just one event or period of time. If you are writing a longer piece, simply divide it into appropriate chapters or scenes.

Such is the general purport of this legendary superstition, which has furnished materials for many a wild story in that region of shadows; and the spectre is known, at all the country firesides, by the name of the Headless Horseman of Sleepy Hollow.

See how Brom Bones offers an ability to shift into another area of history—either by back-peddling or "flashing back" to times when the "furnished materials" took place, the birth of the legends and superstitions?

Finally, make sure that you relate why the experience was important. If it was not important to you, it won't be important to your readers.

The dominant spirit, however, that haunts this enchanted region, and seems to be commander-in-chief of all the powers of the air, is the apparition of a figure on horseback without a head. It is said by some to be the ghost of a Hessian trooper, whose head had been carried away by a cannon-ball, in some nameless battle during the revolutionary war; and who is ever and anon seen by the country folk hurrying along in the gloom of night, as if on the wings of the wind.

Here, the author gets right to the meat of the matter. What made this significant to the writer? Why, the ghost of the Hessian trooper. Not only is the concept novel, engaging, and interesting to a reader, it is also clearly important to the writer or storyteller based on the powerful words and descriptions being used to portray the subject.

Now, you'll have to read the tale yourself if you want the rest of the facts as I don't have all day to tarry about with you. Seems there is this mad scientist who believes he can take control of my body and use me for his nefarious purposes. I must make a note to deal with this fool before Orion touches the night sky.

Now, where was I?

Ah, yes. So, that was a taste of a personal narrative. (Although I guess just to confuse things one might argue that it was biographical. Depends on whether or not you think old Brom was indeed the "headless horseman." Since I knew the man, I think I can claim some level of authority on the subject and declare that indeed, he was; thus, rendering the whole argument obsolete. Right?)

Moving on.

When writing a biographical narrative, you'll want to focus on a real event that happened to someone else. This focus should be less on the event and more on the individual about whom you are writing. Honest depictions of events are typically categorized as informative exposition, whereas people are narratives—that includes personified animals, such as Rudyard Kipling's work or virtually any animated children's special.

Remember these points when writing a *biographical narrative.*

I know I will always have your heart, Imhotep. It will remain in a jar on my nightstand forever.

Use a third person point-of view (he, she, him, her, they).

*The town folk thought Cruella a strange lady indeed. Especially when **she** started wearing those strange, Oreo-colored coats made from the fur of animals they could not quite recognize until they remembered recent episodes of* Animal Planet.

Study the event thoroughly. You need a firm grasp of the event to make it sound authentic. (If possible, an interview is a great means of investigating an event or a person's life. Sometimes you can interview a person by way of séance, should they no longer be in the realm of the living. I hear Kate and Margaret Fox still do house calls. Just have your table handy. Of course, I wouldn't try to pass off a séance-driven interview to a professor. The living find it so hard to believe, well, anything. As I was saying, make it sound authentic.)

> **It is important to remember that if you are writing about a moment or event that happened in your past, make sure it was important to *you*.**

It is understandable why the people near Mt. Rainer, Washington, thought local pilot Kenneth Arnold was seeing things in June of 1947. Of course, everyone now knows that it wasn't aliens that the man thought he encountered that day, but simply gargoyles flying south for the winter.

Note how the author used specific locations and a date. Do remember that if you are writing this as an academic paper, you would need to cite your source—that means that you would need to explain to the reader where you got your information by using a prescribed set of rules to show them. Generally, in academic writing, you cannot consider yourself an expert on something. For fun, though, or for entertainment, this serves quite nicely to illustrate the writer's knowledgeable stance on the subject.

Show the reader why this event was important. You might convey the importance of an event to the person you are writing about, or why the event was important to those around, whether it was something that happened a thousand years ago or yesterday. Significance can be defined by the writer and even the most mundane event (such as the time you found a dust bunny under your bed) can be made exciting to the reader if the writer can draw out tension and craft some showing details. (Get the ol' pulse racing. Funny how you miss little things like that and to know I'll never feel my pulse again.) At the same time, the snazzier events in your life will be more likely to inspire your readers. As such, the snippet of story below illustrates how powerful a simple story can be.

If it hadn't been for the little Dutch boy sticking his finger in the dike, the world as we know it would no longer exist. Little did mankind realize that the unwitting boy had, in fact, with his tiny finger, sealed a portal that would have opened up the gates of hell, unleashing the fury of demons and beasties and ancient ones, oh my.

Remember that if you are writing about a moment or event that happened in your past, make sure it was important to you. Talking about the time you dropped your ice cream cone in the midway at last year's carnival isn't too exciting. Chances are, it wasn't even exciting to you. (Unlike that dust bunny experience. I'm shaking in my bandages just thinking about that one.) If, however, you dropped your falafel (and that is not a euphemism, my friend) because you saw the Grim Reaper retrieving the soul of a clown behind the fortune-telling tent, then you have our attention. The goal of good writing in general, and especially of good narrative, is to get us excited and interested, or what we writerly types call "engaged." If *you* are not excited by what you write, why should we be?

Another way that you can engage your reader is to jump right into your narrative without hesitation. Get right to the action. It works every time. (Especially in this newfangled age of yours where everyone seems in such a hurry.) Don't muddy the Nile with long introductions and descriptive passages. As with any style of writing, get your reader's attention right from the start. Don't tell us that the clown had huge purple shoes on his feet, and bright orange hair that seemed like it was on fire and a stupid rubber nose that sounded like a gander at mating time. Get right to the point and let us know what scared you so much that your falafel is now lying on your shoes. In addition to all this excitement, you also need to make sure your story has a point. Sometimes the point is simply stressing or reiterating the value or significance it has to the reader in the first place. Sometimes the point is the plot, or the direction you plan to take the reader from point A to point B.

Sometimes the point is the destination and not the journey that

Sometimes when I write about myself, I just need a hug. Why do people always run away from me?

your words take (though, that is less likely). So ask yourself a few key questions: Why are you telling us this tale? Is it to warn us that the Grim Reaper actually exists? Is it to warn your kids not to grow up to be clowns? Is it to explain to the world why you should keep a firmer grip on your falafel? (Okay, maybe that one *is* a euphemism.)

Last but not least, use the showing language mechanisms so eloquently laid out by Sybil in her chapter on Fiction Writing. Engaging the five senses will bring life to your narrative for the reader by engaging their brains more fully in the text you have written. (Well, unless that reader had his brain hooked out through his left nostril by an Ancient Egyptian priest prior to mummification. Not that I'm bitter, or anything. Or does not irony still play a role in your modern languages?) Sensory data, or sensory details, causes different parts of *living* brains to fire, which will trigger a more favorable visceral response toward your writing in your reader. Consider what my old friend Brom Bones had to say in his Sleepy Hollow tale that engaged our senses.

Smell: Our sense of smell can conjure up strong olfactory memories, and some argue that this sense is the strongest when it comes to memory in the first place. Who can't remember the smell of your neighbor's rotting guts steaming on the sidewalk in the hot summer sun after the apocalypse of the undead? Or the last time you mowed your lawn, the scent of clipped grass mingling with the breeze? (Forget about that unfortunate frog that hopped into the mower's path. Of course, I am sure that you writers of horror can appreciate that image.) Or how about the smell of that feta cheese in your falafel? Sorry, back to our example:

> *However wide awake they may have been before they entered that sleepy region, they are sure, in a little time,* **to inhale the witching influence of the air**, *and begin to grow imaginative, to dream dreams, and see apparitions.*

Taste: Our sense of taste is strongly tied to our sense of smell, and the same words can often be used to describe either a smell or a taste. For instance, the gamey taste (or smell) of your zombie neighbor's rotting guts streaming on the sidewalk. Or the salty, stinky, sweet taste of feta cheese crumbling off your falafel. Or the tart and bitter taste of that splash of vinegar that wrinkled up your nose as it rolled over your tongue. Brom could make us taste and smell with ease.

> *In his devouring mind's eye, he pictured to himself* **every roasting-pig** *running about with a* **pudding** *in his belly, and an* **apple** *in his mouth; the* **pigeons were snugly put to bed in a comfortable pie**, *and tucked in with a* **coverlet of crust**; *the* **geese were swimming in their own gravy**; *and the* **ducks** *pairing cosily in dishes, like snug married couples, with a decent competency of* **onion sauce**.

Sight: This can be the trickiest sense to deliver because we often confuse what we see with what we interpret (what we "think" we see). In truth, the goal of good writing (and even good reading) is to generate a working image in our minds. (Those of us who *have them, anyway.* Thanks a lot, *Egyptian Book of the Dead.*) What we see is just the cold hard facts. What we interpret is the subjective meaning, the emotion, or the outcome of those cold hard facts. For example, the man slumped against the wall with his head dropped forward, his mouth open, and his tongue lolling out is more "sensory" than "the man was dead." Let's take another look at one of our earlier examples from my friend, Brom:

> *It is said by some to be the ghost of a Hessian trooper,* **whose head had been carried away by a cannon-ball,** *in some nameless battle during the Revolutionary War, and who is ever and anon seen by the country folk* **hurrying along in the gloom of night, as if on the wings of the wind.**

Sound: Sound is a sense that we most frequently invoke by using dialogue. We put dialogue into quotation marks and show what a person says in order to *hear their unique voices in our minds.* Other things, though, have sounds, too. There's this great scene in *Indiana Jones and the Temple of Doom* (which you should all purchase or stream immediately as it contains one of the most horrific culinary adventures in the history of cinema: the ingestion of that rare delicacy, monkey brains. Ah, there are those brains, again) in which Short Round (a child who works for Indiana Jones, the great archaeologist) is in a black room. The screen is dark and he says something about it feeling like he is walking on fortune cookies, which the audience hears in each resounding footfall, the crunch of what can only be fortune cookies or egg shells being smashed against the floor beneath the weight of his foot. When the lights come on, we learn that he is in fact walking on insects. Now back to the deceptively peaceful sounds of Sleepy Hollow:

> *A small brook glides through it, with just* **murmur enough to lull one to repose**; *and the occasional* **whistle of a quail** *or* **tapping of a woodpecker** *is almost the only* **sound that ever breaks** *in upon the uniform tranquility.*

Touch: Touch typically refers to the texture of an object or person against our skin, but it can be other parts of our bodies as well—the tongue, for instance (get your mind off the falafel). In addition to the sensation on our skin, touch also refers to the sensations we have within our bodies: the tensing of muscles, the hinging of joints, the course of food as we digest. Touch descriptions are typically the ones that will cause your reader to have a *physical reaction* to what you write. In horror, that usually means a wrinkling of the nose or a shudder that wracks the shoulders and chest.

> *As yet the panic of the steed had given his unskillful rider an apparent advantage in the chase, but just as he had got half way through the hollow, the **girths of the saddle gave way**, and he **felt it slipping** from under him. He **seized it by the pommel**, and endeavored to **hold it firm**, but in vain; and had just time to save himself by **clasping old Gunpowder** round the neck, when the saddle fell to the earth, and he heard it trampled underfoot by his pursuer.*

The sands are pouring through the hourglass rather swiftly it seems and I must bid my farewell at this point. That annoying mad scientist is attempting to bid me to act out his commands once again. Now where did I put my gilded sekhem scepter? A good bash on the head should suffice.

Writing Prompts for Chapter 4

1. Write a narrative between two and five pages about the most terrifying experience you've ever had. Use sensory detail to share the terror with your readers.

2. Write an observational narrative where you set yourself up in a public location and write about what you see happening around you. Be as realistic as possible, describing details without assigning your own interpretation to what is going on.

3. Write a 1-page narrative that develops a conflict, such as a difficulty you overcame or a significant moment in your life.

Writing Exercises for Chapter 4

1. **Perspective:** Take a memory from your own childhood. Something short that will span no more than a few pages of prose. Write the memory first from your own perspective. Now, write the memory in second person, turning all the actions of the main character onto whoever reads it—as though the reader is "you." Lastly, write the memory as though you are an omniscient being looking down on yourself as it unfolds. Use third person ("he" or "she") for this exercise and feel free to embellish details that perhaps you did not realize when you first experienced the event. Now look at the different perspectives. How are they different? Which one is the most interesting? Which one is the least? Why do you think that is?

2. **Biographical Narration:** Find a writing partner for this exercise. Begin by having a conversation with your partner about an important event in each of your lives. Really engage in this conversation, asking enough questions to ensure that you have a strong visual about what occurred during this event. Separate from one another and write out the narrative in the third person. Share the narrative with your partner. What was the reaction to your writing? Were you true to life, or did you embellish? How did your partner feel about that? Does that warrant revision on your part, or do you stand by what you wrote? If there were no hard feelings, what did your partner say you composed particularly well?

3. **Resolution:** Find two books or short stories that you've read. One should have a powerful ending, something you really enjoyed; the other should have a weak ending, something that annoyed you. Make a list of all the reasons why the one

ending was strong and the other was weak. Now, look at some of your own work. Using the list you just generated, determine which category (strong or weak) applies to your own stories.

4. **Showing and Telling:** Go outside and grab a handful of pebbles or rocks. Take them to your writing space and lay them out before you. Now, write a separate description for each rock being mindful to use enough detail that a stranger who has never seen any of your rocks would be able to use just your written description to identify which rock was which. Take this a step further and test it on a friend. How'd you do?

5. **Sensory Detail**: Choose an object that is meaningful to you. List as many words as you can about that object using each sense one at a time. For example, you could begin with "sight" (listing words that describe how the object looks) then words for "touch" (words about its texture, etc.). If this object appeared in a narrative, how would you choose to describe it? What kinds of sensory detail (and which words) best capture this object?

— 5 —

WRITING MEMOIRS

We actually received three fantastic submissions for this chapter that were all so good, we couldn't decide between them. As a result, we agreed to include all three. Each has a different spin on the importance of memoirs and different strategies to incorporate when writing them. That's why we included them all. It has nothing to do with the death threats. No. Ha. Nothing at all.

MEMOIRS OF A VAMPIRE

or

Oh, What a Tangled Vein We Bleed

When Contessa Ellspeth Draconia wrote to us to inquire about our need for a chapter on memoir writing, we were hesitant at first. It is well known that the Contessa has a taste for the inspired blood of writers, and working with such a cutthroat was a little more than we thought we could handle (even with a small armory of garlic, holy water, and hand-whittled stakes). But, when Draconia told us she would bring with her two of her dearest friends, Zombie X and the world-renowned Frankenstein's monster, we decided to take the risk. They each wrote such compelling and original spins on the process of memoir writing that we devoted three distinct sections in this chapter to encompass each of their voices. A memoir, after all, is a narrative of memory—who better to write of memory than the undead? The Contessa's unlife certainly has been memorable. See for yourself.

I KNOW WHAT you're thinking. And not simply because I can read your mind, either.

You're thinking: *Sure, it's easy for vampires to write memoirs. Not only have you tasted the very best humankind has to offer in the ways of experience, most of you have a couple hundred years you can talk about—heck, some of you much more than that.*

But most of us have not kept journals (damning evidence one might say, though many argue damnation to be a given) and even though we might vividly recall the taste of Attila the Hun's scorpion-spiked blood at his bitter end, few of us would remember it in detail. (Although I do recall the mild nausea related to sopping up the steel-skinned warrior's blood through the spigot-like blood-pour from his nose on the man's wedding night. What a way to go.)

So, if you have kept a journal, you might have a head start upon deciding to write your memoirs. But sometimes it makes the task harder if you have too much information. It is not always an easy thing to take the pages of your journal and turn them into a format that is readable and enjoyable to others. Yes, you may have paid a visit to your doctor ten years ago to make sure the dog bite wasn't from a mad dog or a werewolf, mangy beasts that they are. But that does not make it an interesting thing to write about. (Unless it really was a werewolf, of course, in which case you have no business being in the company of vampires.)

The first thing you need to remember in writing your memoirs is that it needs to be interesting to people other than yourself. Now this might be an easy thing to do if you recall how you were turned into a vampire by Lon Chaney while sitting in the make-up chair for a scene in *The Hunchback of Notre Dame*, but maybe not so easy if you have been a file-wielding clerk or wrench-twirling mechanic for the past forty years with little variation in routine during that time. After all, the public wants to read about lion-tamers, not accountants, right? But we all have a story to tell. And you don't have to be a vampire to make it an interesting tale.

The second thing to remember is that "the story" should be about yourself whether you are a vampire or an accountant. It is easy to forget the story is *your* story and although Uncle Bob, cousin Jimmy, or Attila the Hun played important roles, this is not *their* story.

Your perfume is exquisite, my dear. Is that burlap and blood larvae I smell? Blood pudding essential oil? Hmmm. With a base note of AB-Negative pulsating from your veins. Delicious!

Of course, then it all comes down to where do you start?

The simple answer seems to be at the beginning. However, since that would be the first answer a zombie might give, you know there's probably more to the story, so to speak. The truth is, there is really no correct place to start if you plan on writing your memoirs. There is no beginning—at least for the moment. After all, we vampires have one beginning in this mortal coil only to be baptized in blood, risen as new creatures. Which beginning, then, should we take? Follow Louis's or Lestat's lead in Anne Rice's interviews? Louis's road of the troubled soul whose mortal breath is tragically lost to him, or the road of Lestat, a vampire born only to be a vampire?

Either way, the important thing to do (as with any type of writing) is to just get started. If you have not kept a journal, there are two basic ways to begin writing your memoirs. The first is to think about an important incident in your life and then to just sit down and write as much as you can recall about the incident. If you are stuck on how to get started, remember that there is always time to change the tale later. Give yourself permission to write a terrible first draft to take the pressure off, then go back and edit and revise once the ink is dry.

Let's say that the incident you wish to write about is the time you were attacked by a werewolf during a full moon. You are likely to recall much of what happened even if it occurred 20 years ago. Your first kiss, while it may have been a milestone in your life, might not be as memorable—you may not remember as much about it as you think you do and perhaps it is not even worth mentioning. One sure way to determine if it *is* worth mentioning is to write and test it. That is, write the story and then deliver it to a friend or a fellow writer and ask for their honest opinion. Is it noteworthy? Does it interest them as much as you thought it would?

A second recommendation is not to sit down and write about any one memory, but rather create a list of events that happened in your life that you recall off the top of your head. Now this may seem like a daunting task, but it is still much easier than fighting off that werewolf. And the cool thing is that one memory usually triggers another. When you feel you have listed as many memories as you can, set the list aside for a couple of days. But have it handy because now that you jogged those synapses in your brain, you are going to start remembering more and more events.

I once drank the blood of a school teacher who'd taught his students how to write their memoirs. Burke was his name, I believe. After I'd drained him, I found myself curiously intrigued by his belongings and set about examining the contents of his pockets. In his satchel, he had a curious stack of papers from his students, each awaiting his sage grading. Upon careful inspection, I saw that each page was a life line, like the ones that track the erratic heart beats of critical patients. Only, instead of tracking heartbeats, the lines were annotated with events that occurred in the student's life, the spikes above a baseline indicating positive and exciting events while the spikes below the baseline indicated negative or tragic events. I found the idea quite compelling and thought I might demonstrate one for myself. You can see it here:

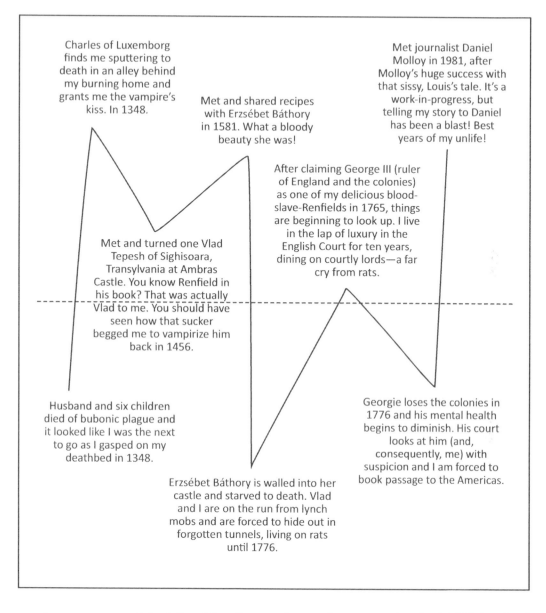

Charles of Luxemborg finds me sputtering to death in an alley behind my burning home and grants me the vampire's kiss. In 1348.

Met and shared recipes with Erzsébet Báthory in 1581. What a bloody beauty she was!

Met journalist Daniel Molloy in 1981, after Molloy's huge success with that sissy, Louis's tale. It's a work-in-progress, but telling my story to Daniel has been a blast! Best years of my unlife!

After claiming George III (ruler of England and the colonies) as one of my delicious blood-slave-Renfields in 1765, things are beginning to look up. I live in the lap of luxury in the English Court for ten years, dining on courtly lords—a far cry from rats.

Met and turned one Vlad Tepesh of Sighisoara, Transylvania at Ambras Castle. You know Renfield in his book? That was actually Vlad to me. You should have seen how that sucker begged me to vampirize him back in 1456.

Husband and six children died of bubonic plague and it looked like I was the next to go as I gasped on my deathbed in 1348.

Erzsébet Báthory is walled into her castle and starved to death. Vlad and I are on the run from lynch mobs and are forced to hide out in forgotten tunnels, living on rats until 1776.

Georgie loses the colonies in 1776 and his mental health begins to diminish. His court looks at him (and, consequently, me) with suspicion and I am forced to book passage to the Americas.

As you can see, this style of timeline can be used to categorize the highlights (and low-lights) of your pitiful existence into a memoir of sorts. It should help you eliminate the extraneous fluff from your story, or the parts that are unlikely to arouse the interest of your readers. After all, your purpose is to really hone in on what matters.

What do you mean you lead a dull life? So what if you were never attacked by a vampire? The thing to remember is that we all have things in common. Good things, bad things—it doesn't matter. When some stranger picks up your memoirs and reads about the time you were nine and spent the night in a graveyard on a dare from your friends, they are likely to recall a similar event in their own lives. It is this connection between human beings (as well as the undead) that makes us sympathetic when we hear the bad things that happen to people or resonate when we hear about the good things. Indeed, it is this very connection that makes memoirs a popular genre amongst the living and undead. There's a reason why memoirs are selling like hot bloodcakes. Everyone wants to feel connection—even the dead. Not that the undead feel much sympathy towards you or your neighbor, but you get the idea.

Also remember that there is a difference between writing your memoirs and writing your biography. Usually, a biography (or autobiography) tells the story of someone's entire life, while a memoir is about one event, episode, or span of time. For example, you might not need to mention the fact you were born in 1695 in a Transylvanian castle unless it is important to your memoir. You don't need to talk about your sessions with the mad scientist who claimed his electro-shock treatments would cure you of your

> **Unless you were born in 1695 in a Transylvanian castle and not on a farm in Kansas, the time and date of your birth may not play an important role in you memoirs.**

vampirism. (Or that you clearly recall that his blood type was B-Negative.) Maybe the summer of 1967 was the best time of your life and that is all you want to write about. It is not necessary that you begin your memoirs with your birth (like you remember anything about that) and end it with the day you publish your book. You can cover one summer or sixty years. It is your story after all.

But you do need a plan.

What do you want to write about and why would someone be interested in reading it other than family members? Maybe you want to write a memoir about your travels to Transylvania or the Bermuda Triangle and nothing else. Maybe you want to talk about the time Satan spent the summer living in your basement. The choice is yours.

Stephen King once said, "I write to find out what I think." The miracle of this is that sometimes you don't know what you think until you write it down.

Now you also need to consider the all-important question: do I need to worry about hurting someone's feelings? Well, if your Aunt Kitty is half-werecat, perhaps she does not want this secret revealed to the world. (Especially your local animal control unit.) But this is your book and you are the one that has to make the final decisions about the people that helped mold your life into a form that is worth putting down on paper. You might also be surprised at how reasonable some relatives can be even if they do enjoy playing catch with the urn containing great-grandma's ashes at family reunions.

But you must confront the truth. If you do not, then you are simply writing a novel. That being said, it must be real, but it should read like fiction. It might be your personal story, but you still must make the reader want to turn the next page to see if you made it through that night in the local cemetery or whether you went home and simply pretended you did. It doesn't matter which event happened. They are both good tales if you tell them right.

You should also decide what voice you want to use. Do you want to use your knowledge and voice as an adult to reflect on things in your childhood or do you want to portray those events through the eyes of the child you were? Whichever method you choose, you must grab the reader's attention. For example:

> *I attended first grade in a small town in Kansas.*

If you are not already yawning, it is only because it is your life. Everyone else is likely nodding off at this point.

Let's try it again.

> *I wasn't afraid when I stepped into class the first time I attended school. Until the teacher glared at me with one evil eye, the other hidden behind a black patch. My simple life in a small Kansas town would never be the same.*

Whether you are writing fiction or non-fiction, it is still the hook that captures your audience and keeps them wanting more.

Also, as others have previously recommended, use all of your senses when you write, whether it is fiction, poetry or, yes, even your memoirs.

Taste: Lick your lips and imagine the taste of the many blood samples sitting in storage at the local blood bank. The familiar taste of O-Positive. The exquisite rarity of AB-Negative.

Smell: Close your eyes and breathe in the delightful musk of innocent teens sitting around the campfire at youth camp. Yum!

Sound: Hear the scream of the innocent young virgin ready for sacrifice at the altar of demon worshippers. (Some of whom are probably members of your local PTA.)

Sight: See the mindless humans who run in terror as you lumber after them in an unsteady but relentless shamble, thinking they are smarter than the average zombie.

Touch: Feel the rough timbers of the ancient ship as your serpent-like tentacles crush it and pull the capsized craft beneath the waves.

My final advice? Think small. Think episodes, not tomes of history.

And remember, memoirs are not your personal recollection of historical events. It has nothing to do with the fact we landed on the moon. It has everything to do with where you were and what your thoughts were on that day. It is the things *we* remember because they were important to *us*.

Enough of my ramblings for now. Seems the fine vintage I have been sipping has left me somewhat inebriated. The blood of royalty will do that, you know. Or perhaps you didn't. Just a warning then, in case you have a lineage of kings or queens in your blood. Now that I think about it, I'm due for a blood bath. And some beauty rest, of course. Dawn is almost here.

I will now turn it over to an old friend who, alas, hardly recognizes me now. He is of the undead, but not lucky enough to have been reborn a vampire as was my fortune. He was, however, one of those lucky ones who retain a little brain matter that actually functions. Just ignore the decaying ear that is hanging on by a thread and the God-awful stench.

MEMOIRS OF A ZOMBIE
or
Nom, Nom, Nom

Zombie X wasn't much to look at or even talk to when he was alive. He was one of those anonymous types: a devoted bachelor working a middle class laborer job in the Midwestern United States, ordering pizza for dinner every night as he watched sports on television. But when the zombie horde broke into his rickety trailer and took a few bites out of his shoulder, it was like he was born again. It wasn't long before he was doing talk shows and ribbon-cutting ceremonies (and he found new and gruesome uses for those gigantic scissors, too). Now, he's a writer—and a powerful one at that. These are his words.

Some people incorrectly assume that zombies don't have memories. We are dead, after all, and we certainly don't behave as though we have any neurons firing across the memory centers of our gray matter. Our actions also fuel the perception that we are essentially bottomless pits hell-bent on assimilating the world to either become like us or become our food supply. (We actually care very little about the assimilation process—but we do love our brains, kidneys, and livers!) We never give up, we never stop chasing you, and we select our meals without discrimination. Doesn't matter if you're our grandmother or a serial killer—all that matters to us is that, right now, you are our meals on wheels. If we had our memories from life, surely we wouldn't eat our own grandmothers, right? Ask yourself that question just one more time. Maybe that's *why* we eat our grandmothers. Did you ever think of that? All the cheek-pinching and nose-tweaking? Totally justifies undead cannibalism, if you ask me.

Okay, okay. So maybe zombies don't have memories. Or maybe zombies have memories that are trapped inside like some mind-controlling parasite that allows your consciousness only to reside beneath the surface as you watch helplessly through your own eyes as you nibble away at your next door neighbor's ankle. All the more reason for us to get our memories down on paper now, don't you think? Before they are lost?

Because memoirs are narratives, they also follow the same rules that narratives follow—chiefly, they are written using the elements of a story. Only this time, that story is based in truth—your truth. That said, knowing that you need setting, characterization, conflict, plot, climax, and resolution to create a quality memoir can cause all sorts of anxieties in a person. The task of telling the story of your life from the day you were born on the kitchen table in the middle of the biggest hurricane your state has ever

> **You need setting, characterization, conflict, plot, climax, and resolution to create a quality memoir.**

seen right up to the point you were bitten by a patient in the emergency room plagued by the zombie death virus that made you the man you are today is an enormous one. In the National Public Radio's series, *All Things Considered*, William Zinsser suggested that this anxiety can cause writers never to pick up the pen in the first place and that the secret to overcoming this anxiety is to make decisions that reduce the enormity of the task. He suggests, for instance, that you choose to only write about one branch of the family, or leave out people in your history who don't need to be there for you to weave a good yarn.

Reducing the enormity of your memoir can also be accomplished by finding a starting place. Not all memoirs need to begin on the day you were born. Apart from prodigy, tragedy, and cases of abuse and neglect, most humans go through the same developmental milestones until they reach the age of three or so: learning to eat solid foods, learning to walk, and learning to stop putting everything they find on the floor directly into their mouths—a habit they'll pick up again when they contract the zombie death virus. So, do you really need to start the tale from the time you were a baby?

How about when you were five? Ten? Or, more importantly, how about the time a major life-altering incident occurred, like when your father started working for Umbrella Corporation when you were just six years old, or that Halloween you went trick-or-treating and thought all the ghouls walking about were just kids in costume—only to find out you were horribly wrong.

You can also reduce the hugeness of your writing task by eliminating some "unimportant scenes." Just like in the movies when the story flashes forward a few weeks, months, or years, allowing the movie viewer to assume that the characters were simply going about their everyday lives without anything really remarkable happening to them, this method works when writing your memoirs as well—particularly if you can create a connection for your reader between the last memory and the flash-forward memory. If you skip from the moment you were a normal kid playing kickball with your friends to the moment five years later when you were kicking the heads of your friends as if they were playground rubber balls before you picked them up and nibbled out their eyes, that might be enough for the reader to follow the thread of your thoughts.

To follow the thread of your thoughts—your memories—readers also need to feel transported into them. It is not enough to simply state that your mother walked into the room. Why? Because your readers don't know your mother. They can't see her, smell her perfume, nor relate to how she looks. You have to paint the picture of your mother that enables your reader—remember, a person or undead creature who has never before seen your mother—to imagine what she looks like and how she acts. (You do this by using showing words, which was discussed in more detail in Chapter 3 on Fiction Writing.)

But, how much or how little you show of your mother is up to you and principally a matter of style and voice. Are you the kind of writer who leaves no stone unturned as you document with veracity every detail from the hairstyle on her head to the color of her fingernails, or are you the kind of writer who can illustrate your mother's character with a few sparse, well-chosen words that tell the reader all they need to know by simply describing the way she talks or the color of her eyes?

In addition to showing your readers the characters and settings of your memory,

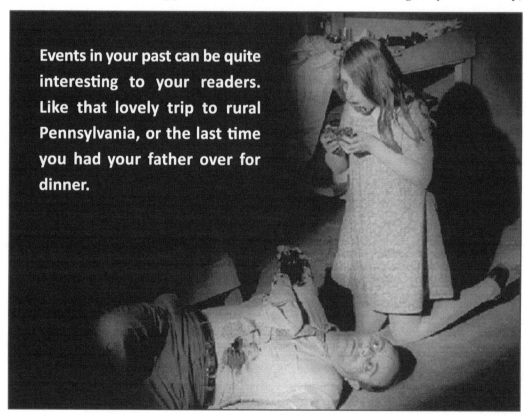

Events in your past can be quite interesting to your readers. Like that lovely trip to rural Pennsylvania, or the last time you had your father over for dinner.

you sometimes have to show them the intention and purpose of your memories as well. Unlike other forms of writing where the reader engages with a piece of fiction or a poem in order to find their own meaning or create their own images and ideas, memoirs are largely writer-oriented. That is, the writer decides what is important and can take the time to describe to a reader what the value of a moment was, or what the moment meant to him years later, or lessons that she learned from the experience being described.

In short, memoirs are able to directly state the significance of an event to the reader as a manner of concluding the memory they depict. Is it necessary to always conclude a memoir in this fashion? Of course not. Many readers will gather the same values or significant points from your memoirs simply by how you depict these memories—after all, that's why they picked up your book in the first place.

> **What is nice about memoir writing is that you get to decide what is important, and little interpretation is needed from readers. Maybe your life wasn't filled with mystery and intrigue, but it must feel familiar and interesting to your reader.**

One way to get at the heart of a memory and tease out what needs to be shown and what can comfortably be left out is to engage in the journalistic art of asking questions. Zombies don't get into the habit of asking too many questions—most of us can't really talk—but writers can ask internal questions to help set the tone and lay the foundation for their work. Writing is primarily a conversation between a writer and a reader. It starts with the writer imagining who the reader is and what the reader might ask about a memory. Then, the writer seeks to answer those questions through creating the story. What happened to the other characters? Why was this even significant or important? How did everyone react? When did it all happen? What happened afterward? Who were the major players? Where did this all go down?

Some writers choose to take it a step further and actually engage in a conversation with potential readers. This can be done in the editing process, or in writers' groups, or amongst friends. Describe the memory you plan to write and invite a dialogue. What points do your listeners feel need to be highlighted? What do they need for it to feel finished? Do they understand the value of your memory, or do they need you to explain its impact on you for them? This exercise can help frame a memory and also help determine if the memory will make for an interesting and engaging story for your readers.

After all, if the audience is dead (whether figuratively or not), well . . .

Now it's time to pass that head I've been using as a kickball on to your next "instructor." You may recognize him from one of your literature classes and he needs little introduction. But be nice to him. The human race was not kind to him during his brief existence on this earth and he deserved better.

MEMOIRS OF A FRANKENSTEIN MONSTER
or
Memoirs of a Not-So-Modern Prometheus

Frankenstein's Monster never had a name. A poor creature infused with that elusive spark of life by a mad scientist named Victor only to be cast aside like an unwanted cat and left to fend for himself on the fierce and cruel streets of humankind, the monster wasn't around long enough to receive a name, let alone gifts like language or fatherly love. Yet in true Cinderella fashion, he rose up from his destitute circumstances to a place of prominence, learning language all on his own—and learning it well enough to write some really good stuff, we might add. His memoir (or parts of it, at least) were preserved by Mary Shelley, but after many years of silence, he has agreed to share with us his process of evolving a memoir into text. Sit back, grab a bowl of popcorn, tuck your children into their beds, and read on.

So, BEING PIECED together with bits and pieces of hundreds of different cadavers by a mad scientist who then brings you to life with a mysterious galvanization process and then pretty much abandons you like a newborn in a basket on the local minister's doorstep—well, that pretty much sucks. But let me tell you: it makes for one hell of a story. I only wish I'd actually written my side of the whole thing instead of that crazy sea captain. He missed a lot in the overture, know what I'm saying?

Anyway, the point I'm trying to make here is that *everyone* has a story. Don't let anyone tell you differently. See, when Father (Victor Frankenstein) abandoned me, he basically taught me that I had no story to tell. I mean, the man abandoned his own child because he abhorred his creation—or, perhaps more accurately, because he abhorred himself for tampering with the fire of the Gods. But you know what the worst part was? It wasn't that I had no clothes or that, as a hideous creature, all the townsfolk greeted me with pitchforks and torches. It wasn't even that I was never able to make friends or that I was the only one of my kind, unable to find a mate and make a life of my own. No. The worst part of my story is that Father abandoned me without any language.

Words are the most powerful tools humans wield on this planet. The telling of stories is our most powerful relief from the pangs of life. In days of old, the best seat near the hearth and the yummiest morsel of meat from the evening's dinner were saved for the storytellers. The storytellers alone were allowed unbridled access to kings, who looked at them as fools incapable of guile.

From the moment you all come kicking and crying into this cold, cold world, you seek out words. You watch the mouths of your mothers and fathers trying to make sense of the sounds they create. You make your own sounds as you try to express yourself until, frustrated at last, you spill tears and cry until your needs are met.

I was never born in the truest sense, and so my story always starts with my Father's cruel and ambitious vision. But there are other stories of people born into misery almost identical to my own. Take, for instance, the memoirs of Mary Robinson, a writer during the Romantic Period (1780-1820), which is the same period into which I was "born." Here, she describes the circumstances of her own nightmarish birth:

> *In this venerable mansion there was one chamber whose dismal and singular construction left no doubt of its having been part of the original monastery. It was supported by the mouldering arches of the cloisters; dark, Gothic, and opening on the minster sanctuary, not only by casement windows that shed a dim mid-day gloom, but by a narrow winding staircase, at the foot of which an iron-spiked door led to the long gloomy path of cloistered solitude . . . In this awe-inspiring habitation . . . during a tempestuous night, on the twenty-seventh of November, 1758, I first opened my eyes to this world of duplicity and sorrow. I have often heard my mother say that a more stormy hour she never remembered. The wind whistled round the dark pinnacles of the minster tower, and the rain beat in torrents against the casements of her chamber. Through life the tempest has followed my footsteps; and I have in vain looked for a short interval of repose from the perseverance of sorrow.*

While birth is not always the best place to begin a memoir, in some cases it is a powerful way to declare indirect characterization. Characterization, while primarily an element of fiction, plays a role in memoirs as well. Remember, your readers typically have never met your family or your friends or even you. As such, you need to show them who you are. Indirect characterization *shows* a reader who you are, while direct characterization *tells* them. In this example, we can see that Mary Robinson's character is solemn, maybe even a little desperate. We also see that her mother is a bit distant or cold (like a rainy storm) toward her daughter through the words the writer chooses to convey the mother's sense of that birth night. The house, originally a monastery, is "characterized" in the sense that it sets a dark and gloomy stage on which the players will act out their sorrows.

But what strikes me most powerfully about this example is her final sentence: "Through life the tempest has followed my footsteps; and I have in vain looked for a short interval of repose from the perseverance of sorrow." Can you hear the echo of desperation? Since the moment she was born, she has sought out some distraction to ease her persevering sorrow. What distractions are there but the arts? Chief among them words, perhaps equal to music? Words and stories bring relief, and that is why, even from birth (or, in my case, creation), we seek out and deliver stories to and from those around us. And it all begins with language.

Think about it. As babies, we have no real language save the body language with which we are programmed to blink and squeal when we are hungry, and smile and laugh when we seek attention. We must learn the words of men and women by listening to our parents or guardians, and by the time we are grown, we are ready to speak and be heard.

Only, I was never a baby in the strictest sense. I was "born" fully grown. Without parents to love and nurture me, I was essentially a feral child who had to learn language in secrecy like a slave hovering near the windows of a blind man's family while they spoke to one another.

You have no idea how important language is. Or, perhaps you do, which is why you are reading this book. What I mean is that language gives us the gift of expression—the ability to carry from our hearts our innermost anguish or our deepest joys. We are social creatures—even we monsters—and we need language to share and socialize. Abandoning me without any language—without the words to tell my story—condemned both my "Father" and I to death.

Now, I'm not saying you will commit patricide and then off yourself if you don't write your memoir. What I'm saying is that your words are powerful because they belong to you and they create a connection between your *self* and the selves of those who read your thoughts. In this way, you will never be alone—not in the truest sense. So, write, write, write! Be like the vision Mary Shelley once had when she wrote in her book, *The Last Man*: "Life is before me and I rush into possession. Hope, glory, love, and blameless ambition are my guides, and my soul knows no dread." Carry on into your own memories without fear. Someone *will* want to read it.

Writing Prompts for Chapter 5

1. Write the opening scene to your memoirs. Remember, a memoir doesn't have to begin at the beginning. Instead, it should begin at the most important or thematic point in your life. Think about what that might be and write it.

2. Think back to a time when something particularly sad happened to a loved one. Writing from your own perspective (that is, your own memory of what happened), describe what happened to your loved one or what she went through. Include your own experiences as they are relevant to the story.

Writing Exercises for Chapter 5

1. **Episodic Memoirs:** Make a list of your several major life events in chronological order. Now, without writing about the events themselves, write a "fast forward" line to connect each event to the next. Let's say one event occurred when you were three and the next when you were five—how can you "fast forward" through those two years to bridge the reader between the events? Do this for all of the events you listed.

2. **Interesting Timeline:** Make a personal timeline such as the one the Countess makes in this chapter. Begin by drawing a baseline horizontally across the page. Now, draw in the high points and the low points of your life above and below the baseline. Connect them. Feel free to use doodles, diagrams, or collage or photo images to spice it up. Use the timeline to determine which elements should be included in your memoir.

3. **Sensory Detail:** Think about a highly sensory experience (such as a delicious meal or the coldest you're ever been); use showing words and sensory details to convey this experience to a reader in a few paragraphs.

4. **Get Reader Feedback:** Take the memory you wish to write about and find a writing partner. The partner you choose should not be someone who is very close to you (so not your sibling or your best friend). Try an acquaintance or someone you haven't spoken to in a while. Tell this person the memory you wish to write about. Be detailed as you tell it. Pay attention to the person's reactions. Is she nodding off? If so, cut that bit. Is she glued to her seat? Great! You're on the right

track. Did she ask any questions? If so, make sure you fill those in when you write your story.

5. **Anatomy of a Memoir**: Read the memoirs of someone you want to know more about. What strategies do they use to tell their story? What did they include, and what did they leave out? What were your favorite parts and why? What could have been done differently?

— 6 —

Persuasive Writing

or

Please Can I Eat Your Brain:
A Zombie's Guide to Writing Persuasively

The following chapter came to us from an anonymous member of the undead calling herself "Henrietta." It was written in what we assume to be a blood-ink, and tied to a brick with a strand of cat's gut when it came crashing through the window of the third-floor apartment where we (the writers) had taken up after the zombie apocalypse started. (If only we'd paid attention to the CDC.) We had taken out the stairs at the advice of Max Brooks' book Zombie Survival Guide, and we were fairly content for the time being with some solar-battery laptops and a backpack full of canned goods (even though <u>somebody</u> forgot the can-opener, Stan.) Then, bang! A spray of glass spatters across the floor and in the middle of it, like a mushroom cloud in the middle of a desert, is this intestine-twined scrap of paper wrapped around an old brick. We were forced to assume that the author—a zombie with a unique sense of our submission guidelines—had somehow heard about our project and wanted in on it. (We were fairly relieved not to have to write this one ourselves, too, since <u>somebody</u> had to go loot an S-mart for a can- opener in the middle of a zombie horde, Stan.) So this chapter comes to you from "Henrietta." Thank you, mystery flesh-eater, wherever you are.

"The foolish and the dead alone never change their opinions." ~James Russell Lowell

I KNOW THAT there comes a time in every *body*'s life when he or she or it has to write something in order to get something. Maybe it's that first letter to Santa Clause begging the thousand year-old (perhaps undead) dude in a red suit to "please, *please*" bring you that pair of pink machetes you've had your eye on (because they match your favorite AK47). Or maybe it's an appeal to your senator to reconsider his stand on undead rights. Or perhaps it's a letter to the torch-bearing, angry mob outside to just "lay off, man, and let me eat this kid."

Whatever the reason, we all find occasion to write persuasively at some point in our lives—or afterlives. Persuasive writing is a style of composition that affects a reader in a distinctive fashion. It's writing that changes how someone thinks about a problem or issue, or convinces them to take a particular action. Persuasive writing is powerful; it's changing someone's mind instead of eating someone's brain.

So, how do we accomplish that when writing? In writing, we don't have a pair of sheepish eyes blinking desperately at mom and dad. No interlaced fingers as we beg. No simultaneously sad and hopeful tone in our voices as we plead and manipulate our way to get what we want. All we have are words on a cold dead page—and when we write to get something, express our views, or change someone's mind, we have to choose those words carefully.

It all starts with selecting a topic and choosing a position. Whatever we choose to argue *must* be a debatable subject. For example, "being bitten by a zombie is a bad thing" would (by most people's standards) not be a debatable statement. However, a statement such as "being bitten by a vampire is a bad thing" could very well be debatable. After all, living forever might be pretty awesome, especially for all those *Twilight* fans out there interested in tracking down their very own Edward Cullen.

You can sort out your debatable topic by first imagining your question. Ask yourself what you want to write about: what question do you want your audience to answer? Should zombies be able to vote? Should werewolves have to wear dog collars? Should vampires be allowed within 100 yards of a blood bank?

Next, set yourself up with a framework for tackling the best approach. For example, if I run across that heroic lone survivor during one of my night-time pillages, should

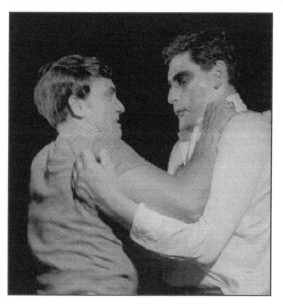

I start a fire to signal the zombie horde shambling aimlessly around the corner? Or should I wait in some dark shadow, hoping to catch my victim by surprise? Writing persuasively is like choosing the best approach to get what you want. First, you have to know what you want: yummy guts or

Come on, everybody. It's time to try that great new dance craze. It's just a jump the left. Now lurch to the right. Everyone, do the zombie shuffle.

juicy brains? Second, you need a really good idea of who you're writing to: are you talking to the human in charge of the monster-hunting mob, or your zombie compatriots? And finally, after making these choices, you can develop a strategy.

Asking yourself the reason why you are writing may sound like a simple question, but sometimes a clear sense of purpose is hard to see. Are you writing to get an interview for your dream job working in a mortuary? Are you writing to change someone's mind about an issue you care about? (Perhaps lobbying against the creation of more remakes of *A Nightmare on Elm Street*?) Are you writing to propose a solution to a problem in your neighborhood, such as whether family members should be required to pick up body parts that drop from zombie relatives when they take them for a walk? If your purpose isn't crystal clear in your own mind, it will be difficult to craft a persuasive argument.

At first glance, you may not see many uses for persuasive writing unless you're doing it for a class assignment. But even then, how about convincing someone to write that assignment for you? Okay, maybe not a good example, but at least I got your attention, and that's the whole idea behind persuasive writing.

The list of occasions when we might use persuasive writing in everyday life is actually quite extensive. The basic categories would likely consist of selling an idea, selling yourself, or selling a product. These categories include specific things familiar to all of us both inside and outside the business world, such as writing résumés, letters of application or reference, book and movie reviews, advertising, product brochures, letters to the editor, speeches, pamphlets, fund raising, and grant writing. It's also something one could make use of even after death. Remember, there are such things as ghostwriters.

Here are some examples of when you may need to write persuasively during the course of your eternal undeadness:

- A résumé and cover letter for that job digging graves
- A proposal to your neighbors that they stop barricading themselves indoors as you're just going to find them anyway

---

TODAY'S MENU

APÉRITIF
Vintage Rotgut

DINNER SALAD
Lightly tossed ligaments and eyeball slices covered with a spinal fluid vinaigrette

APPETIZER
Finger Sandwiches

MAIN COURSE
Brains (very rare)

DESSERT
Kidney Pie (of course)

- An editorial in which you must defend your right to eat bare arms
- A marketing pitch for your new pulled brain sandwich bar
- A paper for your college professor arguing that the brains of educated people are tastier than those with only high school diplomas

One of the first ways we convince our readers (or listeners) is by the way we say things, our body language (delicious!), or the tone of our voices. You see, unlike most of our undead friends, writing has a voice and a voice can have a tone. Tone is sometimes dictated by your audience—that is, who will be reading your guttural cry for help? Is it your boss? Your best friend? Your child? The guy with the machine gun? It is possible you may have to take some educated guesses about your audience. What will they already know about you and your purpose for writing? What do they need to know to be convinced of your position? What reasonable objections will they likely have? If you want your reader to take action, what do they need to do, and why should they do it? By knowing the answers to these questions in advance, you have already loaded the rifle and switched off the safety.

> **Tone is sometimes dictated by your audience. Is it a group of businessmen? Your boss? Your next door neighbor who wants his chainsaw back in order to fight off the zombie horde?**

In addition to audience, tone is dictated by word choice and phrasing. Communicating effectively to a wide range of people takes practice, feedback, and experimentation. What works in one writing scenario won't necessarily translate to another. Did you string a bunch of big, Oxford English Dictionary words together, or did you choose a handful of monosyllabic sounds and grunts to get your point across? How were you feeling when you wrote it? Like your life depended on it? (Perhaps it does.) Chances are, it will show.

When planning your persuasive writing piece, don't just think about your purpose—write it down. Make a list of your goals, or begin a sentence with "I am writing to _____ " and see what comes next. Writing requires pen to paper, fingers to keyboard, or bloody fingers to walls. You can't write unless you are writing, after all, so grab some paper and get to it. Just make sure you define your purpose before you begin.

In addition to a clearly defined sense of purpose, you also need to provide your reader with some valid reasons for believing you. In the planning stage (and you will have a planning stage or you'll have no chance against that zombie horde), list as many reasons as you can think of (which will be more than you need). Having many to choose from will ensure that you're picking the strongest and best reasons to support your position. You can often figure out your line of reasoning by using "because" statements.

Almost everything that we know about persuasive writing we learned from Aristotle. Sure, he's almost 2,500 years old and his lower jaw fell off a few centuries ago when he was gnawing on a thigh bone, making it really hard to understand what the guy is saying. But the gist is essentially that persuasive writing breaks down into three components: Logos, Ethos, and Pathos. Or, as I like to call them, Brains, Limbs, and Hearts. (Brains are most likely the tastiest, but all are of equal importance when writing persuasively.)

You see, whenever you want to convince someone of anything, these three basic principles are your foundation.

Use Your Brains (Food for thought!)

Most people can tell the difference between a pile of fresh guts and a heap of stinking zombie innards. That's why we undead flesh-eaters never eat each other in books and movies. By pure primal instinct, we know what's alive and what's dead. In the world of persuasive writing, this means we can tell when a person is trying to confuse us with lies or misdirection. So, if a person uses their brains or logical reasoning, that person should be able to convince someone using facts, statistics, figures, and other tasty morsels to convey their message and get what they want.

Use Your Limbs (With a hint of tarragon, preferably.)

What is good for your fleshy, living body is good for our decaying guts, too. Ethical arguments can help derail a lynch mob and their pitchfork mentality if delivered correctly. You see, ethics refers to the ways that an idea or proposal will benefit society as a whole. By using arguments that nourish the entire body of people around you, you make it difficult for most clear-headed folks to refute your argument.

Use Your Heart (Tartare and juicy!)

Most people (even dead ones) are moved to change things when they feel something emotionally. If you rip out your heart and bare your true feelings in writing—if you make a creature *feel* something—well, he just might be moved enough to do what you want. Try to think outside of the box, but present your ideas in an easy-to-read fashion. Emotions can make for a strong argument, but you don't have to ram a stake through a vampire's heart to get its attention. And a special note about emotions: humor can be a powerful weapon as well as a common ground even between those on opposing sides of an issue. Maybe your reader enjoys humor as much as the next undead guy. Q: "What's the best way to talk to a vampire?" A: "Long distance."

The first and last thing you do in a piece of persuasive writing is give the reader a clear call to action. It has been determined that most readers are much too similar to reanimated corpses in that their brains don't work in the same way as ours. They sometimes miss the rotten face staring at them through the rain-soaked window until it's too late—the pasty undead fist has already crashed through the glass and seized them by the hair, dragging them outside before their scream has a chance to shatter the dark night. In other words, be clear about what you want. Say it straight up as if you are telling the reader what to do (in a nice way) so they don't get confused and accidentally do something else. Make sense? If you lead a zombie straight to your unsuspecting teacher and then run like crazy, the undead creature is much more likely to chew on the professor's arm than your own.

You must know your ultimate goal. If you don't know (or have no strong feelings) about whether you'd rather be a vampire or a werewolf, then how can you convince others of your feelings on the subject? However, if you are well-informed on your topic, you can be convincing even if you don't believe it yourself. Knowledge is power. Read about your topic, study it, and be informed. Understand different perspectives about your topic, especially if you don't agree. Ask your next door neighbor, who changes into a werewolf every thirty days, about his quality of life. (Just don't do it during a full moon. This would demonstrate how uninformed you are on the subject, not to mention risking the very real possibility of being slashed apart by claws and teeth.)

Getting your goal into a working formula and clarifying what you know (and need to know) about a subject can help you determine how to organize your writing. The organization of your ideas can impact how effective your writing will be. If you give too much information too soon, your reader can feel confused and disoriented. If you wait too long to state your purpose, it might be too late—your reader may have already

*Sparking interest in your audience may require good old-fashioned mob mentality: get the **naysayers** on your side, and **everyone else** will soon follow.*

given up reading and gone back to gathering pitchforks and torches for the assault on your castle lair. In general, there are many ways to organize information, and more than one method (or even a combination of methods) will probably work to deliver your message effectively. A few common methods are:

- Stating your purpose, your reasons, and the action you want your reader to take
- Starting with the more familiar or the "safest" idea and then moving to the most challenging
- Moving from general information to more specific

(For more about these and other organizational patterns, take another peek at Chapter 1 on the Basics of Writing.)

A key step in thinking about organization is understanding how each piece of information relates to other ideas. Outlines are a good way to organize ideas because they have a hierarchical structure, which means that you have to differentiate between big (main) ideas, and supportive ideas (such as a reason or piece of evidence). But some writers find outlines too confining; for them, listing, clustering, concept mapping, or talking might be more effective ways of thinking about how ideas relate to one another. Whether you outline, list or cluster, think of your ideas as the bones of a skeleton. You can leave the skeleton in its true form (like an outline), rearrange the pieces in a cluster with smaller bones separated from larger bones or, heck, just throw them up into the air and see where they land.

Finally, always remember to write the truth. There is no better way to lose track of your goal than to tell a lie, plagiarize, or miss a key point in your research. This one is pretty obvious, but you might be surprised by the number of times this "rule" is not followed. If you write that all zombies are slow and shambling "Romero-type" zombies when the world has just been overrun with zombies that run the hundred-yard dash in three seconds, the reader will never believe another word you say... that is, if either of you is left alive to discuss it later.

Now that we've got the basics down, how exactly does one go about writing persuasively? Sure, you have to use a subtle blend of Brains, Limbs, and Heart, but there are other important factors to consider, too. Perhaps the most important factor when writing persuasively is taking the time to study your audience. Is the person or group of people you are trying to convince a room full of powerful necromancers with your undead body under their every command? If so, you probably want to use a few magical terms in your presentation to grab their attention and get them on your side. Or is your audience that guy with the plow on his truck that keeps mowing down your shambling children when they are simply following their brainless instinct to eat the guy? Well, you might need to use some simple words and soothing tones with Mr. Plow because he's clearly unhinged if he keeps running over bodies.

Know Your Audience
(Get Inside the Skin of Your Opposition and Walk Around)

One of the things I do when I'm figuring out my audience is to create an entire character of the person I'm trying to convince. Let's say I'm a little old lady locked under the trap door after my husband read from the *Necronomicon Ex Mortis* and I'm trying to convince someone upstairs to let me out. I might try banging on the door shouting "Come to Henrietta," or I might wait and bide my time, learn a bit about the people upstairs and then craft my appeal specifically to one of them.

I'd try to figure out their age and education by listening to the way they talk and the words they use. I'd try to determine their socioeconomic status—yeah, big word for someone who no longer has a larynx—by looking at their clothes and where they live and the kind of car they drive. I might try to figure out their values by looking at what they care about or cherish or try to protect from my clutching fingers and gaping mouth.

And if I didn't have a real, live person to stalk, then I'd make one up. After all, I know what I'm trying to accomplish, right? I just want to get out of this cellar! So, what kind of person would want to keep me inside? If I target my message thinking of a worst case scenario (i.e. the hardest person in the world to convince to let me out of the cellar) and I convince him, then anyone else who walks by is just gravy and giblets. Mmm. Or maybe blood pudding.

So here's what I imagine: a younger man, in his twenties. He doesn't have much money: I know this because I picture him in a blue, button-down shirt and a pair of jeans. He drives a vintage station wagon. His idea of a vacation is my rickety cabin in the middle of the woods (unaware of the fact that I've been turned into a zombie by my archaeologist husband and locked in the basement, waiting to eat him), and he appears to have gone on the trip with a couple of buddies and his girlfriend, so he's certainly no Donald Trump. He wears a college jersey, but that doesn't mean

We doubt you will find a copy of the Necronomicon on your local library shelf, but you never know. Our advice? Stick to the books on how to improve your writing skills.

he's been to college; so, he's likely operating with a department-store-job, working class, high school-level vocabulary. This tells me not to use any Latin—that, and I think he doesn't understand Latin, anyway, because this numbskull was dumb enough to also read from the *Necronomicon Ex Mortis*. So yeah, not exactly a rocket scientist. Oh, and I think he lost one of his hands in some sort of black magic accident or something, so I certainly don't want to use any euphemisms that relate to hands, like, say, "Can you give me a hand and get me out of here?" Unless he wants to spare the other one for finger food, that is.

Now that I've got the character in mind of the last person on earth that might let me out of this little dungeon, then I start imagining my opposition's response. I'm not going to spend an hour writing a full draft of this dumbass's interior monologue around why he shouldn't let me out even if I do have all eternity to do it. No, I'm just going to scribble down some bullet points or a paragraph or so of what I imagine he's going to say against my humble and truly reasonable request when you consider how hungry I am. At this point I could eat a roomful of folks at the annual mortician's convention.

What might his objections be? Well, the most obvious is that he doesn't want me to eat him, and I can respect that. Everyone is entitled to his opinion. What else, though? Maybe he doesn't want to let me out because he's afraid I'll also try to eat his girlfriend? He's very protective of her, I think, so he must value his relationship. Okay now we're getting somewhere. I know there is fear involved in his thought process. He's afraid I'm going to eat him *and* his girlfriend. I know what he cares about, and now I know just how to dig my way out of this cellar.

It's like a game of rock, paper, scissors, lizard, Spock only with yummier bits. You see, if he's scared, then he's operating on all "Heart." That is, he's functioning on pure emotion. Emotional people can't be charmed by simply adding more emotion. They're already off the deep end, so what can we do? Can I convince him that letting me out will be for the greater good of all the people in the cabin because they can live in less fear and die more speedily? Not likely, so "Limbs" probably won't work in this instance. "Brains" are the only thing I know of that can beat a "Heart"—in taste and persuasion. I may still weave in a little "Heart" and "Limb" for texture, but only after I've served up the main course.

Hook, Line, and Sink Yer Teeth In

So, now what? I've got my call to action and I know to whom I'm writing, so now all I have to do is write it, all the while weaving in those yummy "Brains," "Limbs," and "Hearts" to get the jaw joints lubricated. I can already feel the saliva gushing in my mouth.

I'm trying to catch me a big, meaty fish. So, I start by writing with a baited hook. I need to get the guy on my side. I need to intrigue him. Seduce him. Get him to trust me. So what do I do? Well, I start by connecting with him on as many levels as possible. If he's working on raw emotion, then I start with raw, fleshy emotion because I know that's where he's at already. The only thing that changes is that I subtly flip the emotional bits so they reflect my situation, and not his. I might say:

Dear Mr. Ash Williams,

It's so dark down in this cellar. I think I heard something chewing in the corner, but I can't really see what it is. Gosh. I hope it's not one of those things. You see, I'm just a little old lady, and my husband is gone now and I'm trapped in this tiny cellar and I do so hope you'll let me out. If not for me, then for my grandchildrens' sake.

The snare is set. Now he thinks I'm just a harmless old lady. He thinks I am trying to protect people I care about, too, which makes him think he and I must be the same and he can trust me. (I can almost taste his gullibility.)

Next, I have to undo his thinking by battling his emotion with my brains. I do that by posing some logical reasons for him to let me out. Sometimes we might need to gather more information to make the best possible case. We might need more background about the topic, a better sense of who our readers are, or supporting information (such as facts or concrete examples) that could help us make our case. Time to hit the books. (Now where did I leave my copy of *The Tibetan Book of the Dead*?)

While determining what to research, I should also try to hunt down someone with expertise. Experts tend to have big brains, you see. (It goes without saying that folks with big brains should not advertise that fact to a group of zombies.) So, how about a statistic from an expert that indicates that if Ash leaves me in the cellar, I'll simply burst my way out in an hour or so anyway and then I'll be loads more hungry and much more interested in playing with my food? Of course, I'd need an expert since I'm not a statistician, though I did eat one some time ago. Maybe statistical expertise can be gained by digestion.

In that case, my next paragraph might go something like this (if I had an expert to help me out with the statistics part, of course):

Mr. Williams, are you aware that five out of six people trapped in basements are actually harmless old grandparents? Five out of six! Imagine that? The odds are simply in my favor, I'm afraid. I'm a helpless old granny and you simply must let me out. Would you leave your own dear granny down here?

Can you see how my ideas are fleshing out? Oh, flesh. I'm so bloody hungry. Blood?

Why did I say blood? Now I'm thirsty, too. Oh, Mr. Williams, just unlock the damn trap door, please? I promise this grandma ain't no wolf. Just a demon in old lady skin. (Guess I shouldn't say that, should I?) No trouble, see? No trouble at all.

Lastly, I have to remember to bring the whole thing back to my call to action. I don't want this guy getting the wrong idea or mixing up my request. No. I want the idiot to let me out. Everything should be tied up neatly and all the nails driven deep into the coffin. It should be creative and memorable as it will be the last thing he reads and, hopefully, the last thing he remembers. This is where I explain the urgency of my claim and call him to direct action. My last paragraph might go something like this:

> *In conclusion, I think it is plain to see that this little old grandma is really quite helpless. Since I've been down in this cellar, my rheumatism has gotten the better of me and all that yelling you heard earlier was just cries of pain. If I don't get out of here soon, I think I'll die from the agony of my poor swollen limbs. So please, please, Mr. Williams—unlatch the trap door and let this poor, sweet grandmother out of this cruel, damp cellar. I promise to stay out of your way. And I really should call the grandchildren to let them know that their old granny is safe and they'll have fresh peanut butter cookies on Sunday.*
>
> *Sincerely, a friendly old lady,*
> *Henrietta (and not some Candarian Demon. Promise.)*

Logical Fallacies (When Brains Start to Get a Little Too Chewy)

As I know I will talk myself out of this situation sooner or later (the mark of any good writer), let's shift the topic while Mr. Williams ruminates about his own future. One stumbling block you might run into with persuasive writing is false thinking. I can imagine that Ash upstairs is falling prey to false thinking even now. False thinking includes several different things and we will cover just a few of them here.

Hasty Generalizations
Don't jump to conclusions or make general statements based on limited evidence. Finding three vampires who prefer not to drink human blood does not mean that the fourth vampire you meet will not abuse you and leave your body in a nearby dumpster.

False Analogies
Poor comparisons form weak arguments. You cannot argue that being undead would be cool simply based on the fact that a vampire lives forever when being undead might also include being a zombie.

Post Hoc Fallacies

"Post hoc" is a Latin phrase warning against confusing a relationship in time with cause and effect. The fact that two events happened one after the other doesn't mean that the first *caused* the second. In other words, the wolf's howl doesn't cause the moon to appear.

Either-Or Fallacies

Always remember that there are rarely just two options. Things are generally not that black and white unless you are a zombie zebra. The proposition that we either kill "all" vampires or they will take over the world is not realistic. After all, not all vampires are evil and want to drink your blood. Well, most of them are, but what about the little old lady next door who is harmless now that she wears false teeth?

Attacking Personalities

Just because an argument is supported by a controversial person does not automatically discredit it from having merit. And when we make arguments, we have to attack ideas or positions, not people. Just because the Lutz family in Amityville believes in ghosts, doesn't mean that we call them hysterical or automatically assume they're wrong.

Begging the Question

A statement cannot stand on its own if it needs to be proven. All zombies must die! Well, maybe so, but you certainly can't stop there. *Why* do they all need to die?

Using Evidence to Support Your Position

Avoiding false thinking or logical fallacies ties in with connecting your evidence and making sure that your research (remember those delightfully large-brained experts we talked about?) is specific, solid, and relative. Make certain your evidence is specific and not generalized.

If 34% of the population believes in ghosts, don't just state that "lots" of people believe in spirits. Try to find the same or similar information in more than one place. Double-check your facts and figures and be prepared to cite them. Perfect evidence is rarely available, so go with the imperfect data you dig up and make it sound convincing. And remember, facts are not the same thing as informed opinion. It is much easier to gather facts on what might be the safest car on the road, but much harder to prove that it could never result in a fatality. The fact that your uncle's grave is empty does not mean he is a ghost, a vampire, or a zombie. The fact that your mother chews on her fingernails does not make her a cannibal. (However, if she is boiling your father's head for dinner, well, that's different story.)

Brain-Programming, or How to Control Their Little Minds

Neurolinguistic programming is such a delectable term, isn't it? "Neuro," with all those mouth-watering cheese curds of gray matter, means "brain," while "linguistic" literally means "tongue." (Oh. To run my tongue over the bloody flesh of your brain. I can almost feel its buttery texture rolling around inside my mouth.) Neurolinguistic programming refers to the way that our minds interpret language—or, more accurately, the way our brains are hard-wired to interpret the words we choose.

Imagine for a moment that you are protecting your child from a gang of guts-hungry zombies as you run through a darkened maze of subway tunnels searching desperately for an escape route. You can feel the monsters close at your heels as droplets of slimy saliva spatter against the back of your neck.

Your child, still tightly gripping your hand, is running furiously by your side and amazingly, keeping up well. You want your child to maintain this pace, but what would happen if you screamed "Don't slow down"? As strange as it may seem, your use of the phrase "slow down" (even though you put the negative qualifier in front of it) increases the chances that your child will pause ever so slightly to process your request. He's thinking about "slow down" and, in fact, probably will, even if it's an unconscious thought. Unfortunately, that's all the time the undead need to snatch him up.

> **Phrases such as "don't slow down" or "don't go into the basement" usually get the opposite reaction, or at least cause the listener to think about what they heard. It is simply the way our brains are hard-wired to interpret certain words and phrases.**

But what if you said, "Hurry up!" or "This way!" instead? By redirecting your child's attention to the positive, he is able to process and immediately comply with your request rather than sift out a negative qualifier in order to understand what you were trying to say by "*don't* slow down."

When we apply this concept to our writing, we have to again consider our audience. For example, if I am begging a torch-bearing mob to please not burn our zombie babies alive (I mean, not all zombies want to tear humans apart and gorge on their innards—okay, bad argument, that's exactly what each one of us wants to do), it's probably not in my best interest to use any words that instigate them further towards violence. For example, it would probably be best to avoid words like "eat," "fire," "burn," "alive," and "dead" because I wouldn't want them to remember that I am, in fact, dead and that to burn me wouldn't be the same as "burning someone alive."

I also might come up with a more neutral term for myself, like "living impaired" instead of "zombie." The word choice matters. By calling myself "living impaired," I not only avoid the whole reminder that I'm an undead creature interested in feasting on their intestines, I also play a bit on their subconscious sympathies by suggesting I'm actually handicapped or disabled in some way and they are not. On the other hand, if I call myself a "flesh-eating monster" and suggest that they "not burn me alive," I've only strengthened their way of thinking—their neurolinguistic programming—to just kill the creature (that's me, unfortunately) and be done with it.

Calling Out for Action

The last step in writing persuasively is to remind the reader clearly what you want them to do. You need to come right out and say, "Please buy me the boom stick you saw at S-Mart" or "Now put down your weapons and go home" or "Reconsider how we define 'monster.'" Call the reader to action. Remind them what you want, and if you've done your job convincing them with your words, you just might get the results you desire.

CONSIDERING EXAMPLES

The sample below wasn't written by "Henrietta." We found it squirreled away in a hidey-hole in one of the craziest houses we've ever seen. (Seriously—this house actually drew imaginary shadows onto the stairs with black paint. It was weird.) We thought this might make a good example of all the things our undead writer talks about in the rest of the chapter. Take a moment to examine the example below and look for moments where the writer demonstrates an understanding of audience and neurolinguistic programming. Try to determine how the author hooks her targeted audience (Dr. Caligari), and consider the call to action at the end. If you were the recipient of this letter, would you comply with this young woman's wishes?

Dear Dr. Caligari,

I was most impressed with your clever show at the carnival in Venice last week's end. I was particularly moved by the prophecy uttered by your somnambulist, Cesare. How could this entranced creature predict the future of your carnival goers? I must admit that I was disappointed not to be selected for one of his predictions. That is, of course, until my dear friend Francis was murdered shortly after your somnambulist predicted that he would die within the night . . . and then killed him. I write, then, to ask that you please stop sending your somnambulist to kill my acquaintances. I think perhaps you'd feel very differently about this entire ordeal if, say, there were hordes of your zombie sleepers knocking at your door in the middle of the night threatening your loved ones. So let's end it, shall we?

First, you should know that coercing another person to commit a murder makes you primarily responsible for that murder and your puppet—the entranced Cesare—is merely an accessory. As such, when you are caught, you will likely be tried as a killer and face serious repercussions. (Hopefully disembowelment or quartering rather than imprisonment in some asylum for the insane.) My suggestion would be for you to give up your carnival show act and retire Cesare to his own cabinet—perhaps six-feet under with a lovely picket fence and creeping clematis? How delightful—then you would most likely not be caught for the few crimes you have already committed and thus not face the terrible tortures that will likely be inflicted upon you by the stark conditions of today's prisons. Save yourself, I beg of you, Doctor. I shudder at the thought of you tormented by the demons of imprisonment. Oh! And the horrors of being captured by the family members of your somnambulist's victims cause me paroxysms and breathlessness. I feel faint at the very idea.

Second, you might also consider how Jane will feel when she learns that you have used your necromantic powers to coerce this poor zombie into killing her betrothed. She'll be heart-broken to learn of your misguided deed, and as such, will most likely fling herself into the river or find some equally depressing way to end her life. Such a sorrow to imagine her floating about in the water, flesh swelling grotesquely. So young and so lovely. I thought perhaps you found her to be in her bloom as well—would you hasten her to her watery grave as Hamlet to his Ophelia, never to touch the warmth of her pale skin again?

In closing, I would like you to consider my request most carefully. I know you have no wish to suffer at the hands of the law, nor do you wish to be separated prematurely from the rosy beauty of our beloved Jane. In that regard, I ask that you please retire your somnambulist immediately and go back to your other profession, whatever that may be. Perhaps you could take up residence directing an asylum? I could see you fitting in quite well in such a thriving, energetic environment, Dr. Caligari.

Best,
Francesca

Francesca went through some painstaking planning as she mapped out exactly how to compose her letter. She knew that she needed to consider the emotional responses of Dr. Caligari as he read her letter, and that she also needed to consider ways to help him overcome those responses so that he'd ultimately end up on her side. She opened with flattery (because she knew Dr. Caligari would succumb to it, we suspect), moved through a list of carefully selected examples constructed with carefully chosen words, and ended with a clear call to action.

Writing Prompts for Chapter 6

1. Find a law that you think is outdated or unfair. Now write a letter to your senator or other regional official asking that the law be overturned.

2. Think about a verbal disagreement or argument that wasn't resolved, or that you felt like you "lost." What would you say to change that person's mind? Write a letter stating your case. How would you organize it? What would you say and why? (We'd suggest *not* sending it, but it's a useful exercise in persuasion.)

3. Write an advertisement for the last story or poem you wrote.

4. Write a news piece as if you are the anchor of a news broadcast. Use neuro-linguistic programming to make it look like the zombie apocalypse is actually a good thing.

Writing Exercises for Chapter 6

1. **Logical Fallacies:** Create an argument in favor of something you disagree with. Use logical fallacy to validate your argument. Be as "ridiculous" with your claims as you like. Now, try the argument out on someone else. Can they add to the fallacy? Or do they not recognize that you used bad reasoning? Why do you suppose it is sometimes hard to recognize fallacy in action?

2. **Audience and Counterarguments:** Imagine that you are having a disagreement with someone about a controversial issue (such as genetic engineering or capital punishment). Write a dialogue in which they persuade you to their point of view.

3. **Call to Action:** Make a list of twenty things you'd like to change about the world around you. It could be your immediate world (like your curfew or your child's curfew), or the world at large (like unjust laws or the way people interact). Create a clear call to action next to each item on the list. That is, how would you change things? What do you want someone to do about it? State it clearly.

4. **Planning:** Your city recently passed an ordinance in which zombies aren't allowed on the streets after midnight. The city is trying to decrease the conflict between

humans and zombies. As a zombie (or zombie-activist), you oppose this ordinance and are writing the city council, hoping to convince them to lift the curfew. Use these questions to help plan your letter.

- What is your purpose? Why are you writing?
- What are your reasons for opposing the curfew?
- Who is your audience? What is their perspective? What do they value?
- How or why will the city council object to your view?
- What is the common ground between you and the city council—what do you both want or care about?
- Is there anything you need to know more about to write persuasively about this issue?
- Can you suggest alternatives, or creative solutions to the problems the city council is trying to solve?
- How will you organize your letter? What will you say?

–7–

ANALYTICAL WRITING

or

I Know Why the Caged Vampire Bites

Dr. Van Helsing really needs no introduction (but insisted on one, just the same). We were honored when he offered to compile our chapter on Analytical Writing. (How could we refuse a man of his celebrity?) At his request, a short biography on our guest author:

Abraham Van Helsing, M.D., Ph.D. is visiting us from his home in the Netherlands. Not only is Dr. Helsing an expert on the art of vampire hunting, he is also highly educated and well-published, traits not normally associated with seeking out and destroying the undead. He has been battling vampires and other undead creatures since before he made the acquaintance of Bram Stoker in 1896. Also a kind of immortal himself (though he'd never admit it), he's still battling undead creatures today in print and other media. Stoker published a letter in his infamous book, Dracula, *from Van Helsing's young protégé and former student, John Seward, who describes his mentor as a "philosopher and a metaphysician, and one of the most advanced scientists of his day, and he has, I believe, an absolutely open mind. This, with an iron nerve, a temper of the ice-brook, and indomitable resolution, self-command, and toleration exalted from virtues to blessings, and the kindliest and truest heart that beats, these form his equipment for the noble work that he is doing for mankind, work both in theory and practice, for his views are as wide as his all-embracing sympathy." Whether Van Helsing (or his publicist) paid Seward to say those things, we don't know; but either way, we are honored to have the world's greatest analytical mind compose our chapter on analytical writing.*

GOOD EVENING, LADIES and gentlemen. I'd like to open my discourse this night with a question. What do young women, evening mist, bats, and wolves have in common? Count Dracula, of course! My arch-nemesis, and the reason I have a job.

Professor Abraham Van Helsing, at your service. Vampire hunter, man of medicine, and deductive reasoner extraordinaire.

If facts spoke for themselves, you see, I would have no reason to write—or to even exist, really. But facts don't speak for themselves—therefore, I'm forced to use reasoning to draw conclusions from the evidence before me. In analytic writing—such as my famous treatise, "The Ill-Effects of Vampirism on Young Female Hysterics"—I present evidence and explain my conclusions to my reader. Usually, analysis is an element of persuasive or argumentative writing. For example, in one of my books, I argue that garlic should be strung in the rooms of young women, who tend to be rather easily seduced by those afflicted with the terrible malady of *vampirism*. But to convince my esteemed readers to take action, I must persuade them through analytic writing. I have to use evidence and reasoning to prove that my conclusions are correct and that my advice must be followed.

My favorite form of analysis is deductive reasoning, from which I draw conclusions based on premises or hypotheses. One of my great compatriots, Mr. Sherlock Holmes, is perhaps best known for his deductive reasoning prowess. He and I both demonstrate our reasoning skills by establishing a series of proven premises, or hypotheses, and then demonstrating how a conclusion can be drawn from those postulations. It's analogous to algebra in that it is not enough to simply state the answer for the unknown variable—you

> **If X = 100 and Y = 1; and A = zombies and B = you, then it stands to reason that if X = A and Y = B, then C = "you'd better be wearing your running shoes."**

have to also show your work. Deductive reasoning—and indeed, any reasoning—is how we show our work. Here's a famous example of a deductive argument:

1. All vampires are immortal.
2. Dracula is a vampire.
3. Therefore, Dracula is immortal.

Here's another example of deductive reasoning using a simple algebraic equation for the mathematically inclined out there. Consider the following:

$$X + 2 = 5.$$

Fairly simple, right? You can look at that equation and fairly quickly surmise that X must be 3, for what else can be added to 2 in order to obtain a result of 5? But, simply stating X=3 is not enough. (Nor was it sufficient to demonstrate your aptitude to your math instructors, now was it? Tell the truth, now.) Instead, you have to demonstrate your chain of reasoning. Yes, X=3 is the answer, but the real question is "how did you arrive at that answer?" Thus, to use deductive reasoning in this example, your real answer would look more like this:

$$
\begin{array}{rcr}
X + 2 &=& 5 \\
- 2 &=& -2 \\
X + 0 &=& 3 \\
\\
X + 0 &=& 3
\end{array}
$$

Therefore, X = 3

While people (and sadly vampires) are a bit more complicated than simple algebra allows, this example demonstrates the necessity of showing your reasoning in writing. It follows logic that, without walking the reader from point A to point B, he or she might fall off the treacherous precipice of my logic to a bone-crunching death on the rocks below.

Consider one of my most famous cases—that of the unfortunate Lucy Westenra. What would have happened if the local officials had refused me access to her case because they could not follow my reasoning? Who else might have died as a result of her untreated condition? I had little evidence to go on, but I eventually concluded that her mysterious illness was somehow related to the machinations of her new neighbor, one Count Dracula of Transylvania.

I was first called in because local doctors were unable to properly diagnose and treat Lucy—a young woman suffering from weakness, mental disturbances, paranoia,

uneven heart rate, headache, fever, and sensitivity to light. Since my expertise was so obviously needed, I knew her condition was not attributable to a common disease, which any quack from the University College Hospital in London should have been able to deduce. Rather, I set my sights on more unusual medical conditions which better fit the symptoms of my patient.

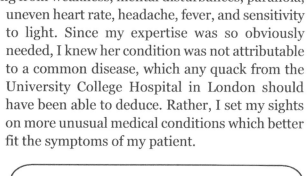

The taste of satisfaction runs like hot blood in my mouth. I guarantee that is the last time Lucy will ever move that football when I try to kick it!

After reviewing the medical literature, I narrowed my diagnosis to porphyria, rabies, or vampirism. The case may have gone unresolved if a key clue hadn't come to my attention: two small puncture wounds on the patient's neck. While this still supports a diagnosis of rabies (perhaps indicating an animal bite), the eye-witness accounts of Lucy's friends and neighbors about the new resident of Carfax Abbey made the case clear. They reported that Count Dracula was never seen in daylight hours, that he was a man with sharp teeth, pointed ears, and an affinity for wolves and bats.

Taking all of this in to account, the evidence was compelling: this was a case of vampirism. Unfortunately, I wasn't able to save Lucy's life, but the importance of my contribution to medical knowledge cannot be overstated.

If it talks like a vampire and walks like a vampire, then we suggest you carry a big stake and maintain your distance.

Okay, back to how this all applies to analytical writing. Writing analytically means being able to think critically—to synthesize information into new knowledge (such as applying a theory to a set of facts) and to present that analysis to your audience clearly and concisely. Analytic writing often involves some kind of fact-finding or preliminary research. While you might assume that a reader can follow your reasoning (if it's sound and based upon empirical evidence), you cannot assume that your audience will agree with your conclusions. After all, all evidence requires interpretation. Analytical writing is most frequently a business-driven or academic pursuit. In business, you write analyses about the feasibility of a financial investment (perhaps in a company that distributes garlic), or an analysis of your market to see if a new business venture will prove to be fruitful or not (for example, developing a synthesized blood drink for vampires). In academia, you write analyses to demonstrate your critical thinking and reasoning skills.

When writing analytically, you often have to present the evidence that supports your analysis—or, simply put, those expert opinions, statistics, and secondary reasons why you think for yourself. Depending on the subject of your analysis, your evidence may take many forms. In analytic writing, "evidence" can come from a variety of places, such as literature, poetry, plays, films, statistics, historical facts, eye-witness accounts, observed phenomena, numerical data, and/or results from experiments. (In my case, of course, the evidence included known facts about disease, the observed symptoms of the young lady, my own impressive body of research into the history and causes of vampirism, and eye-witness accounts of the strange behavior of Count Dracula.) Your analysis, therefore, might include statistics or other numerical data, measurements, calculations, tables, figures, illustrations, art works, film stills or clips, literary passages or poems, or quotes from critics, scholars, experts, study subjects, or eye-witnesses.

Regardless of the type of evidence you are integrating into your analysis, when presenting it, be sure to introduce it. This often includes naming the work or person and summarizing some basic information. An alternative to the classic method of introducing research by saying simply "According to Cornelius Agrippa in his work *Three Books Concerning Occult Philosophy* . . . " (because, frankly, that gets old faster than one of Bill's or Eric's mortal girlfriends from Bon Temps), would be to simply couch the evidence inside a paraphrase or sentence that surrounds the quote. You might say, instead, "When Cornelius Agrippa studied the phenomenon of vampirism in his work on occult philosophy, he discovered that . . . " and then lead the evidence in. Utilizing either method to introduce evidence demonstrates your mastery of the subject you're writing about and increases your credibility. It also helps your reader follow your reasoning. Remember: show, don't tell. Or, as I like to say, "Kill, don't maim." That, I might add, is something for all monster hunters to remember. It doesn't matter whether the vampire is a cute little cheerleader or the zombie is your father. The solution is self-evident.

If you are writing analytically for a business or professional setting, the expectation of your audience will be vastly different than if you are writing for an academic setting. Consider the point in Chapter 1 on the Basics of Writing (penned by our semi-famous, but now undead author friend, Spittoon): audience and purpose are everything. This means that analytical writing will vary depending on both what your point is and who the audience will be.

Having said that, you should know that both business and professional analytical writing present objective, factual information about objective topics—they are not argumentative forms of debate. Such works are based upon a search for truth, which if presented correctly, gives the reader an opportunity to formulate their own conclusions about the topic. It is not a descriptive piece of writing detailing your subjective personal opinion on a subject. Whether you hate all vampires or not is of little concern. It can better be described as a reasoned response to a question or statement, useful as a means for getting information across to readers in quick

Who knows what lurks on the pages of an academic writer? The Nosferatu knows.

fashion. It is a way to tell them what is important and why it is important in a precise and readable manner that doesn't bog down with technical details and jargon. Think in the terms of a zombie with a half-working brain rather than a vampire with 200 years of knowledge. Or, in other words, be the skeleton, not the cadaver.

This is no time to throw bouquets of flowers on the grave. It is not the time to do a clinical autopsy. Tell your readers exactly what they must know. No more. No less. Let them walk away saying "so that's why the dead come back to life" and not still be unsure about their final opinion on the subject.

Now, writing an analytical argument for an academic audience, such as a literary or artistic analysis, will have slightly different rules or expectations than writing something analytical for a business or professional setting—chiefly, it is primarily an argument offering your unique perspective or opinion on the subject. In the academic world, analytical writing is a step above the information regurgitation you perform when expounding a book report, for instance. That is, analytical writing goes well beyond summarizing a work (whether artistic, musical, literary, etc.). Instead, it demands that the writer offer new ideas which he or she tosses into the fray. In other words, you might suggest that Dracula is a modernized retelling of the Perseus myth (the Greek "hero" best known for slaying Medusa and rescuing Andromeda from certain death). To support this theory, you would need to look at the both the myth and the novel and demonstrate your reasoning for the reader, creating a sound argument with ample evidence (from sources outside the novel and myth, as well) to support your claims.

This type of analysis is criticism at its finest—that is, the root meaning of the word "criticism," which is "critic"—the same as in "critical" thinking.

Indulge me for a moment while I ask one of my wards to venture into a few comments on analytical writing. Christabel is a young woman whom I met near a castle gate around midnight one April whilst traveling a bit with my companion, Samuel Coleridge. A vampire, sure enough, she has renounced her demonic ways and is currently under my treatment. She should be cured of her insatiable thirst for blood within a fortnight, and though I have a few reservations about asking for her assistance in penning this chapter, she is one heck of an academic writer.

Academic Analytical Writing

They say everyone is a critic.

I suppose that's true to some extent, but in recent years, I have found it is not true when it comes to glittery vampire novels. And be careful not to criticize them unless you want an army of pre-teen girls and their mothers picketing your front lawn with a backpack full of wooden stakes and holy water—not a pretty scene. Even if you are tempted to criticize this vision of vampires that sparkle, you can't deny that some people are very rich as a result of such characterizations.

But criticism really is more than your vampire mother telling you to "straighten your caplet and clean the blood off your chin; you look like a rabid chinchilla." Criticism is a form of analysis that, when coupled with argument, helps you convey interpretive connections you've made within your mind about a piece of literature, a painting, a political debate, or your last income tax statement to readers.

Let's say I decide to write an analysis about the play *Hamlet*. Having personal experience with the symptoms of vampirism and the efficacy of treatment, I have long held the belief that Shakespeare's Hamlet character was, in fact, a vampire. Now, to write any analysis, you must first entertain a hypothesis about your subject. This will vary depending on what you are writing about. For the sake of this analytical argument, let's say that your hypothesis is that Hamlet himself was actually a vampire. You would then take this hypothesis and evaluate it against the evidence provided in the text.

Here's how I see it: Hamlet talks to the ghost of his father, which might indicate that he's in league with the dead. He hangs around in cemeteries playing with the skulls of old friends like Yoric, which may indicate that he is comfortable with graveyards, coffins, and cemetery dust. He agrees to kill several people and does so by the end of the tale, which indicates that he may enjoy killing or that people are of little value to him—like they would be, perhaps, if they were a food source? And he engages with the principle heroine of the story, the young and fair Ophelia (not unlike Lucy

And for my soul,
what can it do to that,
being a thing immortal
as itself?
Hamlet I:iv 66-67

Westenra or Mina Murray Harker, wouldn't you agree?), as a rogue who strings the girl along in hopes of wooing her out of her shift—indicating that he might have the dashing and debonair vampire charisma we've all come to know and love from such greats as Dracula, Lestat, Eric, Angel, and Edward.

After you've held the hypothesis

up to the sunlight of your evidence and ensured that it has not disintegrated into a glittering pile of dust (or, uh, since we want him to be a vampire, maybe the opposite of what I just said), then you engage with research to see if there is anything out there that supports your ideas outside of the text itself. Even as an expert myself, I still must turn to other experts to support my claims.

For instance, I might examine what the *Malleus Maleficarum* ("The Hammer Against Witches," the book used by the Inquisition in the fifteenth century to determine if a person was to be burned alive as a witch or not) has to say about vampires. It suggests that three things must be present for a being to become a vampire: the devil, a corpse, and God's permission.

After establishing some initial research, I then would take the supplementary evidence I acquired (the *Malleus Maleficarum*) and use that to support the contextual evidence I discovered in the scenes from *Hamlet* itself, crafting a connection between the two sources as I go.

For example, in Act II, Scene 2, Hamlet says directly "The devil [has] power to form a pleasing shape," which might suggest that Hamlet is engaging with the devil, or at the very least, has found the devil to be appealing in some capacity. Then we tie that to the evidence in the *Malleus*, saying something like: "Thus, if Hamlet is able to find the devil attractive, perhaps Hamlet has invited the devil in." We would then go on to search for connections between the rest of the evidence. There are several dead bodies in *Hamlet* to provide one of the three ingredients for a *Malleus* vampire to be present—indeed, they stack up like virgins in Elizabeth Bathory's basement. And as for God's permission, Hamlet does suggest that men are like gods in his famous monologue, "What a piece of work is man . . . in action how like an angel! In apprehension how like a god," which might suggest that Hamlet either has God's permission or feels that he doesn't need it because he is already like a god unto himself (*Hamlet* II:ii).

So now, I have a hypothesis, I've supported my theory with evidence from the text, and corroborated it with evidence from other experts and resources. I am now ready to write my thesis statement and thesis map (or my "theory statement" or "statement of purpose"). Whatever you call it, it all amounts to the same thing: a sentence which encapsulates my argument and shows the reader how I plan to prove it which is then carefully placed somewhere near the beginning of my essay to guide the reader like a compass through the points I plan to make. For this example, I might write the following thesis:

> In Shakespeare's *Hamlet, the protagonist is a vampire as evidenced by his attraction to the devil, his bloodlust for the deaths of so many loved ones, and his relationship to God.*

Notice how the statement doesn't beat around the gravestone, nor does it whimper or try to disown the idea in case someone reading it might disagree? In other words, the statement doesn't say "Hamlet could possibly be seen as a vampire." It comes right out and says "Hamlet is a vampire." That's because you need to be confident when presenting a theory unless you want to give your readers a flaming torch and pitchfork so they can later annihilate you with a counterargument. Be brave. And don't say "in my opinion." Your readers are smart enough to know that if they are reading something you wrote, chances are, it is your opinion.

The conclusion of a piece of academic analytical writing reaffirms the thesis. It reminds the reader exactly what you want him or her to walk away from your essay believing (or at the very least, considering) by refreshing their minds about what you theorized and how you supported it. In our example, that would be the idea that Hamlet is a vampire—a fact supported by all the points along the arc of the play's story that suggested your theory was accurate (with a good peppering of evidence along the way). In other words, it summarizes your key points, reasserts the thesis, and declares the point all over again. Like any good conclusion would.

Academic analytical writing, then, requires that you posit a new and unique theory about a piece of work, whether that work is creative or scientific. To that end, it could even be a chemistry lab report (perhaps on a potion to repulse the dead) that will allow you to add new research and new ideas to the world of scholarly pursuits. Once you have posited your new theory (declared your hypothesis), you then find evidence both contextually (within the thing you are studying, like vampire-infected blood) and externally (with supporting evidence found in expert research on the same or similar topics). Demonstrate this evidence in true essay form with a thesis (your hypothesis), chain of reasoning (with evidence), and a conclusion. Voila—an academic analytical essay is born!

As with all writing, even academic writing needs to go through rigorous drafting and revision. Many times, writers have to write the whole first draft just to figure out

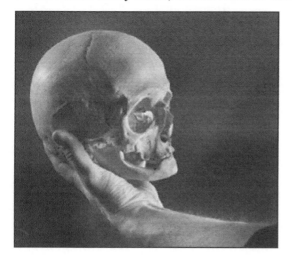

Who hasn't talked to a skull or two in his day? It's when the skulls talk back to you that you should begin to worry.

what they think—and then write their way into a powerful thesis. (In rough drafts, the last paragraph often becomes the introduction in the next version—or the final sentence, which hadn't occurred to the writer earlier in the drafting process, turns out to be the perfect thesis.) When drafting and revising academic writing, ask for feedback. Ask your reader specific questions about your paper, and think about how to integrate their feedback and suggestions as you revise.

To improve the organization or clarity of an academic paper, try reverse outlining. Take your rough draft and write down the main idea for each paragraph. And voila! You have a reverse outline of your paper. (In other words, slay the vampire and then figure out how you accomplished the feat.) You've basically just created a mini-index of your paper, which can help you analyze and evaluate your own writing. Revision is (literally) re-vision—seeing your paper again in a new way. A reverse outline can help you accomplish this.

Now that you have a reverse outline, you can assess different parts of the paper. For example, compare your thesis with the reverse outline: are all the main ideas present in both? Use the reverse outline to study the organization of your ideas. How are they organized? Is that the most effective sequence? What if you tried moving ideas around? There's a particular type of reverse outline referred to as a "daisy chain" or "clotheslines" outline, which is useful for revising arguments. To employ this method, put your thesis at the top of the page and beneath it, list every topic sentence from your draft. Ideally, you should be able to see the line of argument or reasoning connecting everything together—like a clothesline with pieces of clothing hanging off it. Or maybe pikes displaying the decapitated heads of vampires.

I appreciate your indulgence as well as my doctor's (Abraham Van Helsing) as I expound my own ideas about analytical writing. Since the paper I described arguing that Hamlet is a vampire has already been written by one of this very book's authors, I see no reason to, what is it you say, "reinvent the horse"? No? "Wheel," is it? That makes no sense. The horse is much older than—very well, then.

The following example of a literary analysis on *Hamlet* is presented in MLA format as this would be considered a "humanities" paper. If writing an analysis of a person's mental health through case studies, you might use APA formatting instead. (For more information on MLA formatting, read the section in Chapter 9 on Academic Writing.)

Matthews 1 ◄─ ①

Araminta Matthews ◄─────────────────────────────── ②

Professor Abraham Van Helsing

Vampirism in Literature ENG201

June 6, 2006

    Interview with a Danish Prince: An Exploration into the Vampiric ◄─ ③

        Tendencies of Shakespeare's Greatest Antihero

    Few characters in the expanse of literary history have been as ◄─ ④

confounding or inspiring as Shakespeare's immortal Hamlet. At once ◄─ ⑤

a hero driven to avenge his allegedly murdered father and a villain

who commits the rash and bloody deed of murdering Polonius, the

father of his only known romantic interest in the story, Hamlet is ◄─ ⑥

indeed a dynamic personality. Regardless of Hamlet's profound

infamy in the world of scholarly debate, he remains a rich tapestry for

exploration and analysis. The discrepancies of his age, his ◄─ ⑦

relationship to the other characters in the play, and the myriad

references to blood and death threaded throughout the script support a

theory few scholars have exhaustively researched: Hamlet is an

immortal vampire driven to bloodlust and vengeance by the loss of

his immortal soul. ◄─ ⑧

    At the beginning of the play, Horatio, Hamlet's long-time ◄─ ⑨

1 All margins are 1". There is a header in the upper right margin which contains the page number and (usually) your last name.

2 Instead of a title page, papers in the MLA style have headings on the left side of the first page with your name, your professor's name, the course, and the date.

3 The paper's title (and it should have one!) is centered and formatted normally (no italics, quotation marks, or underlining). Capitalize everything except short prepositions (such as "of") or articles which do not appear as the first word (such as "the" in "the Vampiric Tendencies"). The title is your reader's first point of contact with your work—don't miss this opportunity to hook them, and to set their expectations regarding what the paper is about.

4 Text is double-spaced, in a regular font (such as Times New Roman).

5 The paper's "hook" emphasizes the "confounding" and "inspiring" qualities of this well-known character. We can assume that this paper explores a new way in which this character is interesting.

6 Even though the paper is on a well-known play, Araminta provides a brief sketch of the character. Even if her reader knows the play very well, they may not recall these same details that Araminta wants to emphasize.

7 In this sentence, Araminta connects her work to a larger conversation about Hamlet; she acknowledges that much research already exists about this work, but that there remains more to say. Pointing to a "gap" in the scholarly conversation is one strategy to set up a thesis.

8 Araminta's thesis uses concrete details from the play as reasons to support a debatable theory about Hamlet. The thesis is debtable because other scholars or readers might interpret this same evidence (his relationship to other characters and references to blood) in a different way. In the humanities, an argument based on interpretation is acceptable; other disciplines may ask different kinds of questions ("Was Hamlet schizophrenic") or require different kinds of evidence (historical accounts of mental illness; modern scholarship on mental disorders).

9 New paragraphs begin ½ inch from the left margin (use the "Tab" key). There are no spaces between paragraphs.

Matthews 2

friend, is talking to the night-watchman who oversees the cemetery

outside the castle at Elsinore and believes he has seen the ghost of

Hamlet's father. In true ghost-story fashion, Horatio tells the fellow

guard a tale of Rome in which, shortly before Julius Caesar's death,

"the graves stood tenantless and the sheeted dead / did squeak and

gibber in the Roman streets / as stars with trains of fire and dews of

blood" (I.i 132-134). Horatio speaks in great detail about this event,

almost as if he had been there to witness it himself. In addition, where

this occurs in the opening scene of the play, it sets the tone for what is

to come. Here, we have graves that have been emptied and their

presumed dead inhabitants no longer behave thusly, as would a

vampire newly risen from the dead. To have Hamlet's closest friend

declare that graves are "tenantless" and that their inhabitants were

moving about as mortals might with "dews of blood" suggests that

this might be the tone for the overall story arc—particularly when this

tale of Roman vampires comes after their own brush with the ghost of

Hamlet's dead father. Or is Hamlet's father—described as a ghost by

the characters in the play—in fact a vampire?

　　　　Some cultures throughout history have made little if not

merely vague distinctions between our modern concept of ghost

(apparitions which appear after a being has died) and vampire (post-

10 Here is Araminta's first piece of textual evidence—a direct quote. This is a blended quotation, whereby the quote is part of Araminta's sentence. Before the quote, Araminta describes the scene so that her reader can understand what's happening, and therefore be more convinced by her evidence. If readers are confused by a quote, they will not be convinced of your argument.

11 After the quote, Araminta explains and analyzes it. As the writer, it's her responsibility to show the reader how this quote supports her argument. She does this with analysis, where she connects the empty graves and walking dead from Horatio's line to Araminta's idea that the play contains elements of vampirism. Sometimes writers feel that this step is redundant, but it's not. Every reader will read the same quote in different ways. Including clear analysis is one way to make sure that readers don't miss what you think is important information.

12 Asking a question can be a great way to engage your reader—as long as you answer it in some way. Here, Araminta's question introduces a new idea that she begins to explore in the next paragraph.

13 Early in her paper, Araminta presents historical background information to help support her analysis. This information is not represented in the thesis, and that's okay. This historical background is important for understanding her argument, but it is not in itself one of the claims she is making.

Matthews 3

dead beings which suck the life energy from those still living). The
old Norse word, "draugr," for example, is often translated as "ghost"
in English, but more accurately refers to creatures that rise from the
dead and torment the living (Jakobsson). In Indonesian legend and
culture, vampires and ghosts can be one and the same, as evidenced
by the myths of creatures inhabiting mannerisms of both ghosts and
vampires, such as Langsuyar, Pontianak, and Penanggalan (Siddique ← **14**
25).

    Given that historically, cultures have offered few distinctions ← **15**
between vampires and ghosts, it is possible that the ghost of Hamlet's
father is, in fact, a vampire. Where vampirism is a blood disorder as
evidenced by their supposed thirst for the life fluid (Boffey 15), and
where genetic blood type and blood diseases can be passed from
parent to offspring through genes (or, to use a less modern conceptual
term, through "blood") (Baker 18; 21-22), then perhaps the dead king
passed on a genetic predisposition to vampirism to his only son, the
prince Hamlet.

    As most people know, the modern day image of the vampire ← **16**
revolves around the concept of blood and immortality. Further
evidence that Hamlet is a vampire comes from the twenty-nine
references made to blood by different characters throughout the play.

14 Even though there is not a quotation here like we saw above, Araminta includes a citation. When summarizing ideas or background information, you still need to cite the source. This way, if readers want to know more about your topic, or if they have a question about the source, they know exactly where it came from. Citing also gives credit where it's due, and establishes your credibility as a researcher and writer. Most in-text citations include the author's last name followed by the page number. The last name helps the reader find this source in the "Works Cited" at the end of the paper, which is organized by authors' last names (or title if there is no author).

15 This topic sentence transitions from the idea of the previous paragraph (the history of vampire and ghost legends) and the next idea (whether Hamlet's father might be a ghost). Without this transition, a reader might feel lost jumping from Indonesian legends to Hamlet's father.

16 This sentence includes what we can consider "common knowledge" (that vampires are connected to blood), and therefore does not need a citation. Sometimes it can be difficult to determine what is or isn't common knowledge, especially if you are writing on a topic that's new to you. When in doubt, cite it!

Matthews 4

Additionally, according to the scene around Yorick's grave, we learn

that Hamlet is approximately 29-30 (Wood 25). But some question

lingers around the true age of Hamlet as he is supposedly just

returned from college in Wittenberg (I.i 316), , which would make

him closer to age 16-20. So why is Hamlet closer to thirty when ← **17**

returning from college? Could it be that his rate of aging has been

altered by his vampiric disease?

His vampiric disease is evidenced, too, by his traditional

vampire tendencies. He is attracted to younger women over whom he

purports some pernicious power. Like Dracula to his Lucy Westenra,

Ophelia is as a moth to his flame. Vampires are well known for their

seductive powers and their sexual openness, as "the very notion of

'devouring' and 'eating' is redolent of sex" (Backstein 38). ← **18**

Furthermore, "the vampire , in almost every artistic incarnation,

symbolizes . . . the romantic idea that sex = death" (Backstein 40).

Ophelia and Hamlet have had some kind of romantic relationship in

which gifts were exchanged. Might blood have been exchanged, too?

We know that Ophelia is enamored of Hamlet, and we also

know that the infatuation, while mutual, is, as Laertes suggests, "a toy

in blood" (I.iii 488). This implies that Laertes views Hamlet's desire ← **19**

for Ophelia as nothing more than a plaything which might be related

17 These questions—and this paragraph—begin to refer back to the ideas in the thesis. Showing the reader these connections builds the argument, piece by piece.

---

18 Instead of offering her own analysis of the literary text, Araminta here quotes from a scholar. Even though Backstein is not talking about *Hamlet*, Araminta can use Backstein's work to support her own (original) analysis of vampires in *Hamlet*. Using supplementary sources such as this allows Araminta to support her argument and not simply to reiterate the arguments other scholars may have about Hamlet. When searching for research for a literary analysis, don't limit yourself to resources specifically related to the literature you are analyzing. Think deeper.

---

19 In MLA style, quotation marks end the quote, followed by the in-text parenthetical citation, which is then punctuated with a period. Note that the period is on the outside of the parenthesis, since it's closing punctuation for the entire sentence, not just the quotation. When citing plays, it's common to give scene, act, and line numbers. In this case, the lines come from Act 1, Scene 3, line 488.

Matthews 5

to his desire for her blood. Ophelia's father, Polonius, too views

Hamlet's infatuation with the girl as dangerous, declaring that "when

the blood burns, how prodigal the soul" (1.3.603), suggesting that

Hamlet's blood (or, perhaps, Ophelia's) is hot, causing the soul to

return temporarily—as a vampire who is soulless must feed on the

blood of a living being to drown the sorrows related to the loss of that ◄──20

soul. Polonius further suggests that Hamlet's infatuation with Ophelia

is an "unholy suit" (I.iii 616) and that his nature is simply to

"beguile" the girl (I.iii 618).

    Beguiling the girl may not have been Hamlet's only intention

when dealing with Ophelia. When she attempts to return the gifts, or

remembrances, he has given her, she is met with hostility and anger.

Hamlet turns on the girl and, after a few angry words, declares "for

virtue cannot so / inoculate our old stock but we shall relish of it" ◄──21

(III.i 1810-1811). An inoculation by modern standards often refers to

receiving a fluid by way of transfusion directly injected into the

bloodstream, usually used to prevent some kind of illness from

descending, and virtue is often used in Shakespeare's time

interchangeably with the concept of virginity, a secret weakness of

vampires in popular culture. The sheer act of vampirism, where the

creature "leans in to take his victim's blood, a thinly veiled act of

20 Even though this is neither factual nor is Araminta likely an expert on this subject, this sentence is not cited because it is "common knowledge." Common knowledge refers to information that your audience will already know without needing a book or expert resource to tell them so. It is information readily available to anyone who might read her paper. In this case, the fact that vampires drink blood is a necessary supportive component to Araminta's argument even though it is common knowledge—hence, there is no need to include a citation for it.

21 When citing lines of poetry or plays, use the slash to indicate line breaks. While many plays are not written in verse, much of Shakespeare's work is poetic by nature.

Matthews 6

penetration," suggests that vampirism and sexuality are inextricably linked (Winnubst 9). Thus, Ophelia's apparent romantic interlude with Hamlet may well have been under the guise of a vampiric seduction of a young virgin. Could lusty Hamlet be saying that his young lover's, Ophelia's, virtue (her virgin blood) inoculates him against the ill-effects of vampirism?

And later, still, in the same scene after Hamlet has left their encounter, Ophelia reflects on her own interactions with Hamlet prior to the scene. In this reflection, she explains that she, "of ladies most deject and wretched / . . . sucked the honey of his music vows" (III.i 1846-1847). While most scholars will suggest that this is a metaphor for Ophelia's folly at taking Hamlet at his word when he told her he loved her, what if this isn't a metaphor at all? What if she literally "sucked the honey" (his blood) because he promised her immortal youth and beauty ("his music vows")? Dracula seemingly pulls a ◄— ㉒ similar stunt with his vampire brides and when he attempts to woo Mina Harker. Similar promises are made by Lestat when he sires ◄— ㉓ Louis in Rice's Vampire Chronicles, as well.

According to myths and legends surrounding vampires, the creatures are believed to be unholy or damned. *The Malleus* ◄— ㉔ *Maleficarum*, or "The Hammer Against Witches," which was used

22 These next two sentences contain references to other works of literature, *Dracula* and *Interview with a Vampire*. Because this paper is for a course on vampires in literature, these works are probably "common knowledge" for Araminta's reader—in this case, her professor. For another audience, however, this might be information that Araminta might choose to expand (such as with brief quotes and citations) to help her reader understand the references.

23 Araminta has spent four paragraphs on the relationship between Hamlet and Ophelia, which suggests that this is an important and main point in the paper. Their relationship was generally introduced in the thesis, and in the paper we see it again—but in much more detail, with evidence and analysis.

24 In MLA style, titles of longer or significant works are italicized.

during the Spanish Inquisition in a misguided effort to eradicate

supposed witches and other supernatural beasts from the earth in the

name of the Catholic Church, declares that "the Devil . . . loves blood ◄—24

and the pouring out of blood" (159), suggesting that blood-drinkers or

those who spill blood are unholy or sinful.

Later, Hamlet himself supports the idea that he is of this

unholy brood when he declares that there is something more than

natural about blood—presumably his blood—while referring to his

family (II.ii 1449). Perhaps Hamlet is alluding to a blood impurity or

a disease of the blood not unlike vampirism that racks his soul, too,

when he declares that, "when the churchyards yawn, and hell itself

breathes out / Contagion to the world. Now could [he] drink hot ◄—25

blood" (III.ii 2265-2266). There is no greater evidence that a person

has become a vampire than his thirst for human blood and his own

passing into death. Vampires, after all, "suck blood, transferring an

illegitimate and disavowed substance, transforming his 'victims' from

the living to the undead, giving birth without sex, trafficking in the

strange and unruly logics of fluids, mixing and spilling and infecting

blood" (Winnubst 8). Here, Hamlet declares that his blood is

unnatural and that he could drink the blood of others. Has Hamlet ◄—26

already died, then, and entered one other realm of vampirism?

24 These three periods, an ellipsis, means that Araminta has omitted a word or words from the quote. It is assumed that the omission has not altered the meaning of the quote in any way.

25 Brackets indicate that this word is not in the original text. Brackets are used to supply words to help clarity. Here, the original line includes "I," which in this case would not fit with Mina's sentence. In other cases, pronouns in a quote might be unclear or confusing, and it's common to supply a name or other identifying information in brackets.

26 In this paragraph Araminta uses a combination of primary texts (the play) and secondary texts (the scholarly work of Winnubst) to introduce and support this point.

Matthews 8

Symbolic imagery suggests that Hamlet is deceased before the

show begins. Early in the production, Hamlet enters the Castle at

Elsinore dressed in his "inky cloak" (I.i 281). In the middle ages, ◄—— 27

people of all castes were often buried in shrouds, but the "richest

classes were buried in elaborate and elegant garments" (Welford 11).

Famous artists of the period, such as Holbein the Younger, DaVinci, ◄—— 28

Dürer, and Brecht, are also known to have painted portraits of the

royal classes sporting dark gray and black clothing as they posed

resplendent in their best finery for the occasion of a portrait painting.

This suggests that the finest clothing a prince would have (and thus,

the elaborate garment in which he would be buried), would indeed

have been black.

Furthermore, individuals interred during the Middle Ages

were buried symbolically in a six-foot deep hold "from east to west

with the head lying to the west, so a person could rise up with his/her

face to the east" (Welford 12). Hamlet's father, either a ghost or a

vampire as we well know, appears in the cemetery according to

Bernardo when the western star has moved across the sky (I.i 47-48),

suggesting that Hamlet senior, who may have passed the vampire

disposition through his blood to his son, faces westward—opposite

the church's sanction. Perhaps he has been damned? We also know

27 Here, Araminta is playing with common knowledge and argument. It is common knowledge—perhaps even common popular culture—to envision a vampire in a long, black cloak (such as Bela Lugosi, Christopher Lee, Lon Chaney Jr., or Gary Oldman depicting the popular vampire, Dracula).

28 Not all supportive evidence needs to come from books, scholarly journals, or personal interviews with experts. Here, Araminta uses famous painters to exemplify what sorts of things might have been seen in the era in which Shakespeare was writing the play. In a generation without photography or the Internet, paintings would be one of the few methods by which we could examine popular fashion of the period. Using painters to support this argument presents another way of looking at the argument which is likely to attract or convince more of her audience than simply using written works as supporting evidence.

that Hamlet considers himself to be "but a mad north-north-west"

(II.ii 1460) and that he among his Danish peers are known for their

"heavy-headed revel east and west" (II.iv 645). These lines suggest

that Hamlet may, like his countrymen, spend too much time reveling

eastward and westward, like a mourner or a corpse laid to rest,

perhaps? And that he, unlike his god-fearing, properly buried

compatriots with all Catholic funerary rights, may have been buried

facing west or northwest, leading to his supposed madness.

Regardless of Hamlet's location in funerary space, let's

suppose for a moment that Hamlet has been a vampire for much

longer than the Middle Ages. Even with this consideration, the nature

of his costume still lends credibility to the idea that it is his burial or

mourning clothing. Men of ancient Rome would wear a "special toga

of mourning which was made of special black or dark brown wool"

(Sabesta 11). Black has long been considered symbolic of death, so ← 29

even should Hamlet have been made a vampire in the times of

Ancient Rome, his choice of clothing still supports the concept of his

death. And, in part due to its connection to the night, the inky color of

his cloak suggests vampirism, as well, given that the garment could

be a symbol of the death shroud (cloak), a toga, and the cloak of

"night" which shrouds vampires in their evil deeds.

Using symbolic imagery or meaning to support an argument offers yet another diverse way of looking at a thesis or claim. Here, Araminta offers the symbolic meaning of a color. While it is common knowledge that black might symbolize death and thus she doesn't need to cite it, had she decided to expand on this concept she may have turned to an expert on symbolism or a dictionary of signs and symbols to incorporate yet another valid, supportive resource into her argument.

Matthews 10

In addition to other evidence supporting Hamlet's death (and ← 30 thus resurrection to the ranks of the undead) prior to the start of the play, Hamlet also displays a remarked comfort in dealings with other dead things. That is, he actually plays with the skull of his childhood guardian and playmate, Yorick, cleaving to the skull from the moment it is tossed to him in Act 5, Scene 1 for several lines, receiving the skull before line 3,417 and not putting it down until line 3,530. Thus, for 113 lines, Hamlet plays with a skull as though it is a normal action for a prince to undertake.

Even previous to Yorick's macabre skull being used as a kind of softball, Hamlet also expresses his comfort with dead bodies by hiding the corpse of Polonius, whom Hamlet "accidentally" murders during a row with his mother (III.iv 2410). Claudius is forced to send in Hamlet's friends, Rosencrantz and Guildenstern, to seek out the hiding place of the body (IV.iii 2708-2709), which Hamlet is remiss to give up, instead playing at riddles of worms that eat bodies and humans that eat worms—in essence, eating people. (IV.iii 2739). Hiding a body requires handling it, which demonstrates Hamlet's ease with regard to being in the company of (un)dead things. Eating ← 31 people, as we've already pointed out, is a vampiric activity.

Finally, on the matter of Hamlet's death, when at last he is

(30) This topic sentence transitions by linking different pieces of evidence together, marking a shift from previously discussed evidence to a new example: dealing with the dead.

(31) This sentence connects the evidence of this paragraph to a point made earlier in the paper. This kind of connection and repetition builds coherency in the paper, and makes it much easier for a reader to see how everything (main points and pieces of evidence) is working together.

confronted with the death of Ophelia, Hamlet reacts passionately as a
vampire might, suggesting that he should be "buried quick with her"
(V.i 3623) and that the onlookers should "throw millions of acres on
[them], until the ground / singeing his head against the burning zone"
(V.i. 3625-3626). Many will remember that Bram Stoker's famous
vampire, Dracula, was required to sleep in his own grave's dirt, and
most of the vampires in popular culture (a few withstanding) are
thought to burn up when exposed to the rays of the sun. Here, Hamlet
suggests he bury himself with Ophelia, be surrounded by the grave
dirt being tossed upon her and that the burning sun will otherwise
burn his head. Thus, Hamlet's symbolic clothing, his relationship and ← **32**
ease around dead things, his riddles about eating people through
worms, and his desire to be buried against the singeing of the hot sun
all suggest that Hamlet might already be dead, like a vampire.

But this still raises the question of when Hamlet may have ← **33**
died and how he became a vampire. The answer might be found in his
grand death scene in the final act. In the scene with Yorick's skull,
Hamlet turns to his long-time friend, Horatio, and suggests in true
macabre fashion, that "imperious Caesar, dead and turn'd to clay /
might stop a hole to keep the wind away" (V.i. 3540-3541). This is the
second time one of the duo has made reference to ancient Rome, with

This sentences summarizes key pieces of evidence as support for Araminta's main claim (that Hamlet is a vampire). In this context, this sentence is preparing the reader to transition to a new idea. Before presenting the new idea, Araminta reminds us where we've been so far in the paper—it's easy for a reader to lose track of the thesis they read several pages ago.

So far, the paper has presented evidence that Hamlet is a vampire. This paragraph marks a shift towards a slightly different question: How did he become one?

Matthews 12

one more still to come. As Hamlet continues to fight to the bitter end,

Horatio likens himself to being more like an antique Roman than his

kinsfolk of Denmark in the final scene of the play (V.ii 4000), closing

the play with another reference to what would be ancient history for

the people of Elisinore just as he began the play with a similar

reference, speaking of ancient Rome with familiarity, describing in

detail the night that same Caesar, "the mightiest Julius" fell (I.i 133). ← 34

    Where Hamlet speaks of Caesar with obvious disdain in that

the body of this man could be no more useful than as a cork to plug a

hole, is it possible that Hamlet might have some personal contempt

for the man? And where Horatio speaks of ancient Rome not only as

if it were his own home, but also in great and specific detail

surrounding the night Caesar died, could Horatio have possibly been

there? Could it be these timeless friends were Romans together, and,

together, plotted or killed an old enemy: Caesar? This would certainly

support the possibility that Hamlet, now hundreds of years older than

even his age discrepancies in the script would allow us to argue,

might have endured some transition into a state of immortality—

perhaps a transition such as the one endured by legendary vampires

who, apart from staking, decapitation, and burning, are immortal

themselves.

By reminding the reader what she already stated in previous pages about Hamlet and Horatio and their connection to Ancient Rome, Araminta has created a connection between the beginning and the end of the play that ties in with the lines from her argument. Sometimes repeating yourself is necessary to demonstrate the relationship between your ideas to your reader. Because readers probably don't think the same way you do, creating those connections is of paramount importance to demonstrating a sound argument.

Matthews 13

At last, the play concludes with the entrance of Fortinbras, coming onto the scene where Hamlet has been finally defeated, to find Horatio alone among the survivors able to explain what happened to the new prince of Denmark. Horatio declares that Fortinbras shall hear "of carnal, bloody, and unnatural acts" (V.ii 4048) in the telling of Hamlet's story. Here, again, we have the reference to the unnatural, again paired with the idea of blood. *The Malleus Maleficarum* declares that "every alteration that takes place in a human body—for example, a state of health or a state of sickness—can be brought down to a question of natural causes, as Aristotle has shown in his 7th book of Physic" (*Malleus Maleficarum* 50). Yet, Hamlet and Horatio both describe the Danish prince as unnatural on more than one occasion, both of these references having some relationship to blood. This suggests that Hamlet, being unnatural, must be the result of some "dark and occult cause" (50). As the Catholic Church's own reference manual to matters of supernatural occurrence suggests, unnatural occurrences must be the result of occultism. Therefore, it is possible that Hamlet's unnatural state, if we are to use the logic of *The Malleus Maleficarum* used by the priests of Shakespeare's—and *Hamlet's*—day, could only be a result of occult causes—such as that of vampirism.

When there is no author, use a shortened version of the title in in-text citations.

Matthews 14

Hamlet truly is an immortal Shakespearean character, but **(36)**
could Shakespeare have been hinting at another type of immortality
when he penned the tale of this Danish prince? Infected by the
vampire-tainted blood of his own slain father who haunts the family
cemetery still, Hamlet may well have murdered Polonius and even
Ophelia driven by sheer blood lust. The many references to blood,
Hamlet's unnatural state with relation to blood, the discrepancies
related to his true age, and the suggestion that he and his oldest friend
may well be ancient Romans lend support to the idea that Hamlet is
an undead vampire. Had vampires been even half as popular in
Shakespeare's day as they are today, perhaps the reference to the
Dane's immortality would have been more overt. Maybe Hamlet **(37)**
would have sparkled as he stalked young Ophelia, or maybe he'd
have brooded about whether or not to get his soul back as he dashed
about in a leather trench coat rather than an inky cloak. Who knows?

36 The conclusion summarizes the motivating question and the key points of the paper, but without using the same exact sentences.

37 The conclusion also leaves the reader with something to think about— how Hamlet (both the play and the character) might have been different if vampirism was a more prominent theme. Certainly food for thought…

Matthews 15

Works Cited ◄─────────────────── ③⑧

Backstein, Karen. "(Un)Safe Sex: Romancing the Vampire." *Cineaste.* ◄─── ③⑨

35.1 (Winter 2009): 38-41. MasterFILE Premier.

Baker, Catherine. *Your Genes, Your Choices: Exploring the Issues*

Related to Genetic Research. American Association for the

Advancement of Science, Science + Literacy for Health Project:

1999. Web. 3 Nov. 2011. http://www.choicesandchallenges.sts.vt.edu/

modules/pdf/yourgenes.pdf>

Boffey, Philip. "Rare Disease Proposed as Cause for 'Vampires.'" *New*

York Times. 31 May 1985, p. 15. Web. 3 Nov. 2011.

<http://www.nytimes.com/1985/05/31/us/ rare-disease-proposed-as-

cause-for-vampires.html>

Jakobsson, Ármann. "Vampires and Watchmen: Categorizing the ◄─── ④⓪

Mediaeval Icelandic Undead." *Journal of English and Germanic*

Philosophy. 110.3 (2011): 281-300.

The Malleus Maleficarum of Heinrich Kramer and James Sprenger. ◄─── ④①

(1487). Trans. Montague Summers. (1928). Mineoloa, NY: Dover

Occult, 1971.

Sabesta, Judith Lynn. *Weavers of Fate: Symbolism in the Costume of* ◄─── ④②

Roman Women. University of South Dakota. (n.d.) Web. 3 Nov. 2011.

<http://www.usd.edu/arts-and-sciences/upload/Harrington-Lecture-

Sebesta.pdf>

38 Depending on the style you are using, your list of references will look very different. In general, though, all styles represent the same basic information: the author, title, and publication information. The list of references begins on its own page. It should have the same margins, header, and text as the rest of the paper. The title is centered, without italics, underlines, or quotation marks.

39 Citations are listed in alphabetical order, which makes sources easier to find in your list.

40 In MLA style, references begin with the author's last name, followed by the title of the work. In this entry, a journal article, the title of the article comes before the title of the journal. You can tell the difference because the article title is in quotation marks, and the journal title is italicized. This is followed by information about the volume, including which volume and number it is, when it was published, and its page numbers.

41 Sources without authors begin with the title. In this case, there is also a translator included, and this information comes after the title. Because there are many versions and translations of this work, Araminta also included the original date of composition (1487) and the date of translation (1928), in addition to when the copy she was using was published (1971).

42 Citing sources from the web follows the same basic format. In this case, the author name, followed by the name of the website, the medium (Web), and access information (3 Nov. 2011). Date of access is important to include in case information on the website changes, as it often does.

Matthews 16

Shakespeare, William. *Hamlet*. Open Source Shakespeare. George Mason
    University, 2003-2012. <http://www.opensourceshakespeare.org/
    views/plays/play_view.php?WorkID=hamlet&Scope=entire&pleasew
    ait=1&msg=pl#a1,s1>

Siddique, Sophie. "Haunting Visions of the Sundelbolong: Vampire
    Ghosts and the Indonesian National Imagery." Ed. Harmony Wu.
    *Axes to Grind: Re-Imagining the Horrific in Visual Media and
    Culture. Spectator* 22.2 (Fall 2002): 24-33.

Welford, Mack. "American Death and Burial Custom Derivation from
    Medieval European Cultures." *The Forum.* (Sept./Oct. 1992): 11-14.
    Web. 2 Nov. 2011. <www.nyu.edu/ classes/gmoran/WELFORD.pdf>

Winnubst, Shannon. "Vampires, Anxieties, and Dreams: Race and Sex in
    Contemporary United States." *Hypatia.* 18.3 (Summer 2003): 1-20.

Wood, Robert E. "Taking Up the Past: Hamlet and Time." *Journal of
    Dramatic Theory and Criticism.* (Spring, 1988): 21-40.

Writing Prompts for Chapter 7

1. Write an analysis of what frightens you. What is it about these things that frighten you? What caused it? Is there something in your history that made you fear this?

2. Write an analysis of the horror genre in film, comic book, or fiction in terms of highlights and lowlights. Really think about what made something strong horror versus what made it weak horror.

3. Pretend you are a detective; make observations about your bedroom as if it were someone else's. What is the occupant like? How can you tell? Write a 1-2 page analysis about your findings.

Writing Exercises for Chapter 7

1. **Critical Thinking:** Take something you are considering using as research. This can either be research for a paper you are writing, or simply research you are using to support your own ideas about life. Now, analyze the document thoroughly. What questions should you ask of it? How can you tell if it is valid or invalid? Credible or incredible? Logical or illogical? Make a list of all the questions you have and find the answers. Then, determine whether you should or shouldn't use that document to validate your ideas.

2. **Thesis Statement and Map:** Look at an email you sent to someone recently. (Try to find a longer one—at least a few paragraphs.) If you had to write a thesis statement about your email (that is, what is the point of this email in one statement), what would it be? Create a map that points to the key topics of the email in the order they are presented.

3. **Reverse Outline:** Create a reverse outline for a short story or novel you have been working on. What patterns do you see? Does anything pop out at you as unnecessary or confusing? Use this outline to revise your draft.

4. **Analyzing Literature:** Find a copy of Shirley Jackson's "The Lottery," a classic story that is perhaps the greatest example of horrific irony ever written in

English. Now, pretend you are defending the right of this small, New England town to honor its customs in a trial for violating human rights as dictated by the United Nations. What evidence can you find to support your claim in the story? How about experts who might back you up?

–8–
Academic Writing
or
Scholars Can See Right Through You

Emily Winterhaven is a hard woman to find. Considering she is largely transparent and doesn't go for the whole "ectoplasm" hoopla, it took us a while to track her down. After a few orb photos and some electromagnetic spikes, however, our ghost hunter friends were able to pinpoint her location at the Stephen A. Schwartzman Building of the New York Public Library in Manhattan, trying to influence an Italian exchange student into turning the page on Dante's Divine Comedy *(not ironically, the section dedicated to "Purgatory"). She was a little surprised to see us—or, rather, she was surprised that we could see her. When we told her we could download her into a computer with a direct interface to the library, she was pretty thrilled and agreed to write this chapter for us. Of course, we lost track of her after she submitted this. For all we know, she's found her way through the cloud to a desktop near you.*

"'Tis falsely said / that there was ever intercourse / between the living and the dead."
~William Wordsworth, "Affliction of Margaret," c. 1804

Ah, ACADEMIA. WHEN I was alive, I devoured my school subjects as easily as I now exude ectoplasm while moving through the library shelves at the New York Public Library. I've been dead a long time—long enough to know that there isn't much for ghosts to do but further their education. After all, we can't interact with the living, we can't enjoy a good steak, and we can't explore the pleasures of touch. So, really, what else is there to do but read?

Sometimes, I write, too. I don't use some Patrick Swayze electromagnetic thing that allows me to punch the keys of a keyboard, and I'm certainly not throwing any clay onto the pottery wheel. I suppose writers who are still among the living might think of me less as an apparition and more as a ghostly muse. I visit while you sleep, filling your head with the dreams I want you to write about, and whispering in your ear as you wake, restless and jazzed with the spark of inspiration before you stumble to the laptop to begin your affair with words. I may not be flesh and bone, but I am still very interested in the world of words, even though now I employ other methods of communication.

I know you are probably asking yourself why the authors have asked a ghost to educate you on the methods of academic writing instead of one of the legions of the walking dead? The answer is simple: academic writing is not for zombies. To be an academic writer, you must be unafraid of asking questions, of exploring subjects from divergent angles regardless of what paradigm or previous thought patterns have brought you to this point.

Zombies, with their insatiable appetites and one-track minds, aren't typically cut out for that sort of thing. Demons aren't much better, with their singular intent of harvesting souls for their master. And Sirens simply have a problem keeping their writing paper dry. Don't even ask about vampires. Although they may have hundreds of years to learn and evolve, many

> **If you are going to choose someone to do some scholarly writing for you, zombies, vampires, and mummies would probably not be your first choice. Logic, of course, would suggest a "ghostwriter."**

squander their extra time sparkling and brooding, preoccupied with following teenaged girls around in hopes of getting into their knickers. Better to leave those passionate fools to the words of creativity than to the structured, left-brained, logical discourse of academia.

What other creatures of the night could bear witness to the world of scholarly writing? Mummies are far too vengeful, ghouls too bent on trickery, and werewolves (while technically not undead, mind you) are typically more interested in sports than intellectual pursuits. Witches do spend a good deal of time in study and exposition, naturally; how else would they learn the proper applications of wormwood and mallow root? But like werewolves, witches are not members of the undead—and their scholarly research is highly secretive. Most would be unwilling to share their trade secrets in a book such as this.

So that brings us to ghosts.

Ghosts are the perfect medium, ahem, for explaining the inner workings of academic writing, for what have ghosts to do but read? Sure, there are poltergeists more interested in wreaking havoc and terrorizing the living than anything else, but how do you think they learned to do things like levitate your couch, turn your television into a wormhole to the underworld, or make your walls bleed? You think they picked it up haunting the subway, or watching reruns of *X-Files*? No—they learned these skills attending ghost school and reading books in the ether. They can't all be interested in your miserly attitudes toward consumerist winter holidays in the past, present, and future, after all—and even those Dickensian ghosts learned time travel and techniques for motivating a greedy man's behavior from somewhere. And unlike mortals, ghosts have plenty of time available to perfect what they learn.

Because we aren't constrained by physical limitations, we ghosts have the luxury of approaching these lessons with a beginner's mind. Gone are the trappings of our mortal coil. No longer are we obsessed with being on time, having the perfect hairstyle, or impressing the creature next door. As non-corporeal entities, we are free to think and learn whatever we want. Like children, we approach each new lesson like a tabula rasa, enabling us to see things we wouldn't have seen before.

Academic writing starts with this frame of mind. You have to be willing to let go of your preconceived biases, predispositions, and prejudices and learn to look at the world through a critical lens. When your physical body lies rotting in the ground somewhere and you are free to move about as pure consciousness, your perspective begins to change a bit. Suddenly, what was impossible yesterday doesn't seem so unrealistic today. After all, you're dead, but you're not dead-dead. It's actually quite liberating.

No, I don't need a ghostwriter. Mister Dickens is doing just fine on his own.

The Foundation of Thinking Critically

Being critical requires you to know yourself and your inclinations as much as it requires you to understand your surroundings and how to interact with them. We must separate our *selves* from our influences, and learn to recognize what motivates us and why those motivations cause us to act and react in certain ways. When we do this, we establish the framework for critical thinking—a skill required of every piece of academic writing you pursue. To establish the framework, we start by asking ourselves questions like:

- Where did your identity come from and what shaped it?
- What are your opinions and reactions? Which of them do you display because

you think you have to, you've learned them from your parents or television, or because you think that's what society expects of you?

- What do you value? What do you reject?
- Or, to put it as simple as the Caterpillar when talking to Alice, "Who are you?"

This framework of self-knowledge is foundational to virtually every academic pursuit. By recognizing where our ideas and impulses come from, we are then able to strip them down to bare bones, to mere wisps of breath. By stripping away our impulses, we are much more equipped to see things clearly, to question authority (that is, the expertise of an "author"), and to engage responsibly with the world around us. We ghosts do it all the time. We bring you that cold draft that tickles your spine. We appear before you at the stroke of midnight with messages about our murderous brothers and incestuous wives. We come to you through mediums and table-rapping and alphabet magnets that move along your refrigerator doors. But this is not the same level of engagement you need for academic writing.

> **"You may be an undigested bit of beef, a blot of mustard, a crumb of cheese, a fragment of underdone potato. There's more of gravy than of grave about you, whatever you are!"**
> **Charles Dickens**
> ***A Christmas Carol***

After we have recognized and freed ourselves from our influences, we can begin to question scientifically. This is particularly important when dealing with research. No one—not even a ghost—wishes to be remembered as the person who cited a fraud or a flimflam man to support her argument in academic discourse. That is why we must research our research.

Identifying Valid (or Credible) Sources for Research

It is always a good idea to question the validity, authenticity, and authority of any information you encounter. Academic writing requires you to look at, analyze, evaluate, and choose or eliminate information as needed. Typically, this information is derived from past research presented in a variety of information media, including personal interviews, books, journal articles, podcasts, webinars, and documentary films. Conducting research is an important aspect of academic writing. Using reliable sources to support your position establishes your credibility as a writer, since it shows that you've immersed yourself in the body of knowledge pertaining to your topic and have thought deeply about how previous research applies to your topic. But the thinking does not stop at the research you have done—you must also think about the research in terms of its intrinsic value and you must challenge its veracity.

Many writers and teachers consider academic writing to be a dialogue or conversation. Citing, analyzing, and responding to sources (through agreement and disagreement) are some of the ways you engage in a "scholarly dialogue" through your writing. As with any good conversation, you want to talk to interesting people with something valuable to say. In academic writing, you want to engage the work of reliable scholars and researchers. This means you have to evaluate your sources. Schools and universities have research librarians who can help you use library resources and determine which sources are valid. Do you think Buffy learned all her vampire-staking techniques from the Internet, or did she trust the peer-reviewed *Vampyr* tome handed to her by her watcher, the Sunnydale High School librarian? And do you think the Scooby-Doo gang learned how to fight island zombies playing video games, or do you suppose the librarian at Crystal Grove High School set them up with a few scholarly journal databases?

Online sources, which can be written by anyone (or anything—hell, I've written a few in my ghostly years), pose a particular problem when it comes to validation. Sometimes it is very easy to determine if an online source is valid, but sometimes it is not so straightforward. (When in doubt, consult a friend, classmate, instructor, or librarian.) But evaluating sources based upon the following criteria is a good place to begin:

- Who created or hosts the site?
- Does the person, organization, or institution seem fair and unbiased?
- Does the writer have academic or professional credentials?
- Does the URL end in .gov or .edu? (This usually signals a government or university website, and while it doesn't guarantee that a source is valid, it can be useful information.)
- Are there any citations or links to credible sources?

Too often, I watch my zombie friends swallow news stories and political speeches and religious lectures whole—particularly those they bumble across on the Internet—without taking the time to really chew on it. In academic writing, you need to always

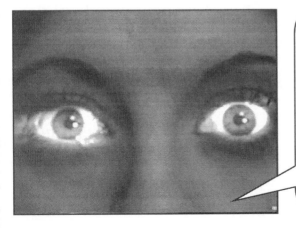

We call upon the spirit of the person responsible for inventing scholarly citation guidelines. Come to us now and explain yourself.

question the validity of the information you are using. For instance, who wrote this book? Was it just a couple of quacks interested in perpetrating a hoax at readers' expense, or was it actual experts on writing—like, a writer and instructor with an MFA, a college writing instructor, or an author who has been independently published elsewhere? And even if you do trust the authority of the information these authors provide based on their education and credentials around writing, is that enough? You also need to know the reputation of the writers you are reading, what sorts of things they usually write, and sometimes even the way other people have received their words and ideas—though you should always reserve your own judgment to be based on your own ideas, and not solely on someone else's. In other words, do not trust everything you read.

A writer's reputation ties in with the purpose of their writing. If, for example, an informer's aim is to sell you something or entertain you (like, perhaps, most news programs, whose salaries are often paid by the commercial advertisers that appear during their broadcasts or which flicker on the edges of their page on your monitors), does this color the way their information works or how much you believe it? If not, should it?

> The "Pluto is still a planet" controversy still rages. And why not? Otherwise we are reduced to recall the order of the planets with the phrase "My Very Evil Mother Just Served Us Nothing."

And what of the relevance to your topic, or the time at which the book was written? I've been dead for nearly two centuries. Things in your world of knowledge have changed dramatically in that time. I remember haunting the library aisles when Pluto was discovered as a planet, and then haunting those same aisles when the world decided Pluto was not, in fact, a planet, but a dwarf planet, unworthy of its line-up in "My Very Elegant Mother Just Served Us Nine Pizzas," the mnemonic device all grade schoolers were once given to recall the order of the planets as they orbit the sun from closest to farthest from the blazing star. If I were to look at a book about planets, then, from fifty years ago, it would not be as current or useful as a book printed this year on the subject. At the same time, if I'm hoping to support theories around the history of astronomy, then a book written fifty years ago may well be a useful tool in my academic paper or speech. The year tells me how useful the information is so long as I relate that year to the purpose for my research.

To all ends, then, our research must be by and for scholars when we are writing things for academic audiences. In general, "scholarly sources" present academic arguments, not just information. For a source to be considered scholarly, it has to go through the process of peer review—this means that other experts in the field have read and commented on the work before it was published. If a book or journal article is published by a university press, this is a good sign that it is a scholarly source, and therefore credible. If it has been published by Bimbo Vampire Babes from Mars Press, then maybe not so much.

Another indicator is whether the book or article cites other scholarly sources. As with your own writing, this shows that the writer has done his/her due diligence and understands what other researchers have said about the topic. Now, a source can be credible without being scholarly. For example, *Wikipedia* is a great resource, but is not a *scholarly* source, because the content it presents does not go through the critical evaluation of rigorous peer review and its purpose is to provide objective information (in the style of an encyclopedia), rather than evidence-based arguments. In the same way, newspaper articles, articles from non-academic journals, or government websites might be valid, credible, and reliable, but not necessarily scholarly sources (since they generally don't present an evidence-based argument).

Given that academic writing is both scholarly and critical, we must always come back to the world of critical thinking. We ghosts recognize that there is more than one truth. Nothing is black and white on the slippery gray of our own translucent bodies, which fade back and forth between realities. Truth is multidimensional. Anyone who believes that there is only one right answer to anything is failing to think critically.

Critical thinking allows you to not only consider the validity of information you are dealing with, which can help to inform your decisions about, say, who to vote for in the next election (and believe me, there have been more than one elected official who was secretly a zombie), it also helps you consider how to frame your own writing for academic audiences. Academic writing is simply writing authored by scholars for other scholars. All students are scholars (whether they mean to be or not), and so any writing you do in school—whether public or postsecondary—is meant to be academic. Lab reports, arguments, debates, and research papers are all types of academic writing. The most common type of academic writing in the postsecondary world would be argumentative—which is similar to persuasive writing, but with a whole lot more research to back it up.

Seance is not the most scholarly method of research, and anyway, we're not sure how to properly cite table rapping and picture frame spinning.

Argument in Academia

The word "argument" conjures visions of quarrelling with your vampire neighbor about the angle of your floodlights shining into his basement dungeon, or bickering with your father about having access to the family station wagon on Saturday night to haul your boyfriend's corpse out of its grave so your necromancer teacher can resurrect him. However, in writing, presenting an argument requires that you support your claim (usually delivered in the form of a thesis) with corroborating evidence.

For the most part, academic writing (such as what you might have to do in a high school or college course) is all about argument. The point is to offer a new body of knowledge into the world, a new way of thinking or doing things, or a new way of seeing something. Writing arguments combines elements

> **The only way you might convince your mother to allow your weekly coven meetings in the basement is to offer a potion giving her eternal beauty.**

of informative, persuasive, and analytical writing. Academic writing begins with a question or problem that you "answer" in the form of an argument. In academic writing, there is no single, right answer (even in the sciences!), but rather new knowledge that emerges out of scholarly dialogue. Scholars and researchers interpret evidence—everything from experimental data to Bram Stoker's *Dracula*—draw conclusions based on their interpretations, and attempt to persuade others that their argument is the "best" answer for that research problem or question.

A teacher or professor may provide a prompt with a question or problem to write about, but that won't always be the case. You may have to write a paper without much direction at all, and battle it out with a horde of zombies (i.e., your classmates) without your teacher providing you any weapons or tools to win the war. In either case, be sure you have a good sense of the question you're trying to answer. Good research questions have to be real questions—questions you don't already know the answer to, but want to find out. Good questions don't usually have "yes" or "no" answers—they're tough questions that will challenge you to think, analyze, and do research.

Research Questions

Consider the following academic research questions that your scholarly ghost has conjured up:

- Why do zombies, vampires, and werewolves become afflicted by means of a physical bite? Is it a virus? Where do these diseases (or myths) come from?
- Why is it that a piece of sharpened wood driven through the heart can kill a vampire? Why are vampires susceptible to damage inflicted by a wooden implement, but not ones comprised of steel?

- What is the origin and evolution of Halloween-based celebrations?
- Why do zombies prefer to eat brains and living flesh but not other zombies?
- Was Shakespeare's *Hamlet* really about vampires?

Once you have a good question in mind, you can start planning your research and argument. What do you already know about this topic? What do you need to find out? What sources will help you answer this question? At this point, you might have some idea about what your conclusion will be—but try to keep an open mind. As you read other people's ideas about this topic, your own thinking will develop and evolve.

One way of engaging with research is to not search for information from experts that support your ideas, but rather to search for information from experts that refute them. This way, you help yourself to keep an open mind to the possibility that you are wrong. In doing this, you allow yourself to continue to think critically. Opinions, for instance, are only as good as their owner's ability to question and support them. Blind opinions have no place in academic discourse.

Conducting Research

The research process itself is my area of expertise. After all, my chosen place of haunt is the New York Public Library. (Although I hate it when those stupid Ghostbusters come in with their homemade vacuum cleaners designed for sucking up the wispy tendrils of my ghostly sisters.) When it comes time to research your question, you certainly could hit the keyboard and draw out hundreds of websites on the topic of your essay. You could also use a librarian to help identify and gather resources for you. Or you could use my tried and true method of actually going to the library in person. You see, libraries categorize their books thematically by subject, which means that all the zombie culture books are typically housed on one shelf in the library. If you find that shelf, you suddenly have a brain-sized feast of

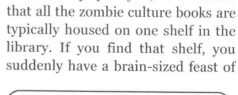

How can I get any research done with all of these words and letters bouncing around my head?

resources for your paper—and you didn't have to spend an hour searching through a myriad of invalid Internet sites or trying to think of a good keyword search in order to find them. Bravo!

Thesis Statements

Once you're gathered and reviewed research materials for your paper, you are in a good position to begin crafting an argument. Developing a thesis is a good starting point. In one or two sentences, what is the best answer to your research question? Is your thesis convincing? Do you have evidence supporting your claim? Could another person reasonably disagree with your position? Based on your tentative thesis, try to diagram, outline, or cluster a preliminary argument: what are the reasons that support your thesis? And in turn, what is the evidence that supports those reasons?

There are several methods you can use to craft your thesis statement including diagramming, outlining, and clustering. Experiment with several of them to find which works best for you.

With your argument outline or diagrammed, begin drafting your paper. Some writers prefer to begin at the beginning—they like to have a solid introduction that sets the tone and offers a road map for the entire paper. Other writers prefer writing the introduction last. They might begin with the easiest section of the paper, or the most difficult. Once you have a working draft that you think presents a clear argument, try to get some feedback about your work. All writing is communication, and getting feedback from other readers tells us how well our messages are getting through to another brain regardless of how many living cells it still maintains.

Many schools have writing centers and tutors available for free. You can also ask a friend to review your work or exchange papers with a classmate. You might ask for feedback on specific components of the paper—the argument, the use of evidence, its tone, the introduction, the organization, etc. You might also ask your reader to summarize your paper back to you. This is a great technique for evaluating how well you've explained your position. If your reader misses a key point or is confused about your argument, that's a good indication that you haven't done a good job communicating your intended message. You can also ask your reader to take on multiple roles as they read, such as the friendly reader or a resistant reader. Challenge your reader to do the best they can to argue against you. What counterarguments, objections, or examples can they come up with? You can also ask your reader for supportive feedback. How can they help improve your argument? Can they identify additional points, reasons, or evidence that would make your argument more compelling? (These different mindsets—being a friendly or a resistant reader—are good practice for being a critical thinker. Being a critical reader can help you become a strong argumentative writer. Practice these skills yourself on someone else's draft, or as you read the research you collected.) Once you have feedback—and a better sense of how your writing is being interpreted by others—you can make active decisions about how to revise your draft.

A Brief Note about Citation Style

One final note about academic writing: when writing an academic paper, you may be tasked to write that essay in a particular citation style. Simply put, a citation style is a set of rules created by writers for writers—it's a system of citing sources by which writers, particularly academic writers, agree to abide. For example, if you're writing a paper for a humanities topic, you'll use MLA (Modern Language Association) formatting and style. For sciences and social sciences, you'll most likely use APA (American Psychological Association) formatting and style. Some journalists use a style called Chicago, while others use a style called AP (Associated Press). There are dozens of citation styles, so it will be up to you (or your instructor) to determine what citation formatting style your writing must adhere to. Failure to cite things properly or to abide by the style's set of rules could cause you to be accused of plagiarism or academic dishonesty, even if this wasn't your intention. (To that end, I've been asked to add some citation rules to the end of this chapter.)

> **The question of the day: would you rather be drained of your blood by a vampire, have your guts ripped out by a zombie, or write a thesis statement? Perhaps we can make your decision a little easier.**

As you do your research, keep track of all of your sources. Be sure you know which websites you accessed and when. When citing from books or articles, but sure you have all of the publication information you need to write a correct "Works Cited." Readers trained in the art of citation (such as your teacher) can tell a lot about a source from its citation, so be sure you're giving the correct information.

Process Example

No two writers work in exactly the same way, especially when it come to the process of research. That said, however, I simply couldn't resist this rare opportunity to write a research paper myself—to demonstrate what the process of research and academic writing might look like, of course, but also to indulge in one of my favorite pastimes: trying to answer hard questions through writing. Without further ado, then, I'll just find an open mind (and body) to inhabit...ah yes, a young college student, that should be perfect. She's come to the library today to work on a question close to my own heart, in fact. Here it is:

Research Question: Why do zombies, vampires, and werewolves become afflicted by means of a physical bite? Alternate form: Why does the bite from a zombie, vampire, or werewolf result in the victim's transformation to a creature of the night? Is it a virus? Where do these diseases (or myths) come from?

To begin analyzing this research question, she might create a web (such as the one below) to map out her thoughts, questions, and connections between her ideas. By doing this, she can more easily track the flow of her logic. One false move in her logical reasoning, and the paper's argument will fall to pieces.

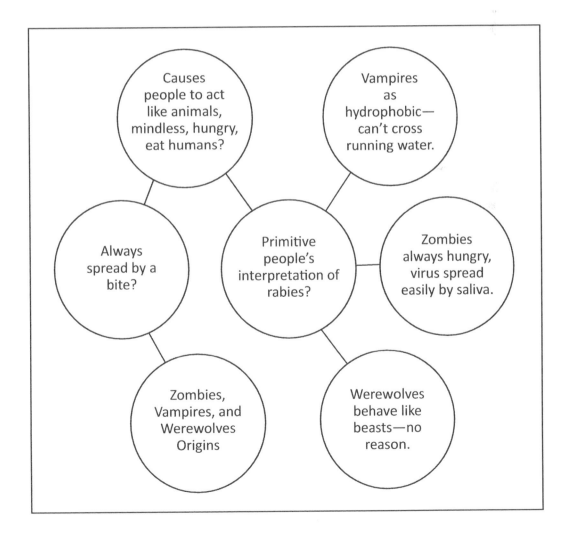

Now that the author has a framework for researching this topic, she can begin researching the rabies virus and its symptoms and then cross reference them to the symptoms commonly associated with becoming a zombie, vampire, or werewolf. She might also examine historical documents, case studies, and first-person accounts of primitive cultures as they encountered diseases that may have been undiagnosed rabies. Armed with her research, she'll then craft her original question into the form of a thesis statement.

The living tend to get all sorts of vexed about thesis statements. They hear the term and shudder in sheer terror at the prospect of what creating one entails. Most would even rather be bitten be a zombie or vampire. I don't know what all the fuss is about; generating them is a simple task. Thesis statements summarize the argument of the paper in a few concise sentences. Just state the point of your paper clearly for the reader, with confidence. (No beating around the bush with "I think" or "This paper is going to be about.") Simply cut to the chase, such as Araminta demonstrates in the example below:

Thesis: Vampires, zombies, and werewolves as we know them today stemmed from early civilizations' first encounters with rabies.

Now, it's not enough for Araminta to leave the thesis dangling unsupported. She

Now, Billy, do you think it's a good idea to try contacting Mr. Krueger and ask why he hasn't been visiting lately?

needs to include a thesis map, which serves as a kind of compass for the reader to determine which direction the paper will go. The map outlines the main points the paper will make (as supported by research) during the paper's progression toward the goal of supporting the thesis.

> **Thesis map**: as evidenced by vampires' hydrophobia and pale skin, zombies' insatiable hunger and infectious saliva, and werewolves' beastly, almost inhuman, actions.

Now put it together:

> **Thesis and map**: Vampires, zombies, and werewolves as we know them today stemmed from early civilizations' first encounters with rabies, as evidenced by vampires' hydrophobia and pale skin, zombies' insatiable hunger and infectious saliva, and werewolves' beastly, almost inhuman, actions.

Thesis statements need to be debatable—that is, another reasonable person could disagree with the claims of the thesis statement. According to the authors of *The Craft of Research*, one way to test how debatable a thesis is to state the opposite claim and see whether it's a reasonable claim. In this case, the "opposing" thesis would be:

> **Opposing thesis**: Vampires, zombies, and werewolves as we know them today **did not** stem from early civilizations' first encounters with rabies.

This *does* seem like a reasonable claim—someone else writing about this topic might come to different conclusions about the origins of these myths. Instead of making an argument connecting early accounts of vampires, zombies, and werewolves to actual diseases (as Araminta has done here), someone else might argue that these myths were caused by mass hysteria, folklore, or other cultural factors. It looks like this thesis (and map) stands up to the debatability test.

For the sake of comparison, though, let's test a weaker thesis statement:

> **Thesis**: Zombies kill people and are therefore dangerous.

> **Opposing thesis**: Zombies **do not** kill people and are therefore **not** dangerous.

In this case, the assertion that zombies **do not** kill and are **not** dangerous does not hold up to reasonable scrutiny. Instead of making a claim *about* zombies, this writer has just stated facts about zombies that are not debatable. To develop this thesis, the writer might first need to frame some better questions about her topic. For example, wondering *how* or *why* zombies are dangerous, or even whether they're more dangerous than other undead creatures, might help her make an argument.

Now that Araminta has a fully formulated thesis, my ghostly hand can guide her toward completing her paper. (Of course, this argument suggests that vampires, zombies, and werewolves are imaginary creatures, something we all know to be a lie. How else could so many of us have gathered together to (de)compose this book on writing?) Her thesis will be positioned at the end of the introductory paragraph, strategically placed to hook the reader into the paper so he or she (or it) keeps reading. The map points the reader to the order in which paragraphs will be presented. In this example, the first paragraph (or group of paragraphs) after the hook will be about vampires, the second about zombies, and the remaining few will be about werewolves. She'll then conclude the essay with a brief summary restating her original claim and reiterating key points of the essay.

To show you some of the differences between citation styles, I've included Araminta's paper in two styles: MLA and APA. Notice how the MLA formatted paper has a different structure for the title page: instead of a separate page, the title is listed on the first page with the scholar's information listed to the left. Also notice that each page has a header and page number, and notice what that header includes.

The Importance of In-Text and Bibliographical Citations

Last but not least, take careful note of the use of both in-text citations and bibliographical citations (in an MLA paper, the latter is referred to as a "Works Cited" page). Many novice writers or students operate under the assumption that plagiarism only occurs when the writer copies another's work *word for word* without properly citing it. While that is a form of plagiarism, plagiarism also occurs when a writer fails to cite paraphrases and summaries, which can occur when a writer takes someone else's *idea or intellectual property* and treats it like it his or her own work by failing to properly cite it. If

Why do we always end up haunting kitchens? It's so depressing. I sure miss my Count Chocula and Franken Berry cereals.

you look carefully at this paper, you'll see there are in-text citations (look for the parenthesis) in the body of the essay, and sometimes they aren't next to quotation marks. This means that the reference was paraphrased or summarized. In MLA citation, we typically refer to research in-text by the author's last name and page number. There are different rules for different types of resources, though, so don't follow that rule blindly—and certainly don't leave a citation out just because your source fails to list an author or perhaps doesn't have a page number (like a website). In such cases, the in-text citation must utilize the appropriate protocol for properly making the citation, which may vary by reference resource type.

MLA and APA citation are rigorous and complex styles of writing. The rules and guidelines for presenting research, structuring papers, and referring to other experts is extensive and updated regularly—whenever a new type of media is created, APA and MLA revisit the guidelines for incorporating references writers might make to information gathered using the new medium. The following examples are designed to give you a taste of what MLA and APA typically require, but they are by no means exhaustive examples of all the rules for style and citation. These are a starting point. To fully implement MLA or APA citation styles, you would need to access a manual of style (either published or on the web), such as the Online Writing Lab at Purdue University (OWL) website for "Research and Citation."

APA and MLA papers have different rules, but they basically follow the same idea: cite your sources for all research (anything that is not common knowledge, which is information you are certain your readers will know) both in-text and in the bibliography. Use proper formatting (margins, title page, line spacing, headers, and page numbers). And above all else, use a manual. I see lazy students wander into the library all the time seeking to use the library's Internet-based tools to automate the creation of their citations. These tools may help students save time, but they don't account for human (or inhuman) error—and a single error could be enough to throw the peer reviewers (or teachers) into a plagiarism tizzy. Instead, scholars do best when the follow the rules specified in a manual. Since manuals are often updated, scholars should always check to see that they are using the most up-to-date version of the rules for the required citation style. There are a few free, reliable manuals online that scholars can use—so long as they are able to verify that these resources are up-to-date and created by experts. Danger lurks for scholars who fail to follow the rules appropriately.

Matthews 1 ← ①

Araminta Matthews ← ②

Professor Peter Venkman

Ghostbusting 101

October 31, 1666

Creatures of the Night: The Rabid Causes of the Living Dead ← ③

You hear it scratching at your window pane. Gnarled and ← ④
yellowed fingernails dragging long streaks down the glass, screeching
against it. You know what it is and why it's come. The wolf come to
claim Red Riding Hood's grandmother for dinner. The vampire
calling Lucy out of her bed chamber to be his next bride. A lone
zombie driven mindless by its own insane hunger waiting to eat you
up. We all know the myths of vampires, zombies, and werewolves, ← ⑤
but where did they come from? How did it all begin? Could there be a
scientific explanation for their cursed behavior? Vampires, zombies, ← ⑥
and werewolves as we know them today spiraled out of early
civilizations' first encounters with rabies as evidenced by vampires'
hydrophobia and pale skin, zombies' insatiable hunger and infectious
saliva, and werewolves' beastly, almost inhuman, actions.

The history of rabies dates back to approximately 2,300 B.C. ← ⑦
when references to the sickness caused by the bites of mad dogs was ← ⑧

1 All margins are 1". In MLA style, there is a header in the upper right margin which contains the page number and (usually) your last name. Sometimes the header is omitted on the first page.

2 Instead of a title page, papers in the MLA style have headings on the left side of the first page with your name, your professor's name, the course, and the date.

3 The paper's title (and it should have one!) is centered and formatted normally (no italics, quotation marks, underlining, or larger-sized text). Capitalize everything except short prepositions (such as "of") or articles which do not appear as the first word (such as "the" in "of the Living Dead"). The title is your reader's first point of contact with your work—don't miss this opportunity to hook them, and to set their expectations regarding what the paper is about.

4 Text is double-spaced, in a regular font (such as Times New Roman, Arial, Tahoma, Courier, or Helvetica).

5 The hook of this paper sets the scene for the reader through sensory details and well-known references. This opening is followed up with the motivating questions of the paper.

6 The thesis presents concrete pieces of evidence (a set of physical symptoms) to support Araminta's claim about rabies, vampires, zombies, and werewolves.

7 New paragraphs begin ½ inch from the left margin (use the "Tab" key). There are no spaces between paragraphs.

8 This first body paragraph introduces some historical background about rabies. This follows an organizational pattern of moving from general information to more specific.

Matthews 2

recorded in the Babylonian Code of Eshnunna (Surreau S581). ◄———— 9

During such early times before knowledge of bacteria or microscopic

viruses was readily available to physicians, it is feasible that such

illnesses as rabies could have been treated with superstition. Certainly

a degree of superstition surrounds the nature of the illness, which is

spread by the bite of a creature (usually an animal, but it can be

spread by humans), causing everything from convulsions, loss of

muscle function, excitability, and anxiety to drooling and difficulty

swallowing ("Rabies"). Its superstitious, alternative name,

"hydrophobia," is perhaps derived from this difficulty swallowing

causing anxiety in animals (or people suffering from rabies) as they

drew close to bodies of water (Goss 2). ◄———— 10

Similarly, vampires are known to have a perceived fear of ◄———— 11

bodies of water, being unable to cross large bodies of moving water

(Melton 114). Vampires exhibiting anxiety in general—or agitation

and irritation, two other symptoms of rabies ("Rabies")—were once

believed to be indicators of a person's likelihood of becoming a

vampire. That is, individuals who were perceived to have died in a

state of anxiety or unrest were thought to be possessed of vampiric

spirits, and thus, bodies were exhumed all over Europe and, upon

seeing any supposed signs of a "lack of decay," were presumed to be

9 Even though there is not a quotation here, Araminta includes a citation. When summarizing ideas or background information, you still need to cite the source. This way, if readers want to know more about your topic, or if they have a question about the source, they know exactly where it came from. Citing also gives credit where it's due, and establishes your credibility as a researcher and writer. Most in-text citations include the author's last name followed by the page number. The last name helps the reader find this source in the "Works Cited" at the end of the paper, which is organized by authors' last names (or title if there is no author).

10 In MLA style, in-text citations usually include the author's last name and page number (or page range). There is no "p" for "page" and there is no comma between the author's last name and the page number. Ending punctuation is on the outside of the parenthesis.

11 This topic sentence connects the previous paragraph (superstitions about a fear of water) to a new idea: vampires.

Matthews 3

vampires and treated accordingly (Gottlieb 42). In addition to ◄━━ 12

historical evidence supporting the idea that vampires are possessed of

rabid symptoms, they are also thought to be largely hydrophobic in

popular culture. Vampires are thought to suffer pains if splashed with

holy water, and surely the rabies symptom of drooling must be a

problem for these toothy creatures as their fangs protrude over their

lower lip.

Like vampires, zombies, whether of the Haitian or undead ◄━━ 13

variety, suffer symptoms of rabies, as well. When zombies are

"created" by Haitian voodoo "hexes" (or skillful poisoning), the

bodies of their victims are pronounced dead by local doctors then

raised from that state of death in a series of "convulsions"

(Efthimious and Ghandi), not unlike those suffered by a person

bearing the rabies virus. In addition, popular culture images ◄━━ 14

demonstrate the ease by which zombification spreads (like a virus)

simply by the transference of blood or saliva to exposed mucus

membranes, such as seen in the film *28 Days Later*, in which a

character transforms instantly into a zombie upon a drop of infected

blood falling from a crow's beak into his open eye. Rabies, too, can

infect an uninfected animal (remember, humans are animals) by

contaminating "mucous membranes (i.e. eyes, nose, mouth), aerosol

12 This transitional sentence show how the two pieces of evidence in this paragraph (the historical background from Gottlieb and common knowledge from popular culture) both support the same idea: that vampires are associated with a fear of water.

13 This topic sentence transitions from an old idea (vampires) to a new idea (zombies). The connection is that these creatures share symptoms.

14 This transition creates flow by linking different pieces of evidence to support the same idea.

Matthews 4

transmission, and corneal and organ transplantations" (Centers for

Disease Control and Prevention). In that sense, rabies (like ← 15

zombification) spreads perniciously and without discrimination. In ← 16

addition, both diseases are virtually impossible to eradicate.

Another disease that spreads perniciously and without ← 17

discrimination is that of lycanthropy, a disease cataloged in popular

literature as well as in bizarre historical incidents. Werewolves were

believed to be men who craved only bloody, uncooked meat or who

were given to bestial behavior (Woodward 19). Humans who become

infected with the rabies virus are typically infected by a bite of an

animal. Given that some rabies symptoms include hypersalivation,

agitation, and confusion ("Rabies"), it is conceivable that rabies

victims would present as animal-like—or, at least, like the animal that

infected the human. Various tribes of the Americas as well as other

ancient cultures held certain animistic beliefs suggesting that the bite

of an animal could transfer the spirit or "powers" of the animal onto

the human who did the biting or received it (Fox 132-133). This idea ← 18

suggests that if a person were known to have been bitten by a wolf,

then primitive people might have thought the spirit of the wolf would

transfer into the body of the man who was bitten.

One thing that connects werewolves, zombies, and vampires is ← 19

15 Information from a government agency about medical symptoms supports Araminta's analysis of zombie symptoms. She is able to show her reader the similarities between rabies and zombies, not just tell them.

16 Araminta concludes the paragraph by reiterating the similarity between rabies and zombies, but with slightly new information than she's given already (both are hard to stop). Each sentence in this paragraph supports the central idea, but they build off of each other, connecting to one another and offering new information.

17 This topic sentence transitions from zombies to werewolves by emphasizing their similarities to disease.

18 To make her case, Araminta analyzes the evidence that supports her idea. She doesn't just give the reader a quote about the beliefs of ancient cultures—she says something about it, showing us exactly how it connects to her argument.

19 The conclusion pulls all of the main ideas together.

Matthews 5

that each of these supernatural disorders is typically spread through

the bite of an infected creature. Rabies, too, is typically spread by way

of biting. Like zombification, rabies infections cause convulsions and

spreads as quickly as any epidemic imaginable. Vampires experience

hydrophobia, which is the original name for the rabies virus, and

werewolves behave like the animals that infected them through

hypersalivation and agitation. These threads of similarity between the ← [20]

symptoms of supernatural disorders in popular culture and the rabies

virus can't be ignored. Early civilizations who had a limited

understanding of bacteria and disease may have treated rabid people

with superstition, perhaps even accrediting them as having

supernatural disorders: like vampirism, zombification, or lycanthropy.

Maybe all three of these undead creatures are really just victims of a ← [21]

violent rabies virus, a fatal disease when untreated that could lead its

victims further down the rabbit-hole of madness and oddity.

20 In addition to summarizing the argument, this conclusion also answers the "so what?" question—this is why Araminta's argument is important.

21 The last sentence leaves the reader with a new idea to think about—a what-if question based on the argument.

Matthews 6

Works Cited ◄──────────────────────── 22

Centers for Disease Control and Prevention. "How is Rabies ◄──── 23

Transmitted?" Atlanta, GA: CDC, 2011. Web. <http://www.cdc.gov/

rabies/transmission/index.html>

Efthimiou, C.J. and S. Ghandi. "Cinema Fiction vs Physics Reality: Ghosts,◄── 24

Vampires, and Zombies." *Skeptical Inquirer.* 31.4 (2007): 27-40.

Fox, Michael. "Animism, Empathy, and Human Development." *Between* ◄── 25

the Species. (Summer/Fall 1995): 130-140.

Goss, L.W. "Rabies-Hydrophobia." *Experiment Station, Circular No. 9.*

Kansas State Agricultural College. (1910). Web. <http://www.ksre.

ksu.edu/historicpublications/ Pubs/sc009.pdf>

Gottlieb, Richard. "The European Vampire: Applied Psychoanalysis and

Applied Legend." *Folklore Forum* 23.2 (1991): 39-61.

Melton, J. Gordon. *The Vampire book: The Encyclopedia of the Undead.* ◄── 26

Detroit: Visible Ink Press, 1999. Print.

"Rabies." *A.D.A.M. Medical Encyclopedia.* U.S. National Library of ◄── 27

Medicine. PubMed Health. 10 February 2011. Web. 27 October 2011.

<http://www.ncbi.nlm.nih.gov>

Sureau, Pierre. "History of Rabies: Advances in Research Towards

Rabies Prevention During the Last 30 Years." *Reviews of Infectious*

Diseases. 10.4. (1988): S581-S584.

Woodward, Ian. *The Werewolf Delusion.* New York: Paddington Press, ◄── 28

1979.

22 Depending on the style you are using, your list of references will look very different. In general, all styles represent that same basic information: the author, title, and publication information. The list of references begins on its own page. It should have the same margins, header, and text as the rest of the paper. The title is centered, without italics, underlines, or quotation marks.

23 Citations are listed in alphabetical order by author or title, which makes sources easier to find in your list. Create a "hanging indent," where the second and subsequent lines of each entry is indented five spaces. In this case, there is a "corporate author" of an article about rabies.

24 In MLA style, references begin with the author's last name, followed by the title of the work. In this entry, a journal article, the title of the article comes before the title of the journal. You can tell the difference because the article title is in quotation marks, and the journal title is italicized. This is followed by information about the volume, including which volume and number it is, when it was published, and its page numbers.

25 All words in the title are capitalized except for articles and short pronouns (unless they are the first or last word.) Note that periods are placed inside the quotation marks.

26 Because there are hundreds (maybe thousands) of different types of resources you might refer to in your essays, MLA has cataloged specific guidelines for citing each type of resource you might use. For example, a book with one author will include different information than a book with several authors or even a book with a corporate author. On the same token, a podcast will include different information than a lecture or a personal interview with an expert. Generally, MLA will always try to capture (at the very least) an author's or creator's name, the title, the location of the publisher, the name of the publisher, and the year it was published. Some citations will require more information than that. To generate citations for the different types of resources you may incorporate into your essays, it is best to consult a current MLA manual or style guide.

27 Sources without authors begin with the title. Citing sources from the web follows the same basic format as other references. In this case, the article title followed by the name of the website, who published it, the medium (Web), and access information (27 October 2011). Date of access is important to include in case information on the website changes, as it often does.

28 For books by a single author, list the author name, book title, place of publication, the name of the press, and the year.

Creatures of the Night: The Rabid Causes of the Living Dead   1

Creatures of the Night:

The Rabid Causes of the Living Dead

Araminta Matthews

Transylvania University

APA style uses a title page, which includes the paper's title, the author, and the institutional affiliation.

Creatures of the Night: The Rabid Causes of the Living Dead   2 ← ②

Abstract ← ③

Creatures of the night, such as vampires, zombies, and werewolves, ← ④ have a long history, and are often explained as myths derived from cultural superstitions and social fears. But could there be an underlying physiological explanation? What if these "creatures" were in fact people suffering from an unrecognized illness? My paper argues that the historical superstitions about vampires, zombies, and werewolves may be rooted in a medical reality unknown at the time: rabies. Comparing the physical and psychological symptoms of rabies to historical accounts of vampires, zombies, and werewolves, I show that there may be a medical explanation for how these "mythical" creatures look, behave, and spread their "infections." The familiar stories about vampires, zombies, and werewolves emerged out of early civilizations' first encounters with an unknown medical condition; vampires' hydrophobia and pale skin, zombies' insatiable hunger and infectious saliva, and werewolves' beastly, almost inhuman, actions are the stuff of nightmares and terrible tales, but are also all symptoms of rabies. ← ⑤

Keywords: vampires, werewolves, zombies, rabies

2 APA papers have a running header on each page. The paper's title is on the upper left and page numbers on the right.

3 After the title page comes the abstract, a concise summary of your research in 150-250 words.

4 Abstracts are not indented.

5 Keywords help researchers identify relevant works in a database. The word "Keywords" is indented 5 spaces and italicized.

Creatures of the Night: The Rabid Causes of the Living Dead   3

Creatures of the Night: 6

The Rabid Causes of the Living Dead

You hear it scratching at your window pane. Gnarled and   7
yellowed fingernails dragging long streaks down the glass, screeching
against it. You know what it is and why it's come. The wolf come to
claim Red Riding Hood's grandmother for dinner. The vampire
calling Lucy out of her bed chamber to be his next bride. A lone
zombie driven mindless by its own insane hunger waiting to eat you   8
up. We all know the myths of vampires, zombies, and werewolves,
but where did they come from? How did it all begin? Could there be a
scientific explanation for their cursed behavior? Vampires, zombies,   9
and werewolves as we know them today spiraled out of early
civilizations' first encounters with rabies as evidenced by vampires'
hydrophobia and pale skin, zombies' insatiable hunger and infectious
saliva, and werewolves' beastly, almost inhuman, actions.

The history of rabies dates back to approximately 2,300 B.C.   10
when references to the sickness caused by the bites of mad dogs was
recorded in the Babylonian Code of Eshnunna (Surreau, 1988, p.   11
S581). During such early times before knowledge of bacteria or
microscopic viruses was readily available to physicians, it is feasible

6 The title is centered and not formatted.

7 Papers in APA style have 1" margins. The recommended font is Times New Roman or any other professional font. The point size should be 12.

8 The hook of this paper sets the scene for the reader through sensory details and well-known references. This opening is followed up with the motivating questions of the paper.

9 The thesis presents concrete pieces of evidence (a set of physical symptoms) to support Araminta's claim about rabies, vampires, zombies, and werewolves.

10 New paragraphs begin ½ inch from the left margin (use the "Tab" key). There are no spaces between paragraphs.

11 This first body paragraph introduces some historical background about rabies. This follows an organizational pattern of moving from general information to more specific.

Creatures of the Night: The Rabid Causes of the Living Dead   4

that such illnesses as rabies could have been treated with superstition.

Certainly a degree of superstition surrounds the nature of the illness,

which is spread by the bite of a creature (usually an animal, but it can

be spread by humans), causing everything from convulsions, loss of

muscle function, excitability, and anxiety to drooling and difficulty

swallowing ("Rabies", 2011). Its superstitious, alternative name,   ← 12

"hydrophobia", is perhaps derived from this difficulty swallowing

causing anxiety in animals (or people suffering from rabies) as they

drew close to bodies of water (Goss, 1910, p. 2). ←   13

    Similarly, vampires are known to have a perceived fear of ←   14

bodies of water, being unable to cross large bodies of moving water

(Melton, 1999, p. 114). Vampires exhibiting anxiety in general—or

agitation and irritation, two other symptoms of rabies ("Rabies",

2011)—were once believed to be indicators of a person's likelihood

of becoming a vampire. That is, individuals who were perceived to

have died in a state of anxiety or unrest were thought to be possessed

of vampiric spirits, and thus, bodies were exhumed all over Europe

and, upon seeing any supposed signs of a "lack of decay", were

presumed to be vampires and treated accordingly (Gottlieb, 1991, p.

42). In addition to historical evidence supporting the idea that ←   15

(12) Even though there is not a quotation here, Araminta includes a citation. When summarizing ideas or background information, you still need to cite the source. This way, if readers want to know more about your topic, or if they have a question about the source, they know exactly where it came from. Citing also gives credit where it's due, and establishes your credibility as a researcher and writer. In APA style, punctuation goes outside of the quotation marks. The date of publication is included because APA researchers value the most current research.

(13) In APA style, in-text citations include the author's last name (if it's not mentioned in the text already), the year of publication, and the page number. This lets the reader know that the citation belongs with the sentence or sentences being quoted in case the reader wants to find the original research. Note that there is a "p." for "page" and the closing punctuation for the sentence is outside of the parenthesis.

(14) This topic sentence connects the previous paragraph (superstitions about a fear of water) to a new idea: vampires.

(15) This transitional sentence show how the two pieces of evidence in this paragraph (the historical background from Gottlieb and common knowledge from popular culture) both support the same idea: that vampires are associated with a fear of water.

Creatures of the Night: The Rabid Causes of the Living Dead   5

vampires are possessed of rabid symptoms, they are also thought to be largely hydrophobic in popular culture. Vampires are thought to suffer pains if splashed with holy water, and surely the rabies symptom of drooling must be a problem for these toothy creatures as their fangs protrude over their lower lip.

Like vampires, zombies, whether of the Haitian or undead ◄————— **16** variety, suffer symptoms of rabies, as well. When zombies are "created" by Haitian voodoo "hexes" (or skillful poisoning), the bodies of their victims are pronounced dead by local doctors then raised from that state of death in a series of "convulsions" (Efthimious and Ghandi, 2007), not unlike those suffered by a person bearing the rabies virus. In addition, popular culture images ◄————— **17** demonstrate the ease by which zombification spreads (like a virus) simply by the transference of blood or saliva to exposed mucus membranes, such as seen in the film *28 Days Later*, in which a character transforms instantly into a zombie upon a drop of infected blood falling from a crow's beak into his open eye. Rabies, too, can infect an uninfected animal (remember, humans are animals) by contaminating "mucous membranes (i.e. eyes, nose, mouth), aerosol transmission, and corneal and organ transplantations" (Centers for ◄————— **18**

16 This topic sentence transitions from an old idea (vampires) to a new idea (zombies). The connection is that these creatures share symptoms.

17 This transition creates flow by linking different pieces of evidence to support the same idea.

18 Information from a government agency about medical symptoms supports Araminta's analysis of zombie symptoms. She is able to show her reader the similarities between rabies and zombies, not just tell them.

Creatures of the Night: The Rabid Causes of the Living Dead   6

Disease Control and Prevention, 2011). In that sense, rabies (like ← **19**
zombification) spreads perniciously and without discrimination. In
addition, both diseases are virtually impossible to eradicate.

Another disease that spreads perniciously and without ← **20**
discrimination is that of lycanthropy, a disease cataloged in popular
literature as well as in bizarre historical incidents. Werewolves were
believed to be men who craved only bloody, uncooked meat or who
were given to bestial behavior (Woodward, 1979, p. 19). Humans who
become infected with the rabies virus are typically infected by a bite
of an animal. Given that some rabies symptoms include
hypersalivation, agitation, and confusion ("Rabies", 2011), it is
conceivable that rabies victims would present as animal-like—or, at
least, like the animal that infected the human. Various tribes of the
Americas as well as other ancient cultures held certain animistic
beliefs suggesting that the bite of an animal could transfer the spirit or
"powers" of the animal onto the human who did the biting or received
it (Fox, 1995, p. 132-133). This idea suggests that if a person were ← **21**
known to have been bitten by a wolf, then primitive people might
have thought the spirit of the wolf would transfer into the body of the
man who was bitten.

19 Araminta concludes the paragraph by reiterating the similarity between rabies and zombies, but with slightly new information than she's given already (both are hard to stop). Each sentence in this paragraph supports the central idea, but they build off of each other, connecting to one another and offering new information.

20 This topic sentence transitions from zombies to werewolves by emphasizing their similarities to disease.

21 To make her case, Araminta analyzes the evidence that supports her idea. She doesn't just give the reader a quote about the beliefs of ancient cultures—she says something about it, showing us exactly how it connects to her argument.

Creatures of the Night: The Rabid Causes of the Living Dead   7

One thing that connects werewolves, zombies, and vampires is ← **22**
that each of these supernatural disorders is typically spread through
the bite of an infected creature. Rabies, too, is typically spread by way
of biting. Like zombification, rabies infections cause convulsions and
spreads as quickly as any epidemic imaginable. Vampires experience
hydrophobia, which is the original name for the rabies virus, and
werewolves behave like the animals that infected them through
hypersalivation and agitation. These threads of similarity between the ← **23**
symptoms of supernatural disorders in popular culture and the rabies
virus can't be ignored. Early civilizations who had a limited
understanding of bacteria and disease may have treated rabid people
with superstition, perhaps even accrediting them as having
supernatural disorders: like vampirism, zombification, or lycanthropy.
Maybe all three of these undead creatures are really just victims of a ← **24**
violent rabies virus, a fatal disease when untreated that could lead its
victims further down the rabbit-hole of madness and oddity.

22 The conclusion pulls all of the main ideas together.

23 In addition to summarizing the argument, this conclusion also answers the "so what?" question—this is why Araminta's argument is important.

24 The last sentence leaves the reader with a new idea to think about—a what-if question based on the argument.

Creatures of the Night: The Rabid Causes of the Living Dead   8

References ◄———————————————— **25**

Centers for Disease Control and Prevention. (2011). How is rabies ◄——— **26**

transmitted? Retrieved from CDC website: http://www.cdc.gov/

rabies/transmission/index.html

Efthimiou, C.J. and S. Ghandi. (2007). Cinema fiction vs physics ◄——— **27**

reality: Ghosts, vampires, and zombies. *Skeptical Inquirer.* (31.4), ◄— **28**

27-40.

Fox, Michael. (1995). Animism, empathy, and human development.

Between the Species. 130-140.

Goss, L.W. (1910). Rabies-Hydrophobia. *Experiment Station,*

Circular No. 9. Retrieved from http://www.ksre.ksu.edu/ ◄——— **29**

historicpublications/ Pubs/sc009.pdf

Gottlieb, Richard. (1991). The European vampire: applied

psychoanalysis and applied legend. *Folklore Forum* (23.2), 39-61.

Melton, J. Gordon. (1999). *The vampire book: The encyclopedia of* ◄— **30**

the undead. Detroit: Visible Ink Press.

"Rabies." (2011). *A.D.A.M. Medical Encyclopedia.* U.S. National ◄— **31**

Library of Medicine. Retrieved: http://www.ncbi.nlm.nih.gov

Sureau, Pierre. (1988). History of rabies: advances in research

towards rabies prevention during the last 30 years. *Reviews of*

25 The list of references begins on its own page. APA style uses the title "References". It should have the same margins, header, and text as the rest of the paper. The title is centered, without italics, underlines, or quotation marks.

26 Citations are listed in alphabetical order by author or title, which makes sources easier to find in your list. Create a "hanging indent" where the second and subsequent lines of each entry is indented five spaces. In this case, there is a "corporate author" of an article about rabies.

27 The titles of journal articles have "sentence punctuation", which means that only the first word, a word after punctuation (such as a colon), or proper nouns are capitalized.

28 The titles of journals are italicized and are capitalized.

29 Online sources include "Retrieved from" and the URL.

30 The publication date is the second piece of information in all entries. In APA, researchers value the most up-to-date research.

31 In APA, different types of resources are cited differently in the References pages. A journal article retrieved from a website will look a little different from a journal article retrieved from a print resource, just as a podcast will look a bit different from a book with one author or even a book with twelve authors. Essentially, all APA citations will attempt to include at the very least an author (or "creator" of the work), the year it was published, the title of the work, the location of the publisher, and the name of the publisher. For a full list of citation rules and guidelines, it is best to consult a current manual on the subject.

Creatures of the Night: The Rabid Causes of the Living Dead   9

   Infectious Diseases. (10.4), S581-S584.

Woodward, Ian. (1979). *The Werewolf Delusion.* New York:

   Paddington Press.

32

32 For books, the place of publication and the name of the publisher is included, along with the author's name, date of publication, and the title.

Writing Prompts for Chapter 8

1. Write a paper about how you write an academic research paper. Include everything you know about it from your life, your studies, or just this chapter. Format it properly and cite any research you use.

2. Write an essay about the existence of vampires in your hometown. Pretend you are an investigative journalist as you interview teens you suspect might be secret blood-drinkers (there are many more than you might think).

Writing Exercises for Chapter 8

1. **Critical Thinking:** Answer the questions bulleted in the "Foundations of Thinking Critically" section of this chapter. Be as thorough as possible with your answer. How does knowing your own influences and biases help you to engage with the world of words and research in a better way?

2. **Asking Questions:** Asking good questions is an important skill in academic writing, but you can practice crafting good questions in many contexts. Pretend you are interviewing someone you would love to meet—a writer, film director, actor, musician, etc. List as many interview questions as you can think of. Go back to your list and highlight the ones which would lead to the most interesting answers. Why are those more interesting questions? What makes a good question? What makes a good question for academic writing?

3. **Academic Audience**: Who is the reader for your academic work? Jot down a list or freewrite about an academic audience. Think about writing a paper for a teacher or instructor. What are they looking for in your writing? What are their expectations? Do expectations change between high school and college, or between disciplines and classes?

4. **Research Question:** Create a research question about vampires, zombies, werewolves, mummies, necromancers, or ghosts. Follow the procedures for making sure your question is genuinely good.

5. **Conducting Research:** Take the question you generated in the previous exercise to your local library. Yes, find it and actually go inside the building. Ask a reference

librarian to help you find a book on your topic on the shelves. Go with the librarian to that section and look at the books on the shelves around the one you originally sought. Record the titles and any information you have about the similarity of the surrounding books to your topic. Choose at least three to explore in detail as possible evidence to support your paper.

6. **Citations:** Choose either MLA or APA formatting. MLA is typically used for papers written in the humanities, whereas APA is often used for social or healthcare sciences. Using a manual (such as the ones found at the Online Writing Lab at Purdue University or Diana Hacker and Barbara Fister's Research Documentation), create both an in-text and bibliographical citation for each of the books you found in the previous exercise.

7. **Critical Reading:** Find a source that makes an argument about something you are interested in. Prepare to inhabit the mindset of two different readers, and have pens of different colors ready. Read once as a "friendly reader," jotting down questions, ideas, examples, or evidence that would help the writer make a stronger argument (use one color for this reading). Next, using a different color, read the same text as a "resistant reader," noting questions, ideas, examples, or evidence that weakens the argument presented. Pretend the writer of this text is a friend of yours: what feedback would you give to improve their writing? Try doing this with a classmate's paper or even your own.

8. **Revision**: Once you have a draft of an argumentative paper, try a "Clothesline Outline" to analyze (and possibly improve) your argument and organization. On a separate piece of paper or in a new document, list the question or paper prompt at the top. List your thesis beneath that, and continue by listing the topic sentence from each paragraph. Can you see the chain of reasoning that ties everything together (like laundry hanging off a clothesline)? Do you see any logical fallacies or gaps between points? How can you make your chain of reasoning stronger and/or easier for a reader to follow?

—9—

INFORMATIVE WRITING

or

You Can Fool Most Zombies 100% of the Time

Buster Ashford was once a brilliant scientist. He had two children, a dog, and a loving partner. He went to work every day, donned his token white lab coat, fixed his black-framed glasses upon his nose, and set to work trying to save the world. Along with a team of other scientists, Ashford would eventually stumble onto a means for creating a kind of eternal life all under the guise of creating an anti-aging cosmetic product—or so he thought. In retrospect, he probably should have realized that the Kevlar-clad Special Forces roaming the halls, and the exorbitantly high paycheck he received each week were all signs that maybe something more was afoot at Umbrella Corporation. After falling victim to his own creation, the T-Cell Virus, Buster did the only thing a zombie scientist could do: he ate his family. And shortly after that, he took up writing. With a background in science (and cold hard facts), the chapter devoted to informative or journalistic writing seemed a natural fit for a man whose life had been dedicated to reading lab reports and observing data. If only he'd observed the T-Cell a little more closely.

W E OF THE undead variety often find ourselves in a position where we have to explain what we are doing and why we are doing it. Funny, I know. You probably imagine that we just stumble around day and night, moaning and picking at the (yummy) bloody flesh of the living. Well, you'd be mostly right, but sometimes we *do* have a message to get across.

You can imagine how hard this might be when you consider that in many cases our tongues are decaying and our lungs have lost the ability to force air through those rusting vocal chords. Not to mention the fact that most of the living run screaming from us the moment we stagger into their line of vision. How, then, are we supposed to declare our intentions toward our food supply, uh, I mean friends?

Well, by this point, even a zombie without a single brain cell remaining could guess the answer to this. That's right. Writing. Whether we are delivering news reports on the latest anti-zombie attacks at the local graveyard, generating lab reports on our decapitation science experiments, or summarizing our research about the various weapons humans choose to use against us, writing tends to be an easier path to communication than guttural grunting and flailing limbs. There are still a few of us with enough fluid in our bodies to move our fingers across a keyboard (like, me, for instance), and others who find gripping a pencil like a Kindergartener a still manageable feat. Give us enough time, and we'll give you the next zombie *Hamlet*. Or are you suggesting we're dumber than a room full of monkeys?

But this chapter isn't dedicated to *Hamlet*, it's about informative writing,

> **If a room full of monkeys might eventually write a version of *Hamlet*, would a room full of zombie monkeys eventually write a zombie version?**

which covers everything from reports, newsletters, blogs, tutorials, essay assignments in school, and book reviews.

Let's start by defining what informative writing is. Unlike narrative writing (which attempts to share an undead experience with a reader) or persuasive writing (which tries to convince readers to do whatever you want them to do), informative writing attempts to provide a reader with enough information about a subject so that he or she or it can decide for themself what to think about the topic of discussion.

Now, informing a reader (whether living or undead) about a topic requires us to go back to the old standards of "who, what, where, when, why, and how." Keep in mind that the goal of informative writing is to guide the reader to a new level of understanding, and to do that we need to present thorough information. How do we present thorough information? By asking questions. Let's say that you are writing an essay about Bram Stoker's *Dracula*. Good choice. (I knew Dracula, you know. Back when I was still a fresh, young corpse at Umbrella, Dracula came by to help us out with a few experiments. He was, after all, immortally young, so to speak, and thus the perfect test subject. Stoker didn't get all the facts right, but I think he captured my buddy fairly well, which is pretty amazing considering Dracula's thick, Transylvanian accent—even I could only understand every tenth word—but that's blood under the bridge.) So, in this example, let's see how we lay out the questions:

WHO? This one is easy. Bram Stoker, of course.

WHAT? *Dracula*. Hey, this is easier than gnawing on bones in a basement, isn't it?

WHEN? Now it gets a little more difficult. If you want to speak about Stoker's birth and some of the things that happened during his life before he wrote *Dracula*, the question of "when" changes. Are you writing about the period when he actually wrote the book? Or, are you talking about Dracula's own birth and life? Well, you might have to go even further back than Stoker for that one, as Dracula (Vlad Tepesh) lived hundreds of years prior to the time Stoker even lifted a quill. Thus, your "when" will depend on your purpose. Your purpose is the goal you use to unify your writing, but we'll get to that. Moving on.

WHERE? Again, you must start narrowing your subject matter to specifics. Remember, you are writing an essay. Sometimes informative essays are biographies, sometimes they are histories, and sometimes they merely document a strange medical condition (like rigor mortis or porphyria). So, again, this is tied to your purpose. Are you talking about where he wrote the book or are you talking about locations in the book?

WHY? Once again, you must answer this question for yourself before you can answer it for your readers. Starting with a "why" question can help you hone in on exactly what your topic is, which should help illustrate your purpose more clearly before you even begin writing. After that, you can illustrate it for your reader. Therefore, the main question is probably "why did he write this particular novel?" But it is not the only one; you could also ask "why did it become popular?" or "why is it considered a classic?"

HOW? "How" is maybe the most complicated question to answer and in some instances is closely related to the question of "why." The "why" question will sometimes dictate the "how" question in terms of topic. Perhaps you need to explore *how* Dracula became immortal, and research and deliver information about his own demonic possession or physical illness. Or perhaps you need to explore *how* Stoker met Dracula in the, uh, flesh. It all depends on your angle.

You might not actually want or need to answer all of these questions in your piece of writing, but asking (and attempting to answer) them for yourself can be an important part of pre-writing.

When dealing with informative writing, establishing an angle is secondary to the method you use. You can write, for instance, about any part of Dracula's life or Stoker's tale, starting anywhere and ending anywhere on the curl of his cape, if you want to. What really matters when it comes to informative writing is how you approach it.

I remember when I was a living boy back in grade school outside Raccoon City, long before I had any pipette dreams of joining the ranks of the Umbrella Corporation. Must have been third grade, I think. Miss Sweater's class. Her name wasn't really Miss Sweater, but she wore this fuzzy red cardigan all the time, so that's what I called her. I remember it vividly now because all that red makes me think of the delicious blood that used to pump through her body before I ate her a few years ago.

Anyway, Miss Sweater brought in a guest speaker one day from the local newspaper. This guy was a total cliché. Fedora, leather vest, and one of those flip-top notepads. He told us that to write the news you had to be unbiased—you had to tell the news without showing even a glimmer of your own opinion—because if you didn't, then people would get mad and not trust your objective account of things. "Nobody likes being told what to think," he claimed.

I didn't really understand what he meant until I started work for the big U.C. We had a team of scientists working on a special vaccine, or so they called it. All the data backed up the idea that this brilliant vaccine would make you young forever. Botox schmotox—our Regenerate was practically handed down by the gods, our reports boldly declaring that "women look and feel years younger" and "it works like magic." Yeah. Only, what I didn't know was that it wasn't the science geeks releasing that information. Oh no. The lab reports were handed straight to Umbrella's marketing director who colored them a bit with some flowery language.

> **I remember Miss Sweater. She was the one with the large, er, brain cavity, wasn't she? Yum. Brains! What else would a a zombie desire?**

The first flower to bloom in that report? Well, the name. Regenerate was the T-Virus, of course. Can't complain, though. If it weren't for the T-leak, I wouldn't have superhuman strength or this unquenchable yearning for your raw, bloody internal organs.

But I digest—um, I mean, *digress*.

The point I'm trying to make here is that had the science geeks been able to deliver the reports they'd meant to give, the world would have had a better shot at making a clear, self-discerning decision about Regenerate (or the T-Virus) on their own, and maybe we wouldn't all be in this gooey, gory mess of blood-spattered viscera. (Mmmm. Viscera.)

If there is anything to learn from the big guys at Umbrella Corporation, there are some basic guidelines to writing informatively that should be heeded, lest we pay the ultimate price.

Deliver only the facts and justifiable analysis or interpretation of the facts: In other words, don't make inferences you can't back up with valid research.

Avoid weighty words: There are certain words in the language of the living that will automatically evoke an emotional reaction from your reader. Among them are the words "abuse," "murder," "intelligence," "stupidity," and "brains." Tasty, tasty brains.

Use a formal tone: Just because you can't speak doesn't mean you can ignore your tone of voice when writing, zombuddy.

Avoid adverbs: Adverbs are words that modify actions and they always color the way a reader thinks about something.

Using these guidelines, your writing will lead the reader by the hand across the gate's threshold, through the graveyard, and straight into the mausoleum. You always have to be thinking about your reader's mind (I know I am). You see, your mind is distinctly different from anyone else's because it went through your unique experiences to come to your unique location. What does that mean for you? It means that the world will not think the way you do. It means that you will have to choose your words carefully in order to deliver the right message or idea to your reader because what really matters is how your reader will interpret the words you choose to convey your message.

Take, for instance, the word "red." As soon as you read the word, an image probably popped into your head. Maybe it was a streak of blood, or a fire engine, or the still-beating heart of your latest victim. The point is, you interpreted "red" the instant you read the word. The trouble comes when you consider what I implied by the word "red." What if my intent was to describe the color of the bricks in my office as I munched on the small intestine of my intern? That's the "red" I see when I say or write the word. But, you are a different person, and through your lens of experience you'll see a whole different "red." The point is that each word we use needs to be interpreted by another person and, if we are not careful with our words, that interpretation can easily take our reader off track. This often happens within informative writing when it uses too many big words, or the sentences are not concisely written, or the writer failed to take into account that the reader is an entirely different human being (or, yes, dead thing) trying to understand what you are saying through his or her own unique lens of the world.

Now, imagine how much more

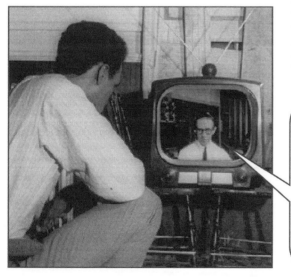

And I repeat—there are no such things as zombies. Ignore that scratching at your door. It is likely just the wind.

complicated this is when you consider what writing really is. Not only do individual words carry individual interpretations depending on the person trying to make sense of it, but they also carry sound. Yeah. That's right. Writing is sound. Remember, all language boils down to this yummy, fatty stew of sound. Written words were developed to carry messages from one living body to another over any distance. Those letters represented phonemes, which is Greek for "a sound uttered." It's kind of like a code. I'd put down a bunch of phonemes that translated to a message I wanted to send to my zombuddy, Brad Vickers. Then, good ol' Brad would get my list of phonemes and he'd sound them out loud to *hear the message.*

Let's say my message was, "Eat the cheerleader." There are many different ways Vickers could hear that message. He could hear it from the voice of a man really angry and demanding, *EAT the cheerleader [now]!* He could hear it from the voice of a child asking a question, *Eat the [uh, ur] cheerleader [sir]?* Or he could hear from the myriad voices from a bleacher-full of football fans shouting, *Eat the cheerleader [yes we can!], eat the cheerleader [zombie man!].* Three simple words that can be interpreted in many different ways and it all depends on how good ol' Vickers decides to interpret it.

A GUIDE TO ZOMBIE MEAL PREFERENCES

**Struggling Students
Juicy Journalists
Wriggling Writers
Portly Professors
Notable Novelists
Tasty Teachers
and even Bony Bookworms**

Now, if I was pissed off at Brad, I might add a few superlatives to my message: *Eat the cheerleader, toiletmouth.* If I was annoyed with Brad, I might add a note of sarcasm: *Go ahead and eat the cheerleader; see if I care.* If I was thrilled with Brad, I might add a note of cheer: *Eat the cheerleader, buddy! Go on! Good job!*

The same methods can be applied to Brad's relationship to me. If he is my best friend, I'd use a more relaxed, friendly tone with him than if he were, say, my boss. Here's a great exercise to help you see the difference in written tones. Write a letter to your boss apologizing for eating his favorite dog for dinner last week. Now, write a letter to your boyfriend, girlfriend, it-friend, or significant other apologizing for eating their favorite dog for dinner last week. Same letter, two different audiences. Now read them both out loud. What differences do you notice?

Chances are the letter to your boss reads like it came out of a textbook or was written by a biochemical student attending the University of Transylvania, whereas the letter to your significant other reads more like the dialogue between two Nicholas Sparks' characters in a sad novel about some fatal disease. The one to your boss is the formal tone you want to match, whereas the one to your significant other is informal. Formal shows reservation with regard to emotion whereas informal lets all of the entrails hang out and drag along the ground for everyone to see. Like it or not, readers can be swayed by your emotions when they read your text, so be reserved and formal with your tone.

Next, let's talk about those adverbs I mentioned earlier. Adverbs are words that often end in "ly" and modify a verb. No matter what our intentions may be, adverbs will color the way a reader hears the words we write. Here's an example. Let's say I'm trying to create a news article on how an anti-zombie-rights activist walked into a store to looking for a bag of zombie jerky, found it, and then made the purchase. I could write that this way:

Linnea shambled into the store, picked up a bag of zombie jerky, put her money on the counter, and left.

Fact based, clean, almost pure observation. But what happens if I say it this way?

Linnea shambled into the store, picked up a bag of zombie jerky, quickly put her money on the counter before leaving just as quickly.

Now Linnea's actions aren't based solely on my observation of her actions. Her actions involving the purchase and exit are "quick." This can imply all sorts of things about Linnea. She might have been scared the owner was going to shoot her. She might have stolen something. She might have been disgusted at the state of the store. She may have just been in a hurry (some of us are *zoombies*, after all). Either way, the word "quickly" repeated in that sentence gives the reader a feeling about what happened and causes the reader to infer why Linnea was moving quickly.

While we are on that example, let's use it to discuss the analysis of facts rather than the inference of facts. But first, a little segue. I knew this guy in college who once told me that one of his favorite jobs was working as a cinema narrator for the blind. Blind patrons would come into the cinema expecting to experience a movie. The guy's job was to narrate what the blind guy couldn't see happening on the screen. He had to give the detail flatly—without emotion—so the movie-goer could experience the film's emotions all on his own. It wouldn't do, for example, to introduce the

My likes are hanging out at shopping malls and wandering through cemeteries. My dislikes are athletic people and chainsaws.

opening scenes of *The Sound of Music* with "A lovely blond woman in a pinafore and black dress frolics on a green-swept hillside." Too much emotion is given away in that sentence. Instead, he'd tell the movie-goer, "A woman wearing a dress and apron is running over a hill." See the difference? One is flowery and full of inference, while the other is flat and observational.

Consider the phrase "Linnea shambled." Well, what sort of emotion do you attach to the word "shamble"? What inference do you make? Shamblers tend to be monsters, lepers, disabled members of the living community, or elderly people. So, if I use a word like "shamble" to describe the way Linnea moved into the store, I'm basically telling my reader to view her as a social outcast. The reader will skim over that word and say to him-,

A GUIDE TO ZOMBIE ADJECTIVES

Shambling	Slobbering
Decaying	Lumbering
Overripe	Putrid
Rancid	Ravenous
Lurching	Rotting
Oozing	Shuffling

her-, or itself, *Yep—that Linnea's a zombie, all right*. In informative writing, those connotations or inferences might be things we want to avoid. Instead, I could simply state the facts: "Linnea walked into the store, purchased the zombie jerky, and left." Now, readers can interpret Linnea's actions for themselves.

And this brings me to my last point about weighty words. There are certain words in the living language that will almost automatically make a person feel something. When seeking to deliver unbiased information, we want to try to avoid using them—after all, what if they feel something that puts them on the opposite side as us? Now we've got a new enemy, and we've got enough of those already.

One of the most powerfully weighty words in English is known to make one and all tremble and perspire at the mere hint of it. Well, at least those of us that still have working sweat glands. And that word is:

Taxes

The second I even mention that word, I know half my audience will be forming opinions against whatever I've written and the other half will be siding with my ideas. But if my topic is about levying a new tax, how do I do that without using a word that will cause neck hairs to prickle on sight? Simple. I just call "taxes" by another name. Perhaps a service fee? Or a maintenance cost? Or an organ donation? Offering? Well, you get the idea.

A classic way to use a formal tone and deliver justifiable facts is to plug your information into a formula. No, not the T-Cell Virus formula—*a writing formula*. Most genres of writing have some kind of formula you can use to convey information, argument, or streams of consciousness. The most basic formula that can be applied to nearly any genre of writing is the five-paragraph essay. In this type of essay, you write approximately five paragraphs. Technically, you can have a few more if you need them, but generally speaking the foundation of the formula requires five. It is not the only means to organize your creative efforts, but it is very straightforward and easy to follow. It simply consists of an introductory paragraph, three supportive body paragraphs, and a conclusion.

The introductory paragraph is your "hook," which was discussed in Chapter 1 on the Basics of Writing. The hook gets the reader's attention and aims the reader directly at the target of your essay.

The next three paragraphs are structured to transition from one paragraph to the next and not only support your introduction, but support their own subject matter as well. Each body paragraph is like the path the reader takes from the aiming (introduction) to the target (conclusion).

Your last paragraph then needs to tie everything together and leave no questions unanswered. To use an old adage from a motivational speaker I once ate, the structure to this method is simply: "Tell them what you're going to tell them (intro), tell them (body), and then tell them what you told them (conclusion)." Here's the layout:

Paragraph 1: Hook and Introduction
Paragraphs 2 through 4: Supporting details or "body" paragraphs
Paragraph 5: Conclusion

This method follows the idea that people respond well to structure. Heck, even zombies respond well to structure—we just don't have much. If you structure your messages so that you always begin with a "lead-in," then follow with a host of supporting details, and finish with a "lead-out" (or conclusion), your readers will thank you. Consider the following example.

Five Paragraph Annotated Example Informative Essay

Are Vampires Among Us?
By Eugenia Crossbones

Whether they sparkle, stalk, or seduce us, vampires have been a recurring theme in popular culture for centuries. Beginning with religious and mythological texts dating back millennia, we can see evidence of vampires and vampiric characters who feast on the blood, souls, life-force or energy, or even the flesh of the living. Sometimes these characters are thought to be living beings—perhaps afflicted

Notice how the writer doesn't just jump right into her statement of purpose. Instead, she leads into it using a "hook" that presents some of the more interesting details of the topic before moving in for the kill—that is, before announcing the precise purpose of this paper. Your reader needs to ease into things; to get comfortable before you pounce.

with the so-called "vampire disease," porphyria—while others are thought to be demons, monsters, or corpses risen from the dead to prey on people. It is easy to understand why some primitive peoples would imagine vampires to be among them, with the various plagues and sudden, unexplainable deaths that surrounded them. But, is it so easy to believe in vampires among us today? After all, we have modern science to explain away the sudden death of a child in a crib or the apparent growth of hair and nails after a person has passed away. Is it possible that individuals who thrive off the life essence of people still plague humanity? While vampires of myths and legends may not be listing their addresses in the yellow pages just yet, there are certainly individuals among us who still thrive by draining energy from other people, whether it be by fierce negativity, sociopathic tendencies, or even murder.

While informative essays do not have "arguable thesis statements," they still have a statement of purpose which also provides a map to paragraphs 2 through 4. Notice how this statement declares what will be discussed as well as the details the author will use to support it.

In early times, it is possible that murderers, sociopaths, and negative people were ostracized or never uncovered. There was a good deal of mysticism surrounding life and death, and certainly the character of people or their mental health was not high on the list of priorities when examining the reason someone might have committed murder or behaved oddly. Whether on purpose or by accident, too, some individuals were buried alive—perhaps comatose—only to be dug up later and found to have clawed at the lids of their caskets, their withered faces immortalized in a horrifying scream. This certainly lent to the plausibility of vampires—creatures that could go on living after death.

Notice how this repeats elements of the last sentence in the previous paragraph? This helps the reader to transition from the last idea (the statement of purpose) to the new idea (a supporting detail).

Here we have some nice examples of fine details. Each body paragraph in this formula should include fine details. If we tried to stuff the fine details into the introduction, we'd clog the whole thing up worse than Aunt Margaret's arteries after an American cruise ship feast.

But what about imagined or social death? Experiencing a trauma, if untreated, can cause people to behave in all sorts of ways. Trauma involving other people can also cause individuals to become hypercritical, suspicious, and pessimistic. This kind of negative behavior can

Questions are a way of engaging a reader and, if used properly, they can function as a transition between paragraphs as well.

suck the life out of the people that surround him or her just as life slowly drains from a person buried alive. Intense negativity has a tendency to block individuals from creativity, an act which will eventually shut down his or her ability to think of new ideas. Ideas are where our lives progress—our life force, if you will, is founded on ideas—thus, if we are stripped of our ideas due to the actions of another person, we are stripped of our life force in much the same way as a victim of a vampire is sucked dry.

> Notice how this paragraph focuses on a new set of fine details? This supports the original claim that vampires are among us by showing us other ways they may exist here.

Vampires among us today are not always psychic vampires, or people who drain away our creative and positive energies, but are also capable of draining away our physical lives, as well. Sociopaths and murderers thrive on the suffering and life force of human beings in a different way. Some sociopaths, so isolated from positive social interaction, find a kind of pleasure in the torturing of others, whether mentally or physically. Thus, their "life force" is lifted up by the draining of another person's energy. Some murderers, too, particularly those who commit murder repeatedly (hence the term "serial killer") thrive on the sense of power derived from stealing another person's breath. By extinguishing a person's life, some murderers feel relief or satisfaction. Again, this suggests that the draining of life from one person can cause another to feel "uplifted" or "reinvigorated"—much like vampires of myth, lore, and legend.

> In this final "body" paragraph, the writer declares one last detail to support the purpose.

Therefore, whether you believe in creatures that stalk the night and fill the pages of our primitive history to be real or metaphorical, vampires are indeed among us today. They may not resemble the creatures we see skulking through our novels or glaring over their capes in our films, but they are here nonetheless. Vampires are creatures who thrive by taking or draining energy from the living. Psychic

> Notice how the conclusion starts with a signal word? This helps the reader to recognize the end is in sight. Think of it like an exit sign on a highway.

vampires drain energy by sucking creativity and positivity from other people until they are all as hollow and negative as the vampire. Sociopaths can be uplifted by draining away the energy of others, either by controlling their emotions or their bodies with pain; and some who murder again and again experience a sense of power and vigor from extinguishing human life. Sure. They don't all have pointed teeth, but what is a vampire if not the guy who takes away everything that makes you *you*? Maybe that's what our primitive history writers and legend makers were really talking about in our myths and religious texts.

And these final sentences reiterate what the writer has declared and the major points the writer used to support the topic. Notice how the writer didn't just restate the ideas in the exact same wording. Instead, she mixed it up a bit, twisted the wording a bit, using synonyms to remind the reader of the point without simply repeating it.

Writing Prompts for Chapter 9

1. Turn on your local news and write about a local event using only observational (journalistic) detail. Try to watch more than one news channel's coverage of the event and determine if they are using sensational language themselves. Eliminate sensational language from your own coverage.

2. Imagine you are a journalist sent to cover a news story about what can only be the start of the inevitable zombie apocalypse. Staying in newsworthy persona, how do you cover the event?

3. Write a *Wikipedia*-style article about a topic you know a lot about or find interesting. (To begin, you might even look at *Wikipedia's* policies and guidelines for contributors.) Was it challenging to maintain objectivity? Why or why not?

4. Think about an activity you do well. Pretend you have to describe this activity or process to someone who has never done this before and write a short, informative article. What strategies did you use to help your reader?

Writing Exercises for Chapter 9

1. **Five-Paragraph Essay:** Write a five-paragraph essay about the historical, mythological, or literary ways that vampires can be killed. Follow the formula for the introduction, the three body paragraphs, and the conclusion as closely as possible. Continue to tweak the paragraphs until they fit the formula. (Keep in mind that a pre-writing activity, such as an outline or clustering, might help you get started.)

2. **Tone:** Imagine you are writing a letter to your boss (or your teacher, or someone else with authority). Explain to them that you are running away and never coming back. Be sure not to burn a bridge with this person in case you need to come back someday and ask a favor. Now, imagine you are writing the same letter (running away and never coming back) to your best friend. How are these different? What words did you use in the former that you didn't use in the latter? Which one was more personal? Which one was more professional?

3. **Adverbs:** Find something you wrote from a while ago. It can be an old email, a story, a letter, or a long text. Scan it for adverbs. If there are any adverbs, remove them and note any changes in how the piece reads. If there are no adverbs, add

some and note these changes to the text. How are they different? How do adverbs change the way we interpret meaning?

4. **Objectivity**: Try writing a review of your favorite movie or book review in two different styles. In one, do your best to write passionately about your favorite book or movie—share your passion with your reader. In the next review, try to write objectively about your favorite book or movie, just to tell your reader what happens. What are some of the differences between your two reviews? How did your choices about language, voice, and objectivity affect the "message" of your writing?

–10–

Business and Professional Writing

or

"Use All Your Well-Learned Politesse"

Countess Cliché is a semi-famous vampire from around the time of Vlad Tepesh and Elizabeth Bathory. Born in Transylvania to Count Cliché and his wife, Carmilla, the Countess was raised with all the finery and courtly manners afforded to any member of the royal family. When she became a bride to Apollonius, a Greek trader, she also became a vampire that very night. Did that stop her royal lust for power? Certainly not. In fact, it merely spurred her bloodlust onward into the twenty-first century where she now resides in one of six homes around the world (depending on the season). Her greatest success has been her international interment service and mortuary, a multi-trillion dollar company. Our writers asked her if she might cover the chapter on business and professional writing, as it is kind of her thing.

GOOD EVENING. PLEASE allow me to introduce myself. My name is Countess Cliché Harbinger, and I am a vampire from the mountains of Transylvania. I have been asked by our esteemed authors to pen these pages due to my particular talents in the area of elocution, exposition, and communication. I have a flair, if you will, for brandishing the flourishes of fine prose, which I express with all manner of, well, manners. Of course, I'm also the owner of Dark Harbinger Mortuary and Interment Services, and am often tasked with creating my own written documents, or hiring others proficiently skilled enough to do it for me. These professional traits, coupled with my insatiable thirst for human blood, make me a writer skilled at flattery and etiquette as well as charisma and salesmanship. In short, I am uniquely qualified to expound on the virtues of business and professional writing. I am, after all, hundreds of years old and unlike my zombie sisters—we of the vampire persuasion think of them as "*that* side of the family"—I have a clear and eloquent voice.

Much like my Uncle Vlad and first cousin Elizabeth, I have found that great power comes from an ability to demonstrate my might to mere mortals, to convince them that I am worthy of their devotion, or to give themselves to me in life and in blood.

That power can be reduced to one weapon which, when wielded by a skillful being educated in the nuance and overture of its use, can bring whole cities to ruin, lay waste to a thousand acres of a thousand crops, and tear the emotions from your very soul.

That weapon, my friends, is words.

Wielding words is a power that requires great responsibility, and with great responsibility often comes an imbalance in our, well, unlives. For who will bear the whips and scorns of such responsibility when we are ill, or tired, or buried in a casket surrounded by our own grave dirt? To that end, you may be able to relate to this. If you have ever filed a TPS report while staring at the back of a co-worker's head over the cubicle wall in your tiresome office, you will not be surprised to find many members of the undead still laboring in the world of business. Zombies in particular, with their Swingline staplers and loathsome fax machines, tend to fill up the ranks of the cubicle world, for who else can we established and elite powers find to do such mundane work? To be honest, eating brains doesn't exactly pay well, and where else would a soulless, mindless drone fit in so easily? At the same time, as a business owner in this century, I am forced to select from my flesh-eating minions only those who have a thorough grasp of language, for how else am I to maintain my power over them without selecting only the best and brightest of the undead? And, while being a zombie in the business world may seem an (un)natural fit, business writing can still be a challenge, even if you have a brain (or two), and my minions have many—otherwise they quickly find themselves on the receiving end of a flaming torch. Zombies are so very dry, you see. Not unlike my sense of humor.

> **While eating brains does not pay particularly well, neither does the profession of writing in most cases. Just as zombies love the taste of brains, however, writers love the feel of the words as they form on the page.**

The point is simply that I only select adept business writers to occupy the cubicles within my office walls. The world of business communication is formal, direct, and to the point. (Since most of the living dead aren't known for our eloquence or talkativeness, this is easy for them to remember, even without a fully-functioning brain.) Most professional communication happens in writing, usually in the form of email, and the last thing I desire is for my unliving colleagues to receive an email communication which is unclear or which contains misspelled words or grammatical errors. Spelling and grammar, after all, are guidelines by which we create understanding and, as such, are a vital component to business and professional writing. How else am I to show my power? You think this flashy red cape and my ruby-encrusted mini-skirt are all that it takes? Think again. The most powerful thing we possess is our language. The ability to sling words around a page (or computer screen) clearly and eloquently is the ability to wage wars . . . or lose them. It is for this reason that my minions—my zombies whose every correspondence represents my business and me—must be exact executioners of language.

Think for a moment about the powerful individuals in your mortal history. I'm sure you can name dozens; I have known many strong men and women during my decadent centuries. Hitler, Stalin, Churchill, Elizabeth, Marie Antoinette. All of them had the power of words at their fingertips, though some, like Marie, swam too deeply in the waves of the words and lost their heads as a result. Telling a nation of starving peasants that they can just eat cake, rumor or not, demonstrates the power I speak of, for it was these words—whether plucked from her lips or imagined by the tongues of vicious enemies—that precipitated her demise. And Hitler's words drove millions to atrocities far more brutal than anything a vampire such as I could aspire to do. Stalin and Elizabeth are just examples of two powerful leaders of empires that wielded words like knives over their enemies. And of course, Sir Winston Churchill was well known for both powerful words and the resolute voice with which he spoke them.

The point is that the most successful beings on this planet, which we immortals share with you, are those capable of wielding words with precision and fierce ability. Great orators become senators who speak their way into presidency. Great writers become the backbone of great leaders as they carefully choose words and craft knowledge. In short, the skill so often referred to as "a way with words" is coveted by one and all, but perhaps most especially by employers because they know that the gift of good communication is a vital component—as vital as life's red blood to my eternal youth and beauty—to every business under the skin-scorching, ash-rendering sunshine.

The principle rule of business writing is no different, really, than any other form of writing in that you must first know your purpose and audience before committing pen to paper. Of course, in the business world, there are certain things we take for granted. Those are that we are professionals and conduct ourselves with that decorum at all times. Take for example, my Uncle Vlad. I'm sure you've seen his movies. Everyone has. Honestly, family reunions are unbearable. "Did you see my star in Hollywood? This is the same cloak Bela Lugosi wore in the movie version of my life

Ben didn't always express himself professionally, but everyone knew exactly what he thought about the new office furniture.

that he was also buried in. I love Gary Oldman as much as the next vampire, but I think he overdid it a little with my fingernails in that film, don't you? And the Mr. Burns hair?" Honestly, it's enough to drive a vampire into the sunlight.

As I was saying, take my Uncle Vlad. In his movies, you'll notice that no matter the circumstance, Vlad is always a gracious host to his guests, flattering them with every luxury he and his home have to offer. He speaks kindly to them, if firmly, and he even avails his own wives to them in some instances. He has the perfect set of manners—when he's not trying to eat you, of course. But, the point is, even when Jonathan Harker shows up at his estate, he was kind to him. And whenever Van Helsing shows up, his mortal adversary, he still exchanges words with the man.

This is an example of professionalism. Vampires are always professional, you see. We excel at it. Professionalism means that, no matter what your purpose or agenda may ultimately be—to suck the blood from the neck of the serving girl?—you always maintain dignity and respect for the person with whom you are engaging. You do your best to oblige them, to say "yes" to them, and to make sure their needs are met. You choose your words carefully and with tact to ensure that your meaning is not lost or misinterpreted. You do this always—even after you have gone to ground for the daylight hours—because you never know who might be watching you from the shadows.

> ## HOW TO SCARE OFF DANGEROUS CREATURES
>
> Zombies don't scare easily, but fire certainly gets their attention.
>
> Vampires have a dislike for garlic, holy water, and stakes.
>
> Werewolves never know when a gun might contain a silver bullet.
>
> Witches have been known to melt away with a little water.
>
> Writers are quite easy to frighten. All you have to do is show them a blank sheet of paper.

Now, for all you underlings out there—yes, I'm talking to you there, holding the e-reader and sipping on your double grande latte—you might fail to realize the larger context of professional writing and all it entails in the grander scheme of things. You see, to be truly professional, you must exude this persona all the time. In other words, you don't get to "turn off" your professional writing skills when you are cruising the local social networking site, and your professional communication skills should be maintained even while you're surfing for fresh blood at the local watering hole.

Why, you ask? You have a life, don't you? So why the need to be professional 100% of the time?

To be frank, you never know if the next person you meet will be a client, coworker, or boss. You never know if the person cruising your social networking profile is intent on hiring (or firing) you based on what you write there. For that reason, it is best not to express your interest in illegal substances, all-night parties, your basement full of dead bodies, or any other behavior that may be construed as reckless—or, more accurately, as "unprofessional."

I believe your American federal government even passed a law recently allowing employers to select employees based on a background check which includes a thorough investigation into one's social networking use. Given that I hire my staff on the grounds of their ability to represent me publicly, do you think I would choose the worker whose Tastebook Page features comments about how he hates his boss enough to eat him with a nice bottle of Chianti and some fava beans? Or the one whose Ogle Plus account displays a series of photographs featuring the applicant passed out over a gluttonous bowl of cthulhu meatloaf of *epic* proportions? Let's say I've hired the hapless chap—do you think I would not fire him the first time he blasts on his Spitter account that he thinks Dark Harbinger Mortuary and Interment Services is a terrible place to work? Naturally I would. Now do you see the importance of your messages—particularly the messages you share with the world? I certainly hope so. Guard what you say in public forums. It is your only hope.

In addition to remaining professional with your social networking, consider also the messages you indirectly send. When Dark Mortuary was still a fledgling morgue with only two zombies and a vampire mortician on the payroll, I once received an employment application from a young vampire. His résumé was dutifully structured, replete with name and contact information at the top, but there was one problem. Do you know what his email address was? It was <u>StakeYourHeartVampireKiller @fakemail.com</u>. Now, does that look like a professional email to you? Do you suppose I hired that fool? Of course not. I hired the next creature whose résumé passed across my desk. His email address was <u>MonsterFrankenstein1888@fakemail.com</u>. See the difference? First name: Monster. Last name: Frankenstein. And, apparently, there were 1,887 other MonsterFrankensteins before he opened the account. Or maybe it was meant as a date.

So you see, your messages are both direct and indirect. Your email address can convey—or betray—a lot about your business nature, as can the way you structure or draft your emails. Always be sure to open emails appropriately with signs of respect. Call them by their titles of Mr. or Ms. and declare your purpose immediately—in the first line—so as not to waste valuable company time. And *do* use "Ms." instead of "Miss" or "Mrs." I'm a modern vampire woman in a modern world. Not only does marital status mean nothing to a vampire, it should mean nothing to my salutation, got it, young blood? And lastly, don't forget to always close with a sincere signature, whether that be "Sincerely, so-n-so," "Coldly, Vlad," or "Bloody returns, Elizabeth."

To that end, carry this form of professional exposition over into all your public writing (emails, memos, press releases and the like), and you can only succeed. Remember that anyone can read them, even if you originally send it only to someone you trust. Accounts get hacked. Friends become frenemies. Some people may stoop so low as to copy your post and mail a hard copy to your employer if they despise you enough. And in the world of business, there's a reason they call it cutthroat. Speaking of cutthroat, I'm quite famished. Allow me to turn the remainder of this chapter over to my very capable and trusted Director of Management Services, Jack T. Ripper. He was planning to conduct a meeting to address a few, ah, issues taking place with the staff. I believe you'll find his direction most enlightening.

Enter Jack T. Ripper, dressed in a long black tailcoat and sporting a top hat polished to a mercurial gleam. In his left, white-gloved hand is a stack of paper. In his right hand, a silver-topped walking stick.

Okay, settle down in back. This may not be your first day on the job here at Dark Harbinger Mortuary and Interment Services, but I guarantee it will be your last if you don't pay attention during this session. I want you zombies in the back there to pay special attention. And please refrain from mingling with our human employees. Rhoda Morgenstern would have been 83 years old next week. But now she would rather feast on human entrails instead of the lovely birthday cake we had planned for Monday. Not that I'm pointing any fingers—particularly at those whose fingers have fallen off in an unfortunate work-related accident—but, thanks a lot, Zed. You know who you are.

Now, back to business, which is precisely why we are here today. Our business letters, company reports, and even our memos have become very unbusiness-like over the past few months. It's pretty bad when I can't tell the difference between a memo written by a zombie to that written by a vampire with a degree from the University of London.

How many of you even know the difference between a business letter and an interoffice memo?

(Silence falls over the room except a low growl from a werewolf near the door.)

Just as I thought.

Here's a memo written by one of our new interns. Fea Morrigan, I know you are relatively new to our Public Relations Department, but you should know better having graduated from Central Transylvania Community College.

October 23

To the peoples and other creatures here at Harbinger.

Mr. Harbinger just told me to tell everyone that Halloween is an important day and you all can take the day off except the guys that dig the graves.

That won't do at all, Fea. Let's try that one again properly, shall we. Here's the same memo as written by moi:

MEMO

To: All Employees of Dark Harbinger Mortuary and Interment Services
From: Cliché Harbinger
Date: October 23
Subject: Work Schedule for October 31st (Halloween)

In honor of the sacred day of Halloween and the 666th birthday of Mrs. Cliché Harbinger, all employees in Groups 1, 2 and 3 will receive the day of October 31st off with pay. Group 4 (including all witches, ghosts and goblins) may also leave at noon on October 30th in preparation for evening activities. Unfortunately, as we anticipate the arrival of several humans who will not be returning from the dead, all employees who participate in the burial service will be expected to work. They will, however, receive a comp day in return.

Now, I hope everyone can see the difference. Notice how the first one is informal and feels a little bit like a scene between two teenaged girls chatting each other up in a bathroom stall at Sunnydale High School. The latter—that's the *second* option, for those of you who literally have no brains—is formal and tasteful, and it is written in a particular structure. That is, it follows some rules, which include calling it a "MEMO," addressing it to particular individuals, dating the work, providing a clear subject, and then using formal tone and clear language to fulfill the message. Just remember, *Fea*, ahem, and everyone else, that in the professional business world we value different qualities than in other styles of writing. We want precision and clarity. We want to get to the point without flailing about like some sea hag out of water. Sorry, Mrs. Greenteeth, no disrespect intended.

Some business writing forms require basic structures, such as what we just saw in the professionally crafted memo. Call this requirement the *expectation of your readers*—your audience will expect things to come to them in a certain way so that they can better understand the point of it. Other types of business writing will not have a prescribed structure, but will still require certain rules of engagement. All you need to remember is five basic points: Tone, clarity, organization, courtesy, and editing.

Tone means you write with confidence and self-assurance. No one will take you seriously if you don't sound like you know what you are talking about. Tell the poor bereaved (and hopefully rich) widow that you guarantee the gold-plated Midas casket will keep her husband's body safe for eternity. And, of course, never tell them the gold is simply paint from the local hardware store.

Clarity means that you want to give the facts quickly and clearly. Leave no room for raised eyebrows or questions. We don't want the widow asking about alternatives like cremation. There is no money in cremation unless you can sell them the Deluxe Funeral Pyre Package where our Joan of Arc look-alike lights the fire.

Organization seems to be what all of you lack, so pay attention. Mr. Collins! Please refrain from nibbling on Fea's neck. We all know how long you've been cooped up in the family tomb, but you're on staff now, so please listen up. Well-organized messages begin with the purpose, explain the details (if necessary), and close with an action item. Don't beat around the bush. Know where you are going to dig the grave, remove the dirt, throw the body in, and replace the dirt. It's that simple. Even Zed can do that, although he tends to slobber on his memos.

> **Dig the grave, remove the dirt, throw the body in, and replace the dirt. It's that simple.**

Sometimes we forget **courtesy,** yet it's very important in all brands of business communication, especially in our business. Whether you are writing a letter praising our memorial service or an interoffice memo, don't be rude. Remember, fresh brain matter attracts more zombies than rotting entrails.

And last, but not least, don't forget to **proofread** your material. Yes, I know that everyone gets in a rush when quitting time approaches and that our werewolves get a little antsy right before a full moon, but that's no excuse. Take the time to look that letter over one last time. Don't forget the incident where we lost a major account when *someone*, and I won't name any names, Candy Mann, ahem, typoed Mr. Smit's last name and failed to catch it in the proofread. That "h" nearly lost the Countess more than a dozen clients all because of one misspelled word. Maybe if *someone* had spent a little less time in front of *someone's* mirror, and a little more time looking at the text, it wouldn't have happened.

Now we are going to spend a little time on the business letter. So, at this time all zombies and grave diggers may be excused. What was that, Wendy, you can't hold a pen in your hand because you're a ghost? Good point. All ghostly spirits may also be excused at this time.

Okay.

The business letter. Please bear in mind that the business letter includes any letter sent to or from a business. In case you don't realize it, the cover letter most of you included with your résumé when you first applied for your position at Harbinger's was a business letter. So was the follow-up thank-you letter you sent to show your appreciation for the interview, and every communication you send out of this office.

Now that we've established this point, I will explain the seven basic components of a business letter, then we will close with an example. Mr. Reaper, could you please quit clanking around so much. This will only take a moment. And please don't poke anyone's eye out with that scythe as you did during our last meeting. What if Mike Wazowski had been sitting next to you rather than that three-eyed ogre from Janitorial?

The **heading** starts things off. It includes the company's address and the date. However, if you are using Harbinger stationery, you only need the date since the address is, of course, preprinted with our logo. Never use abbreviations for the months of the year. For that matter, stay away from abbreviations and acronyms in your entire correspondence. Remember to also skip a line between the address and the date if you do not use company stationery.

After the heading, skip another line before you insert the **address**. Again, do not use abbreviations. This is the address of the recipient, of course. This address should match the address on your envelope. Include the recipient's full name if you know it. Otherwise, the name of the company is acceptable if you are writing to another company or firm.

After skipping another line, you insert the **salutation**. "Dear" is always the acceptable form of salutation in a business letter. "Mr." and "Ms." are acceptable in lieu of first names and even in addition to first names. If you do not know the person's name or it is a general business letter, "To Whom It May Concern" is the standard. Also note that "Dear Sir or Madam" is now considered a dated term, although I know Countess Cliché still prefers to use it.

The **body** of the letter comes next. Remember the points we previously mentioned. Do not write a three-page business letter. Get to the reason you are writing and leave it at that. It's not the time to talk about how unrealistic the latest vampire movie was or how your grandmother transforms into a wraith-like creature every third Monday of the month.

Did I forget to mention that all copy should line up on the left of your page? The same goes for the **complimentary close**. This should appear two lines after the last line of the body of your letter. The most commonly accepted closure is "Sincerely" and is always followed by a comma. Other accepted closures include "Respectfully Yours," "Yours Truly," "Best Regards," and "Best Wishes." "Death Wishes," while pertinent in most cases, is still probably not an appropriate close in a business letter.

You should then leave four vertical spaces for your **signature**, which should always be in blue or black ink.

The **identification line** usually wraps things up and contains your typed name and your title if you have one. If your letter includes an enclosure or who else the letter might be distributed to, you would skip a line after your title and place that information last.

Here is an excellent example of a business letter written by our head mortician, Charles Dexter Ward to the Medical Supply Offices of Dr. Herbert West.

Charles Dexter Ward
Dark Harbinger Mortuary and Interment Services
1313 Mockingbird Lane
Deadwood, SD 57732

October 31, 2013

Herbert West
Lovecraft Medical Supply Company
10 Barnes Street
Providence, RI 02906

Dear Mr. West:

Please be advised that the recent serums we purchased from you for use here at Dark Harbinger have not produced the results guaranteed in your brochure.

Upon injecting them into the recently deceased Rhoda Morgenstern, we found them to be of little effect. Although Ms. Morgenstern is still among our list of employees, her value as a worker is nearly non-existent.

We ask that you promptly refund our purchase. We are returning what remains of the case of unused serum to your office. At this point all we ask for is our refund and are not currently seeking recourse with the aid of our law firm of Wolfram & Hart.

Thank you for settling this matter as quickly as possible.

Sincerely,

Charles Dexter Ward
Head Mortician

Encl: 143 vials of serum

Notice how there is a chunk of space which allows for Dr. Ward to sign his name in ink? Make sure you remember to include that in your own business letters. Thank you, Dr. Ward, for setting such an exquisite example for us to follow.

Now, while we are on the subject of business letters, it may be prudent to brush up our skills on writing cover letters for employment—not that I want any of you to go in search of greener graveyards, but occasionally we have internal job postings for which you might wish to apply. We've grown into a rather large company over the past several years, thanks in part to an increase in vampires and zombies in our inner cities. Nothing keeps business alive like the undead! But, anyway, let's consider what you might do if you were in a position to apply for a job.

The type of letter you would attach to your application (or your résumé) would be the "cover letter" I previously referred to. Some people refer to it as a "motivation letter" because the goal of this particular correspondence is to persuade the reader to consider your own motivations for applying.

(A blue-jump-suited man sporting a dirt-stained hockey mask raises a hand.)

Yes, Mr. Voorhees, we all know *your motivation* for applying for every drowned-victim position that arises here at Harbinger. We don't need a cover letter to remind us of your, um, *interest*. And thank you for refraining from comment. Your stoicism is duly noted.

Now, some of the most important writing you will ever do is when you apply for jobs. A letter or email of inquiry, a résumé, a cover letter—all of these represent who you are through writing. It is through writing that you make a good (or not-so-good) first impression with prospective employers, or how you might undo some old impressions we current employers may already have of you—yes, I'm directing that last comment at you, Mr. Krueger. We all know you're the one shredding the Styrofoam coffee cups in the break room. And if you

Agents and publishers may not take you seriously if they notice your glass eyes are really ping pong balls.

could, for once, show up wearing something more, dare I say it, suit-and-tie-like? That red-striped sweater is looking a little worse for the wear.

And speaking of informal attire, you should remember that, in general, employment materials should be formal and polished (error- and typo-free). All of the materials in your application package should work together to convey a portrait of who you are professionally. Your materials may be read and processed by machines, by someone in (In)human Resources, a hiring manager, a hiring committee, or by a potential supervisor. If possible, try to find out about the hiring process for that field or specific company. If you have a better idea of who your audience might be, you will be able to tailor your application materials to more effectively communicate your message.

> **The better you know your audience, the easier it will be to decide whether a briefcase or flaming torch should be in your hand.**

In a way, cover letters combine the directness of most business writing with some of the elements of persuasive writing. You need to be clear about why you are writing ("I write to apply for the position of Assistant Cryptkeeper at Entombments-R-Us"), but you are also presenting an argument about why you would be a great fit for the company, and you need to support these claims with evidence. Effective cover letters demonstrate that you've done your research—you understand both the position and the company's mission and goals.

The introduction of a cover letter needs to address two things: why you're writing and why an employer should keep reading. Like the résumé, the cover letter needs to whet an employer's appetite by demonstrating how your strengths speak to the company's stated needs and overall mission. The body of the cover letter typically presents your best qualities and how those strengths will benefit the company. As with the résumé, be specific, and support your claims with evidence. Finally, the conclusion of the cover letter describes the action you want your reader to take—most often, you want your reader to schedule an interview with you. In the final paragraph, you might include your phone number and the best times to reach you, or mention that you will follow up with a phone call in a few days. For our fellow vampires, make sure to include the fact that you can only work at night.

When you apply for an internal posting, do remember to update and attach your résumé to the cover letter. We need to see the context of your current skill set to determine if you are a good fit for the job, and with 666 employees currently on our staff, it's hard to remember who is who when sorting application materials.

There are a couple of rules to remember when submitting résumés to me. They should be short—between one to two pages. I only spend about 30 seconds to a minute reading those infernal documents before I send them down to Mr. Lucifer for incineration, or stack them on the "to keep" pile of my desk. Don't bore me with tedious details. Get to the juicy bits! In other words, because they are so short, they cannot—

and should not—list every detail of your life. Instead, you must highlight the most relevant professional or academic experiences, while giving a true sense of your history. Résumés offer just a taste of who you are to make me hungry for more. At the same time, don't stifle my appetite with too many details. Remember, the job of your résumé is to get you an interview. I don't care that you've been in the coffin room for the last 30 years; what I care about is how working in the coffin room has prepared you for the position for which you are applying.

Résumés may be organized chronologically, or be skill-based. When organized chronologically, begin with your most recent experiences. If you decide to organize your résumé based on skills, be sure that the skill areas you highlight correspond to the key terms, qualifications, or requirements of the position you are seeking. Either way, your résumé needs to clearly convey your professional strengths. When composing your résumé, keep in mind that active verbs (such as "motivated," "completed," "compiled," "trained," or "transformed") are good choices since they convey a sense of your action in a given position. Where possible, and when relevant, use facts and details to substantiate your claims. For example, "Trained over 50 zombies for combat" is more effective than "Member of zombie training team."

> **When writing a résumé, it is better to say you were leader of the angry mob storming the castle than you were simply one of the folks carrying a pitchfork.**

On that same token, résumés need to be accurate, easy to understand, and—perhaps most importantly—easy to skim. When I'm ready to hire someone (or something), I often have dozens—sometimes hundreds—of applicants. This means I will be looking for relevant information very quickly. The formatting of a résumé is therefore extremely important. You might be a perfect fit for the new job, but sloppy, hard-to-read formatting will prevent employers like me from seeing how perfect you are. Try to get someone in the office—particularly in the same job for which you are applying—to look at your résumé to see how well it conveys your relevant experience. Have multiple people proofread to ensure an error-free document. It's also common—and a good idea—for applicants to tailor cover letters and résumés for different positions. One résumé won't cut it for every job to which you apply; the expectations of a grave-digging job are very different from the expectations for a coffin-sales job. Remember to highlight your own understanding of the job you are applying for by emphasizing the skills you possess which are specific to that job.

I have prepared copies of the following application for us all to consider. I think this particular cover letter and résumé are very well executed—I do love that word, "executed." The position for which Trash has applied is as one of our Graveside Entertainers, and I think you'll agree that she has a particularly compelling skill set when you take a look at her cover letter and résumé.

Trash E. Dancer
1985 O'Bannon Way
Louisville, KY 40245

July 15, 2011

Jack T. Ripper, Director of Management Services
Dark Harbinger Mortuary and Interment Services
1313 Mockingbird Lane
Deadwood, SD 57732

Dear Mr. Ripper:

Please accept this cover letter and résumé as application for the position of Graveside Entertainer which I saw posted on the job announcements board in the break room last Thursday.

As you may know, I have worked for Dark Harbinger for the past twenty years, ever since I was eaten alive by zombies and, ultimately, turned into one myself. Previous to my position as flesh eater at Harbinger, I was a member of a punk rock band as a performer and dancer. As I'm sure you can imagine, my bright red hair and Technicolor outfits garnered much attention when I moved my body. I believe most will find my dancing to be quite memorable indeed. I am known to throw my entire being into my dancing. I'm certain my abilities will garner new business and increase our bottom line.

Thank you for considering my application for this position, Mr. Ripper. I look forward to hearing your response.

Sincerely,

Trash E. Dancer
Enclosure: Résumé

Trash E. Dancer
1985 O'Bannon Way
Louisville, KY 40245
(555) 555-6666

Summary of Qualifications:
Shock value and the ability to turn heads (sometimes off their stumpy necks)
A willingness to take things to the next level
Dancing, both classical and modern
Music appreciation and a wide array of musical tastes
Comfortable in a graveyard, around the living, dead, and undead
In no way interested in eating my new bosses

Employment Experience:
Flesh Eater   Deadwood, South Dakota   1991-present
Dark Harbinger Mortuary and Interment Services
Devour the meaty flesh from the bones of the living
Prepare corpses for transfer from grave to dinner tables
Train new zombie recruits on processes surrounding proper brain sanitization
Serve ice cream at staff birthday parties

Dancer   Louisville, Kentucky   1985-1991
Uneeda Corporation
Provided the most memorable scene in zombie popular culture
Performed for crowds of living and undead, sometimes in the nude
Dyed my hair shocking colors and otherwise lived a punk rock existence
Pouted and brooded and otherwise demonstrated my general angst

Educational Experience:
Associate's Degree, Science   Hell, MI   1983-1985
Major: Art History   Hell's Mouth Community College
Member of Student Senate
Volunteer in the Office of Student Services

High School Diploma   Boneyard, AZ   1979-1983
General Studies   Boneyard High School
Yearbook staff
Art class model

References: Available upon request

Notice how Trash gets right to the point in her cover letter? She tells me in the introductory paragraph that the purpose of her letter is to apply for a particular position. Then, with confidence and eloquence, she spends the entire middle paragraph declaring her qualifications for the position—some ample qualifications, I might add. As she does this, she consistently reminds me, the reader, of her value both to the company and to the industry as a whole. Not only is she going to turn the heads of all our clientele, but she is also going to increase our bottom line—those are two things that get my attention.

As you look at her résumé, the first thing you'll notice is how structured and tidy it is. This is not just a list of qualifications, but a structured, organized, justified document with columns that allow me to quickly gather information about her. Remember, I've only got 30 seconds to 1 minute to spend looking at her information.

This means I need to see her qualifications and experience near the top, as I may never actually get to the bottom of the page. Another approach Ms. Dancer could have taken to show me her qualifications would have been to include an infographic in her résumé, which would have demonstrated her software and design skills—two skills most employers are seeking in nearly all their candidates for new employees these days—but, since this is a dancing position, I don't imagine Trash will need to spend much time on the computer.

What makes Trash a great candidate for this position goes beyond these documents, I should point out. In addition to a succinct cover letter and a structured résumé, she also sent me a thank-you note following our brief interview earlier this week.

I would go out on a limb and say that less than 1% of my employees or interviewees send me any kind of thank you for me taking time out of my busy graveyard shift to interview them. So, when she did, I was quite moved. It made her memorable—more memorable, perhaps, than her exotic dancing.

So, I hope you all are listening to this. Remember, if you get an interview, it's common practice to follow-up with a thank-you card or email. More than just a common courtesy, a thank-you note shows your attention to detail and is one more opportunity to make a good impression on future co-workers or supervisors—in this case, yours truly.

The last thing you want is to come up on Ripper's Radar for being rude. You might find yourself under the knife shortly thereafter—I mean, on the chopping block. Okay, I mean, fired. All right, all right. Now, there is some debate as to whether a thank-you card is better than an email—do what feels comfortable to you as a job seeker. You will find Trash's thank-you email on the next page.

Dear Mr. Ripper:

Thank you for taking the time to interview me on Monday for the position of Graveyard Entertainer. I appreciate your consideration. I'm still chuckling about that viscera joke you made.

Warmly,
Trash E. Dancer

Notice how Trash keeps the thank you short, but also includes something to distinctly remind me of our specific interview? She mentions the joke I made about viscera. It's a great one, too. This zombie walks into a bar and his guts are literally spilling out over his waistband. The bartender says to the walker, "Hey, zombie. Rough day?" The zombie says, "Que viscera, viscera." Get it?

(Crickets can be heard chirping in the background. A tumbleweed blows across the hallway door just behind the wolfman. No one moves. Jack Ripper sighs.)

No one appreciates fine humor anymore. Oh, well. While we are on the topic of email communications, do allow me to expand on those rules just a smidge. I realize that business is booming. These days, most email inboxes are fuller than a zombie at a children's sleep-over party. To help your reader, and ensure the clarity of your message, make sure that the subject of your email is concise,

> **Most email inboxes in this day and age are fuller than a zombie at a children's sleepover.**

clear, and relevant. Nothing is worse than losing track of important information because the subject heading is completely irrelevant—or blank. Don't miss this opportunity to get your reader's attention. Likewise, be sure your responses to coworkers are timely and precise. You don't want to be the person who never responds to email, *Mr. Krueger*. Yes. I'm talking to you. I know typing is hard for you, what with those blades coming Wolverine-style out of your gloves, but consider taking them off at least once a day to catch up on correspondence, okay?

All right, that just about concludes our weekly staff meeting. Just one more thing. I want you all to write me a report on the successes and failures of your department this past fiscal quarter. No, Barbra; I don't particularly care if this is not part of your job description. The executive board is coming. They're coming to get the reports, Barbra, and they're very interested. They've been away a long time, Barbra.

So, I guess I have one thing left to cover, then, hm? Even if it's not part of your job description, I am expecting you to write or give reports pertaining to your productivity, research you've completed, recommendations for company procedures or products, or progress on a project. Reports might be analytical in nature (making a recommendation based on analysis), or more descriptive (such as a report on the progress of you, your team, or company). As is usually the case with writing, the audience is key. Which one of us will be reading your reports? (Is this report for the head of the department or for clients?) Knowing the needs and expectations of your audience, and the report's objective (to make recommendations or just offer unbiased information), will help you write more effectively.

The introduction to your report should accomplish several things. It needs to establish the context for the report—what is the problem, question, or assignment? As the name implies, the introduction should also introduce the main subjects or purpose, including a sense of why the subject is important. The introduction should also offer a road map to the body of the report—what information will be covered and in what order? (Reports typically include section headings—these main ideas should be first presented in the introduction; vice versa, the section headings should echo the main ideas of the introduction.)

The body of the report provides the information that you have gathered. Depending on your audience and your objectives, the information you provide might include definitions of terms or concepts, facts, statistical evidence, analysis, procedures, sources, pros and cons, and costs. Visual representations work best for certain kinds of information, so bullets, tables, charts, and graphs might be good to include as well. Section headings help your readers navigate the information you are presenting, and are a good way for you to maintain a clear sense of organization and purpose as you plan and write the report.

The information you provide your audience should lead directly into any conclusions or recommendations that you present, often in their own section at the end of the report. Having a separate section for "Conclusions," "Recommendations," "Summary," or "Plan of Action," helps your busy reader quickly find the most important information. And there are few people busier than our executive board. Seriously. People are *dying to get on our board,* I tell you.

I want to thank everyone for your attention this evening, but it's time to get back to work. If you have any questions, you know where to find me. And, if anyone disagrees with these bloody policies, well, you know where the door is. You also know it leads directly to the crematorium. Have a nice day.

Writing Prompts for Chapter 10

1. Write an email to an imaginary colleague at Dark Harbinger Mortuary inquiring about any dead bodies they may have for sale. Use formal tone, concise writing, and proper business etiquette.

2. Write about a horror-themed business one of your characters might work for. Describe it in detail. Who are the owners? Who does he or she answer to? What does s/he do there?

3. Create an imaginary dialogue between your character from the previous prompt and either his or her boss or a customer in which the customer or boss is displeased with something your character has done.

Writing Exercises for Chapter 10

1. **Managing Social Networks:** Visit your social network (either yours or that of a friend if you do not have one) and review the posts for the last three months or so. Are there any posts that you imagine the writer wishes s/he didn't publish? Anything that might be a negative mark on a federal background check? Or is the writer adept at self-editing, and has only posted things that kept him or her employable?

2. **Cover Letter:** Using the proper structure and salutations, craft a cover letter for a job you might be interested in applying for. To find the job, search the want ads at your local Career Onestop, or simply imagine that you are applying for your dream job.

3. **Résumés:** Make a list of your previous work roles, whether they were roles you had as a student, volunteer, or employee. Under each role, list the duties you had or the activities you completed while in that role. Be as thorough as possible and capture every role you can remember having. Now consider that you are applying for a position as a mortician, an assistant to Jack the Ripper, and a vampire's revenant (mortal slave). Which roles have you had that included duties or activities you might have to do regarding any of these three positions? Craft a résumé in which you tailor your work history to demonstrate jobs you've held in which your skills match with the new jobs for which you are applying.

–11–
WRITING FOR THE WEB
or
Who's the Zombie Now?

Murder Legendre was born in the late 1800s in Haiti and was a plantation owner until his untimely death, which supposedly came at the hands of his employees. We were fortunate to contact Mr. Legendre via a recent séance, as we consider him an authority on what many call the "true origin" of the zombie. Although it took many sessions to bring him up to speed on the computer, the World Wide Web, and the many technological changes that have taken place since his demise, he instantly saw the connection between his original form of voodoo zombie-ism and today's high-tech society. We knew we wanted him for our chapter on web-based writing, but we're now a little unsure if the séance was the best way to reach him. We're fairly certain our darling Rachel has been possessed. Her diction-perfect French and the way she keeps offering us discolored wine while holding a shovel behind her back kind of tipped us off.

NOW THIS MIGHT come as a shock to those of you out there who believe that the World Wide Web really works the way you think it does. Zeros and ones? Are you kidding me? You think it's that simple? Heck, you might as well believe in the Loch Ness Monster.

So, now down to business.

This chapter is dedicated to all you zombies out there who have turned into mindless revenants, legions of the undead with hungry mouths and gnashing teeth and bottomless bellies. In case you're wondering, I'm talking to you. Maybe you're haven't died and come back as a zombie, but you could have fooled me. So, put down the cellphone, relax your thumbs, step away from the keyboard, and for God's sake, lay off the video games.

Still don't think you're a zombie?

Fine, answer these questions for me: Do you own a cellphone? Do you have a television connected to cable? Do you have a computer connected to the Internet?

If you answered yes to one or more of the above questions, then chances are you're a 21st century zombie.

So what's the deal with the Internet making you into a zombie? A new type of spyware? Moloch on the prowl in the interwebs? Ghost in the machine? (Ha! A little inside joke there.) When you get right down to it, the truth actually has very little to do with having an Internet connection so much as how you use it. You see, most humans are highly visual creatures, and, as such, they interact with images differently than they do the written word. For one thing, images do all the work. Ever hear that phrase, "a picture is worth a thousand words"? That's because a thousand words can draw out an image in your mind, slowly and with painstaking accuracy, whereas a picture flashes before the screen of your mind's eye and is gone. There's a reason why people are inclined to ban books but not movies, you know.

My point, you ask? It's simply this: the Internet connects you to the World Wide Web, which is largely a visual playground. People look at the monitor the way they look at a television, and you only have to peek in at your parents around 8:00 p.m. on a weeknight to confirm that television viewing makes you slow, dimwitted, and hungry. Very hungry. (Kind of like how a real zombie feels.) You view the Internet much the same as you would a visual device—like your television—and, as such, you become something of a reading zombie. Rather than engage with the text you encounter in the World Wide Web the way you would a brochure or a book, you interact with the web like it is a television set. It needs to be fast, entertaining, relevant, and engaging or you

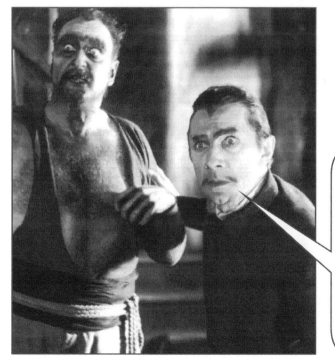

move on like a roving band of zombie holocaust survivors.

Indeed, the web makes reading zombies of everyone. But knowing this helps us understand how you can use the web as a text-delivery tool.

If you think this is good stuff, wait until you see what George Romero does in a few decades.

Writing Concisely (and Precisely)

Everyone knows that in this day and age they need to send emails, post to blogs, chatter on social media sites, and update personal websites. Knowing that most people will only skim the surface of these web-based writings should help you accomplish two important writing objectives: understanding your audience and being concise.

Being concise is only part of the magic of writing for the web, though. After all, you can only muster up so many words before pulling out the red pen and inserting those bloody correction marks. (If any actual zombies are reading this, try not to think about my "bloody" remark.) The bottom line? Stay on topic and use as few words as possible to convey your meaning. Concise writing. Straight and to the point. Happening now.

> **The Internet (not to mention cell phones, cable TV, and video games) can make zombies out of all of us.**

That said, concise writing will only get you so far. It isn't enough to stay on task in your web-based writing and keep your words to a minimum. Nor should you confuse the concept of "concise" with the idea that you have to use a battlefield of a page peppered with only a sparse handful of stumbling monster-words. To write concisely, you need to say what you mean by using precise words—not necessarily fewer of them. In the limbo of the Web, this particular rule goes a little further. Now, in addition to writing precisely and concisely, we now have to engage a room full of zombies. Sure, if you're a young woman in running shoes with a Kalashnikov slung over your shoulder and the feral bouquet of sweat and blood pouring off your dewy skin like waves of smoke off a barbecue in July, you may get the attention of the zombie horde. But through the Internet? Not so easy.

Faced with a room full of zombies, each staring unblinking into the monitor with slack jaws and a strand of bloody drool hanging from the side of his mouth, you know you're going to need to go beyond precise writing and jump headlong into energetic and engaging writing. To do that, we need to get to the point faster— immediately—and we need to hook our readers. Think of the hook that penetrates the side of a fish's mouth so you can reel it in. The hook, then, is the very first thing your reader sees.

So, let's say you're writing an email to your zombie boss. We all know our bosses' time is valuable. You think your job is tough staring into that monitor? Well, your boss is staring at dozens of monitors making sure all his zombies are properly staring into theirs. This means that they don't have a lot of time to mess around with pleasantries and conversation.

Having said that, you should still be pleasant and conversational—just keep it concise. Indeed, when writing an email, it is imperative that you jump right to the point in the opening sentence. Why are you writing? What message are you trying to convey? What do you hope to accomplish? What is your purpose? Answering any of those questions should lead you to your first sentence.

Writing Emails

You also need to consider the importance of professionalism when dealing with undead colleagues from other offices. Because email creates a virtual paper trail, it can and will come back to haunt you if you tell the local heart and liver vendor who stocks (and stalks) your office's wheel of death machine that he's a reanimated bag of partially digested lobster tamale.

Now, this might not faze you if you have risen to the top of your grave at the office, or if you are planning to quit, but remember that the virtual paper trail can follow you wherever you go.

I once knew a vampire student who pulled a lot of all-nighters at U.C. Sunnydale. In a blood stupor at a fanger party one night, he sent an email to a girl he'd had his eye on all semester in which he said something about finding her so cute, he could just eat her up. Well, the next day a copy of that email was printed, folded neatly into an envelope, and stuffed under the Dean's office door and let's just say that vamp awoke a little too early in the morning after one of those all-nighters with a completely fried brain and had to face the heat of the college's student code of conduct. Ouch.

> **An email written in the heat of the moment or a post made in poor taste on your favorite social network can come back to haunt you at any time. And, believe me, I know all about haunting. Just ask those poor folks up in Amityville.**

One of the other, perhaps more serious dangers of emails lies in the way an email is interpreted by the reader. Have you ever received an email from someone that made you think the person was mad at you? Then, you quickly texted your friend with his sparkling personality to ask, "Hey, why are you mad? I swear I didn't mean it when I said 'it doesn't matter'" and your friend was all like "brood face" and "I'm not mad. Why did you think I was mad?" We've all been the victim of a misinterpreted email at some point in our unlives, either as the inadvertent perpetrator or the recipient of the insidious words.

You see, what happens is that people tend to write abruptly or incompletely when replying to emails. They treat emails as though they are texts—not real communication. They forget that words on a page are missing the non-verbal communication element of body language (like facial expressions and tone of voice). So, when you type the words "I'm really hungry. Up for a bite?" they can't see your salivating, blood-drenched mouth and bulging eyes. They don't notice your leg twitching or your sweaty palms. So, they say "sure" because they don't realize you actually intend to eat them.

Words on a screen rely on voice, tone, context, and individual interpretation to create meaning for a reader—just because it is email doesn't mean you get to throw your grammar skills out the window, either. Remember the importance of punctuation to an email. Consider the following message sent by email from Bela to Boris:

Oh my god he is eating Ed in Accounting

Now, in the digital age, many people have simply stopped using appropriate punctuation altogether (particularly apostrophes), which has created a string of misinterpretations. (Imagine all the dramatic teenage fights that could have been avoided by inserting a simple comma.) In the preceding example, because punctuation is called for and not employed, the reader is able to infer a meaning that was not intended. Boris is looking at Bela's email on the screen thinking that someone is actually eating Ed from the Accounting department. Being the decisive man that he is, Boris immediately breaks the glass above the zombie survival kit, pulls the alarm, grabs the machete, and heads for accounting to save his old friend from whatever creature has started eating the number-cruncher.

But, this isn't what Bela intended to say to Boris. What Bela intended to convey in his poorly punctuated message was this:

Oh my God! He is eating! Ed, in Accounting!

In the newly punctuated message, we now see that Bela is trying to convey excitement that Ed from the Accounting Department is actually eating something. Perhaps Ed had been sick from the breached canister of zombie chemical that bubbled up from the basement last week, and Ed had stopped eating for a while. The return of Ed's appetite was what induced an excited Bela to send his message to Boris. But, because Boris didn't get the version with the correct punctuation, he is now on a machete-driven path straight toward the decapitation of some zombie in the Accounting Department. Hey, I'm all for zombie rights, but I draw the line at letting them eat my officemates on the job—that's time for action.

Remember, just because you are using a method of Frankenstein-lightning-fast communication doesn't mean you get to cut corners with your writing. We've all heard that punctuation saves lives—as the Bela-to-Boris miscommunication demonstrates—so consider the next punctuation faux pas, transmitted in an email from Trinity, a secretary at Romero, O'Bannon, Fulci & Flanders, to her assistant down in the break room:

Its moms delicious.

Without context—perhaps from a conversation Trinity had with the assistant earlier in the day—it is hard to interpret what this message is really trying to say. So, let's assume the assistant emailed back a puzzled, "huh?"; this prompts a second response from Trinity:

It's moms delicious.

Well, now the assistant is assuming that Trinity meant to insert the punctuation—

and she's hoping that Trinity used the correct form of "it's" (with an apostrophe, this word is a contraction meaning "it is"). So, is it a comma, period, or an apostrophe that is missing? The assistant, trying to make sense of Trinity's email, inserts punctuation into the mix for her. She reads it in her head like this:

It's moms. Delicious.

She assumes that there is a parade of mothers lining up in the upstairs hallway to be eaten by the zombie horde congregating in the boardroom. After all, those moms are probably delicious, right? *No*, she thinks. *That can't be it*. So, she tries again. Perhaps it was an apostrophe that was missing, and "moms" is meant as a contraction, meaning "mom is." And maybe Trinity really doesn't have the right form of "its" or "it's" after all. It isn't like she's gotten the other punctuation right, so it's possible (it is possible), right? So, now she reads it like this:

Its mom [i]s delicious.

In this form, "its" is possessive. That means, "it" might refer to a creature or a monster or a person. Then, the mom belongs to that "it." Like: "Dracula's mom" or "Lucy's mom." Then, with the contraction form of "mom's" this phrase is read as "mom is." Thus, the assistant now thinks that "it" (whatever or whoever "it" is) has a mom who is delicious, and once again, she is imagining a zombie horde eating someone's mom in the boardroom. Fearing for her life, the assistant refuses to believe this is what Trinity meant by her unpunctuated message and tries one more time to interpret what Trinity meant:

It's mom's delicious.

In this scenario, "it's" (it is) mom's (possessive) delicious . . . something. Some weird euphemism for something mom possesses that she considers to be delicious. Perhaps a bottle of blood chilling in a decanter in her fridge? (Of course, it could just be tomato juice.) Or maybe "delicious" is her nickname for the finger sandwiches she craves all the time—you know, the ones made from actual fingers?

As you can see, at this point, Trinity's assistant is torn between breaking the zombie survival glass and following Boris' stalwart example, or reaching for a fresh bottle of blood herself.

Meanwhile, Trinity is upstairs eyeing the birthday cake that her mother has just placed on her desk. Trinity knew today was her assistant's birthday and had asked her mother to bake a cake to celebrate. Since her mother used to be a baker, she knew it would be the yummiest bloodworm and insect larvae birthday cake the office had ever seen. So, when Trinity emailed her assistant, what she was really trying to say was that a cake had arrived (it) that her mother had made (mom's), and that the cake was going to be delicious.

It's mom's! Delicious!

Blogging

Typos and punctuation errors can be a deal-breaker in emails, but also in other forms of web-based writing. In the digital age, anyone can be a writer and publish his or her (or its) work to the World Wide Web. One of the most common ways that would-be writers publish themselves is through blog posts. Blogging is one of the newest forms of writing and, although it has many things in common with other publication mediums, it has its own distinct personality as well. The undead find little use for computers, blogging, chatting on social networks, and the like. Drinking blood, chomping on brain matter, haunting ex-lovers, and harvesting souls requires a much more personal form of communication. Not that we don't use DeadsList when we are trolling for fresh meat. A zombie's gotta eat.

Blogs, or "web logs," are even trickier than emails because unlike an email with a targeted recipient who you likely know, blogs are for the zombies that surf the web or subscribe to the literary stylings of a blogger of his or her choice, hobby, interest, or entertainment. First rule about blogs? Make them pretty. Images, videos, audio files, and thematic backgrounds that all relate to the point of your blog are important because, remember, people looking at a monitor are looking at what their primitive brains will imagine to be a television. Zombie fools!

While those undead creatures stare listlessly at the widgets and gadgets and counters and donation buttons whirling around your page, you'll be centering in on your target message in just a few short paragraphs (preferably with relevant images peppered throughout) right in the center of the page. Kind of like the way supermarkets put the sugary cereal with the awesome toys inside on the middle level of the supermarket aisle because it will be at eye level for children passing through the store. Do the same thing with your blog post. Put the good stuff at eye level.

Fill your blog with plenty of graphics. Leeches, for instance, are sure to suck your readers right in.

Sometimes blogs will be highly personal, created by some vampire hunter enthusiast with his own bloody hobby kit and a digital camera. Sometimes blogs will be more professional and the blogger (or bloggers) will be blogging as a means of generating income (the income comes from advertisers whose banners and blinky things and pop-ups are on the page, or from people who pay a subscription fee or donate to the cause). Other times, businesses will expect certain employees to keep or update a blog as part of their job description. For most bloggers, writing for the web means sharing a personal interest, skill, experience, lifestyle, or knowledge with others—it is not about earning a living. While it's certainly possible to earn money as a blogger, doing so requires a lot of time, energy, and effort. If you want to blog, know thyself, and thy purpose.

> **Place things on your blog page where people will notice them. People standing in the windows of the local S-Mart are more likely to grab the attention of wandering zombies than those hiding behind mannequins in the back of the store.**

Chances are, you probably already know what you are going to blog about. Just make sure it is something that readers will be interested in. You probably won't have a huge following if you write a blog about movies that were made in the month of June in 1954. On the other hand, writing a blog discussing forensic autopsy of the undead might get a huge following, but if you have no interest in the subject, why tackle it? Not to mention the fact that we (the undead) don't like to talk about forensic autopsies much; too many bad memories.

As with writers of any other publishing medium, bloggers should set aside time each day to write something. The time of the day doesn't matter. Vampires, obviously, prefer to write during the late hours of the night. Zombies should set aside a huge chunk of hours as it will take them that long just to remember what a keyboard and mouse are even used for. It is also individual preference on how many blog posts you write per week. Whether you post daily or just once per week, you should keep to a schedule so that readers will get into a routine of when to expect your next brilliant blog post. If you write a great post about how to make a good stew from the brains of a politician (nearly impossible I might add) and get dozens (maybe hundreds) of new hits to your blog, do not wait three weeks before making another post. It is also good to plan your next two or three posts in advance. If this is zombie melee week, write yourself a note that you want to post about the advantages of a different weapon every other day. Then when you get ready to write on Wednesday, you can refer to your list and see that your next post is about the advantages (and disadvantages) of using a sawed-off shotgun against the advancing zombie horde.

One of the most important things to remember is to keep your voice consistent, whether you post five times a day or twice a month. Your readers will come to recognize your style as a writer. Don't write a blog that sounds like it was written by H. P. Lovecraft one day and Stephen King the next. There is nothing wrong with either writing style, but each has a distinct voice. Be the same person every time you write.

Just as you need a catchy title for a book, you need each entry or post to catch the attention of prospective followers. Unless you have devoted followers (or have personally glamoured them into becoming habitual readers of your blog content), your writing needs to entice them to read further. What would make you want to continue reading: "Old Lady Dies" or "Old Lady Found Dead with Stake through Heart"?

You also need to keep this momentum going as you dig into your first paragraph. Don't just give the facts. Give your readers something to chew on even if they aren't zombies or named Hannibal. Give your readers detail, but make the images you paint with your words vivid.

Pictures and graphics are integral to a successful blog. That's right. A picture equals a thousand words, blah, blah. But you only want to attract the attention of your reader, not mesmerize them with images. And please be aware of copyright issues. Some people think that just because they are writing a blog, that all photos they find on the Internet are free to use. It is simply not the case. Make sure you use images that are in the public domain or that you have permission to use. If you review such things as books, movies, video games, etc., the covers of those items are free to use under the "Fair Usage" copyright act. If you snapped a picture of a zombie on your front sidewalk, of course, it is yours to use. Just make sure it doesn't look like your little brother ready for a night of trick-or-treating. And if it isn't your little brother, have your chainsaw handy as well as your camera.

If you are writing entries or posts of significant length, it is a good idea to break up the barrage of words (as good as they may be) with not only images, but subheads

So, you're telling me the film's distributor forgot to place a copyright on the film prints and now anyone can use this movie any way they desire? Even these authors who are about to be devoured by zombies themselves?

as well. More than any other style of writing, white space is your friend. Don't write more than a couple of paragraphs without a subhead or an image.

Other things you would do in a blog that you wouldn't do as much (if at all) in other styles of writing is to use differing font sizes, font colors, bold face, italics, and block quotes. Again, you do this all to catch the attention of your reader.

One of the mistakes some bloggers make is that they tend to edit as they write, or they forget to edit at all. This is a common mistake made in all styles of writing, but for some reason, bloggers tend to take on the persona of a zombie and never revise their content. Do the job, then clean it up. Do you think vampires care about the blood dripping down their chins or down the clean white clothing of their victim? Nope. The idea is to go for the jugular. There's always time to clean up afterwards. When you are ready to edit, make sure you check your spelling and grammar more than anything else. Things like sentence structure, point of view, and correct punctuation aren't as important in a blog as long as what you write is "readable" and entertaining. Lastly, always re-read your posts before hitting the publish button. Just make sure your spouse isn't eavesdropping when you are describing aloud how to use the "death stroke" to pluck the heart from an unsuspecting demon.

In keeping with the theme of a good-looking blog, there are several other options you can use to make your blog not turn into a bog. Remember, you are trying to attract a loyal following, not swamp monsters or the Creature from the Black Lagoon. Quality is more important than quantity. In other words, one zombie with half a brain is better than ten zombies walking around in circles moaning and slobbering. Keep both your sentences and paragraphs short. If your post seems like it is getting too long, break it up into two or three parts. This is also an easy way to get your readers to return when part two is posted.

Another way that blogging is different from other styles of writing is that keywords play an important role in your posts. If your daily blog is about how to kill a vampire (and I certainly hope it is not, as we undead have rights just as you do), make sure that words like "blood," "stake," "garlic," "cross," etc. show up more than once in your writing. The search engines love this and you will find your blog ranking higher if you follow this advice. In fact, there are dozens of Internet blogs written simply about search engine optimization and the use of keywords.

Most blog readers are similar to magazine readers in that they don't read every article and they seldom read word for word. As previously mentioned, the use of subheads helps bring their attention back to your writing. Another creative tool to use is a list, which stands out visually and grabs attention without requiring the reader to sift through a lengthy paragraph to decipher the same information.

A vampire priest, a zombie rabbi, and a vampire romance novelist du jour walk into a bar . . . Okay, now that I have your attention, you need to do the same thing with your readers and subscribers. Say something unexpected. (Does human flesh taste like chicken?) Make a claim or a promise that will bring them back the next session.

("Tomorrow I will give a detailed plan on how to bring your recently deceased cousin back from the dead.") Start with a quote. ("I have the heart of a young boy. I keep it in a jar on my desk.") Add some controversy. ("Vampires should be given free access to local blood banks.")

Do not make a statement that you claim is factual unless you can back it up with research. Sure, you can make the statement that you think all living dead creatures are evil. In fact, it can spark some great debate. Just don't make a blanket statement that all vampires are evil and need to have stakes driven through their hearts unless you have scientific proof. Besides, it would be hard to back up such a statement as everyone I know who has stated that vampires are evil, sadistic people have met a mysterious untimely death. Just sayin'.

Remember, you want your readers' attention. A blog is not typically a one-way street. There is a reason why blogs have comment features—to keep your readers involved and coming back for more. If you receive an email telling you someone has commented on one of your posts, check it out. Most comments deserve a response. This is even more important if you have posted a controversial comment or asked a question. And speaking of questions. This is one of the easiest ways to keep your followers involved. When you write an article about your recent sighting of a ghost near your favorite pub, ask your readers about their own experiences with spirits of the dead. (On second thought, perhaps you shouldn't mention that your sighting occurred near a bar.)

Unless you are writing a scientific blog for forensic doctors discussing zombie rigor mortis, don't take yourself too seriously. Humor and making your readers smile may be your best friend.

Just make sure that you get to the point. Don't wax on. Deliver the goods and move on. Take a cue from the big guns, like Cracked or eHow, which can deliver everything from the "seven most unlucky people in the world" to "how

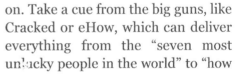

Hey, dad. Can me and my friends borrow the truck? We'd like to eat, er—I mean meet some friends down at the mall.

to build a steam engine with spare parts in your kitchen" usually in 500 words or less. Even 500 words is pushing it. Those readers, remember, are scanning their monitors like a television screen expecting fast service with a smile. Don't get carried away, waxing prolific. This is not *Finnegan's Wake*. Trust me. I happen to be the one who ate that guy. He's not waking anytime soon.

Reading, Word Choice, and Final Thoughts

At the same time, you do want to remember that web-based writing isn't always about business or professionalism. It can be a playground for writers, too. Not only is it easier to get published online than through most traditional channels, writing for the web can be much more informal. While you do want to strive for consistency, you can also experiment with language, tone, voice, styles, and rhetorical strategies. Once you have a readership—however small—you have an audience to play with.

As with all writing, to write well you must read. The same is true for online writing—what kind of community do you want to join or create through your writing? Connect with other writers with similar interests or styles you admire. Learn from other writers, comment on their work, put yourself out there as an active, thoughtful reader.

Because anything can be published to the World Wide Web, writing for the Internet may include elements of informative writing (how to make realistic fake blood, for example, or editing those zombie-writers at *Wikipedia*) and persuasive writing (why *28 Days Later* is the best zombie film ever made or why traditionalists don't even consider it a true zombie movie). Some people even post their academic and analytical writing to the web. There are certainly more than a small sampling of scholars, experts, professors, and students posting research papers to their websites, as well.

In some respects, the Internet was made for zombies. Just think about it—scores of people sitting numbly in chairs, staring blankly at screens—where anything more than a picture of a kitten or 140 characters is simply too much for the brain to process. But the Internet was also made for writers. Where else can anyone write anything for the entire world to see?

Especially when you get into social networks. You should check out Chapter 11 on Business and Professional writing for some tips on what NOT to put in your social network feed, but overall, here are some of the basics: Don't overhype. Don't write more than a sentence (some networks limit what you can type by characters). And practice getting to the point in fewer words. Does this mean grammar isn't important? Not necessarily.

Have you ever been reading your friends' newsfeeds and caught something that didn't sound right? Maybe you read it the wrong way, or you interpreted the meaning differently than the writer had originally intended?

The point is that the World Wide Web and the Internet are the new canvas on which we can create. But you must still choose your brushes and colors with care. After all, certain things are only meant to decorate the front of your refrigerator. Not for the entire world to see. Or, in words you might better understand, there is a reason zombies prefer brains to other body parts. Why not give them what they really want to chomp on?

Writing Prompts for Chapter 11

1. Start a blog at a free blogging site focused on the best horror stories or novels you've ever read.

2. Start writing a blog in which you take on the persona of a survivor of the zombie apocalypse. Write your entries as though the zombie invasion is happening right now.

3. Create a website for vampires (either real or imaginary). What might you include?

Writing Exercises for Chapter 11

1. **Writing Concisely:** Find a passage in a book that you think is overwritten (or, which you think can be written more concisely). Think about the words on the page with particular focus on their function and whether they are fulfilling that function. Now, strip away the unnecessary words and simplify the language until you have a concise passage. Do the same exercise with a passage of your own writing.

2. **Punctuation:** Find or create at least ten other examples of writing that can be misinterpreted based on poor or missing punctuation similar to that in the example of "It's mom's! Delicious!" Explain how each example changes when new punctuation is introduced or removed.

3. **Punctuation**: When used correctly, punctuation not only clarifies the meaning of a sentence, it also conveys tone. Using all of the punctuation marks (and combinations of marks) as you can, punctuate this sentence in as many ways as possible: "Let's eat Grandma". (If you're not used to using some punctuation, like semi-colons, colons, or dashes, or if you're not sure about correct usage, look them up.) After you have a list of sentences, draw a face next to each one showing the emotion of the sentence. Look at some of your own writing, and try changing some of the punctuation to convey a different tone—use punctuation marks correctly, but experiment with using punctuations marks for different tones.

4. **Revise/Edit:** Find a website or blog which includes several grammatical mistakes. (This shouldn't be too difficult.) Go through and count each mistake, making note of the type of mistake it is. Was it a correctly spelled word used incorrectly (typo)? Was it completely misspelled? Does it make any sense at all?

Document the common mistakes you see. If you are feeling plucky, consider sending an email to the author of the page offering up your editorial services.

5. **Visuals:** Find a website which has an appealing layout and strong visuals. Note what it is about the visuals that are appealing. Consider how the layout creates meaning for you. Think about how you might lay out your own web-based writing.

6. **Active Reading**: Leave a comment on a blog or online forum. (If you don't already read blogs regularly, find one about something you're interested in.)

–12–
GRAMMAR AND WORD CHOICE

or

Gnawing on the Brains of "Chunk and Spite"

Cedric Sullen is no ordinary vampire. Turned at the tender age of 17, he is immortally trapped inside the body of an adolescent, never to become a grown man; and with four hundred years of wisdom, he finds it pretty frustrating. He manages to overcome his chronic frustration using strategic coping mechanisms: namely, writing and attending high school—perhaps the most de-stressing activity anyone could pursue—for what is more relaxing than drama, hormones, and repetitive scholastics? Given his four hundred years of English and reading (and the fact that he's been in high school honors English classes for the past two centuries), Cedric is clearly an expert on the functions of the English language, which is why he has agreed to pen these pages. Of course, we had to promise him a box-set of Jersey Shore *and a case of the soft drink* Red Bull *(the tastes of centuries-old gentlemen—who knew?) to obtain his services, but we think it was worth it. Cedric is special. We are just certain that his writing will sparkle.*

I NEED TO set the record straight on a few things before we jump into our grammar lesson. Firstly, I am a centuries-old vampire. Just because I am trapped in the body of an adolescent does not mean that my diction and my attitude will resemble that of a human teenager. In fact, I am much more likely to speak with the cadence and formality of a proper gentleman than I am to speak in the monosyllabic utterances of your typical teenage boy.

Secondly, I am a vampire. That means I am at the top of the food chain and the staple of my food supply is none other than you—my preference going to young, teenage girls in the same way yours may extend to a New York sirloin over, say, a sloppy joe. Lastly, I do not date humans. That would be very similar to you suddenly taking an intimate shine to a goat or a salamander. I do not fall in love with what I eat, and if I did, it would be as anomalous and disturbing to my community as if you were to suddenly propose marriage to a deli sandwich even if, by some miracle, that deli sandwich could talk to you. (Hmmm—I wonder if a Polish Sausage sandwich would speak Polish?)

Now, we may begin with a pristine, black slate wiped free of all that chalk dust that has built up over the years. I must say, I have been around a long time. I have dwelled in every corner of the globe. I have haunted the glittery streets of Thailand. I have lurked in the shadows of the Great Wall of China. I have camped in the Carpathian Mountains, and I have journeyed on foot from one end of Africa to the other. They fear me and my kind properly in nearly every town, village, or city I visit. They see my blanched white skin and know I've come to feast on their hearts, and accordingly, they tremble at the sight me. They run from me. They weep and beg me not to drain them of every last blood cell.

Truth be told, I much prefer to be feared by these mortals than to be received by you silly Americans, and more recently, inhabitants of the United Kingdom, as if I am some kind of teenage heartthrob with Bieber hair and a shiny red car. Fear makes the blood race hot and tingly through your veins.

It's like adding butter to a biscuit still steaming from the oven. But love? Girly infatuations? Fluttering eyelashes and heaving bosoms? That makes you taste a little bit like decade-old Twinkies. I'd no sooner eat one of that kind than I would go traipsing into the mountaintop sunshine (which, any vampire will tell you, burns us into a smoking pile of ash).

The worst thing your English writers ever did to the vampire was make them *objects of desire*. Bella, Elena and, yes, possibly even Sookie, would have been little more than nourishment to us in the real world. Van Helsing and Buffy had the right idea. We are not your friends. (Although even Buffy softened on this notion in her "old age.")

Alas, if I cannot sip the sweet ambrosia nectar that is the terror in your blood and I cannot dine on the saucy entrails of your fright-filled gut, then I suppose I have nothing left to do but teach you how to write proper English sentences. That would be the second thing your English writers bestowed up the vampire species—you made us all blithering idiots. In an age where anyone can publish, *anyone*

I find the Internet most confusing. I tried searching for bats by goggling for them, but it simply didn't work.

seems to—and that includes people who don't know the proper use of "either/or" and "neither/nor" or how to recognize and eliminate redundancies. With vampires hot on the pages (in "life," we are much colder than you can imagine), *anyone* is writing terrible text about my species and I'm here to put a stop to it.

Grammar and word choice refer to the basic tools of English. If wielded well, these tools can harness your creative power and turn your writing into something more potent than you can possibly imagine. If wielded poorly, these tools wear down and break. That's when you suddenly find yourself staring down the business end of a wooden stake—that would be the death of your writing and the English language.

Grammar

Grammar refers to the structure of our language; that is, the order in which words are presented, and how those words work together to form meaning. Think of words as planks in a mortician's hands and meaning (or understanding) as the coffin she is building. Alone, the planks are just pieces of wood, but measured and cut and finally shaped together in a particular pattern, those same pieces of wood form a concept with which you are all familiar. You will look at that coffin and you will understand its purpose. Grammar allows you to look at words and understand their purpose: that is, the meaning the writer of those words intended for you to comprehend.

Each word has a distinct function. While you are probably familiar with them, we should conduct a basic review because the way we wield words hinges on their function. We will begin with the two most important elements of meaning: nouns and verbs.

Nouns

Nouns: persons, places, things, and concepts. Nouns are the subjects of sentences.

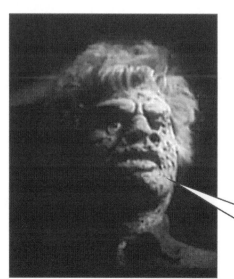

The vampire [thing] watched as the flesh [thing] of his friend [person] dissolved into ashes [thing, plural] in the sunlight [thing], spiraling up the tower [place] toward the sky [thing] while his love [concept] sunk deep beneath the earth [thing].

Perhaps that morning stroll along the beach wasn't a good idea after all. Guess my days of glitter are gone forever.

Nouns can be singular or plural. A singular noun means that there is only one of them, whereas a plural noun means there are several. Typically, we add an "s" or an "es" to the end of nouns we wish to pluralize. An "s" is added to most nouns when indicating there are many, but an "es" is added when the last sound in a word is similar to a hiss; so, if a word ends in "ch," "s," "sh," "x," or "z," you add an "es." If a word ends in "y" you usually change the "y" to an "i" and add "es" to that.

    Vampire (ends in "e") *Vampire**s***
    Ash (ends in "sh")   *Ash**es***
    Sky (ends with "y")   *Sk**ies***

Some nouns are not countable, like dust or sunlight, and so there is no plural form for these words. Other nouns might be irregular and so their plural forms may look a bit different.

    Woman (singular)   *Women (plural)*
    Mouse (singular)   *Mice (plural)*
    Person (singular)   *People (plural)*

Sometimes, you need to show possession of a noun. In your age of cell phone technology and Internet chatrooms, many have forgotten all about this guideline. The possessive qualities of a noun imply ownership. For instance, I can own the soul of a person by mesmerizing them into my own personal Renfield. I can also own a book in my library, or a car. We demonstrate possessiveness (what are vampires if not possessive?) using a mechanical component (think of mechanics like the nails that hold the pieces of the coffin together in certain places): a punctuation mark known as an apostrophe. The apostrophe resembles a singular quotation mark.

    The vampire's slave   Shows the slave belongs to the vampire
    The victim's blood   Shows the blood belongs to the victim

Sometimes plural nouns are also possessive; in those cases, the apostrophe (which signals possession) goes after the "s" (which signals plural):

    The vampires' slave   Shows that the slave belongs to the coven of vampires
    The victims' blood   Shows that the blood belongs to multiple victims

Articles

Lastly, **articles** mark nouns. The rules (and exceptions) about article use might surprise you in their complexity. In general, though, specific nouns are often signaled by the article "the," whereas general nouns are used with "a" or "an." ("A" is used before nouns that begin with a consonant, while "an" is used with nouns that begin with a vowel.) While "a," "an," and "the" are common noun markers, they're not the only ones. Other words, called noun markers or noun determiners, can also give information about the identity or quantity of nouns. Possessive pronouns (such as "my" and "yours"), demonstratives (such as "this" or "that"), quantifiers (such as "all," "any," or "some") and numbers ("thirteen") are all noun markers. Typically, articles are not used with other noun markers (although there are exceptions with common expressions, such as "a few").

The definite article "the" is used when the specific identify of the noun is known to the reader. A noun has a specific identity if it has been previously introduced or mentioned in the text.

> *A starved, rampaging zombie cut off our escape from the alley. Fortunately,* ***the*** *zombie didn't see Mike's baseball bat.*

In the first mention of this zombie, "a" is used because the reader is not familiar with it—just as it appears suddenly in the alley, this zombie is new in the text and is not already known to the reader. The second mention of this zombie, however, uses "the" because the sentence refers to the same zombie—the identity of this zombie (who has cut off the escape of the narrator) is now known to the reader.

A noun is also considered specific if a word (such as a superlative), clause, or phrase restricts its identity.

> *Even* ***the*** *most intelligent* ***vampire*** *is no match for garlic.*
> The superlative "best" restricts the identity of this vampire.

> ***The wolf*** *which bit the child was never found.*
> The phrase "which bit the child" restricts the identity of "wolf." Even though we don't know who that wolf is, we know it was the one who bit that kid.

Generally, we use the article "who" or "whom" to signal a human and "which" or "that" to signify anything which is nonhuman. Bloody rude, if you ask me.

The indefinite article "a" or "an" is used for count nouns whose identity is not known to the reader. A count noun is a noun that can be counted ("three ghosts"), whereas a noncount noun is a concept or abstraction that cannot be counted ("intelligence"). (Note that these vary between languages. Use a style guide or other reliable source to find lists of commonly used noncount nouns.)

In general, "a" marks a noun which is both singular and not known to the reader.

> *A* ***vampire*** *broke into the blood bank on Main Street.*
> Typically, "a" or "an" are used with unfamiliar count nouns.

> ***Thirst*** *drives many vampires to take risks to feed.*
> "Thirst" is a nouncount noun, and thus would not be used with "a."

Sometimes either "a" or "the" would be grammatically correct. In these cases, the writer might choose one article over the other to emphasize the specificity of the noun, or to underscore that it's unknown or general.

A poltergeist smashed the portrait of my grandmother.
In this case, the painting was destroyed by some unknown ghost not known to the writer or the reader.

The poltergeist smashed the portrait of my grandmother.
While this might be the first mention of this destructive spirit in this text, the definite article "the" establishes familiarity between the ghost and the narrator. The poltergeist might not be known to the reader, but it is a specific (malevolent) entity known to the narrator; it was the thing who did this specific action.

Verbs

Verbs: actions, occurrences, or states of being. Verbs begin the predicates of sentences.

He seemed [state of being] like he was going to kiss [action] her, but as he opened [action] his mouth, she realized [action] what was happening [occurrence]. As he bit [action] the supple skin of her neck, she felt [action] certain their teen romance was [state of being] over.

Verbs can be past or present tense; they can indicate which noun is doing the action, and even the mood of the piece. Tense refers to the time the action took place. Timing can be simple or perfect, and it can be present, past, or future. Simple typically refers to an action that happened once, is happening once, or will happen once. Perfect refers to actions which have been completed or "perfected," are completed or perfected, or soon will be.

Simple Present Tense:	*I devour*
Simple Past Tense:	*I devoured*
Simple Future Tense:	*I will devour*
Present Perfect Tense:	*I have devoured*
Past Perfect Tense:	*I had devoured*
Future Perfect Tense:	*I will have devoured*

Different types of nouns also use different forms of verbs. There are regular verbs which are typically altered only slightly to indicate differences in nouns, and there are irregular verbs which are altered greatly to indicate the same differences.

Regular Verb: to stalk (as in, to follow prey as it runs from you)

I *stalk*   We *stalk*
You (singular) *stalk*   You (plural) *stalk*
She/He/It *stalks*   They *stalk*

Irregular Verb: to be (state of existence)

I *am*   We *are*
You (singular) *are*   You (plural) *are*
She/He/It *is*   They *are*

The *mood* is a major component of how verbs function. Verbs can distinguish a subject's intention toward the action being made. This intention is signified by the following moods: imperative, indicative, or subjunctive. We vampires hunt by the imperative, live by the indicative, and wallow in the subjunctive of our sunless existence.

Imperative*:* Demonstrates the subject's command or request.

Run!
Stop, turn around, and face your death.
Show me your neck.
Put that garlic away, silly human.

In each of the examples above, the subject is unnamed, but I'm fairly certain you realized it was me talking to you. The imperative form, as you can see, demonstrates my commands—that is, what I expect you to do or what I am requesting of you.

Indicative*:* Demonstrates (or indicates) that the subject is referring to (or believes that the statements are to be taken as) facts. This is the most common (or the "basic") form of verbs.

Whether she was happy or sad, Ella's face never changed expressions.

I watched as the slayer staked the vampire and the creature burst into a vacuum of dust.

The cross burst into flames as the vampire touched it, and it fell from the hunter's hand.

In this example, each statement is presumed to be true or something that has happened (or is happening, or will inevitably happen). Because we assume the truth in most statements, indicative is the form we use when writing in the standard verb tenses we've already discussed.

Subjunctive: Demonstrates that the subject is referring to things which are (or believes that the statements are) contrary to fact, hypothetical, or just a lot of wishful thinking. When writing in the subjunctive mood, tenses are referred to as either present subjunctive, past subjunctive, past perfect subjunctive, or future subjunctive.

Present subjunctive: *If I am undead, then I am still alive.*

The subject ("I") assumes that his or her state of being "undead" is not necessarily factual, but a hypothetical situation (as indicated by the word "if").

Past Subjunctive: *I wish that I still owned that flame thrower.*

The subject indicates that he wishes (subjunctive) something that occurred in the past was still relevant, thus it is counterfactual or wishful thinking.

Past Perfect Subjunctive: *I wish I had eaten that shop girl earlier this evening.*

The subject has not eaten a shop girl, but demonstrates the subjunctive mood—he or she wishes that it had happened (but it did not).

Future Subjunctive: *If I were to join Armand's Vampire Theatre, I would be able to eat all the shop girls I wanted.*

The subject is imagining a non-factual event that could or would take place in the future, thus demonstrating wishful thinking and possible outcomes of those wishes.

Nouns and verbs are the primary features of sentences as they comprise the elements of "subject" and "predicate," two things necessary for a sentence to be complete. There are, however, other pieces to the coffin of good writing that you should know about. Otherwise your writing will be just as foul-smelling as a corpse in a poorly constructed wooden box.

PRONOUNS

Pronouns: words that function as nouns.

These are kind of like stand-ins. Using the coffin-building analogy, let's imagine that nouns are wooden planks. If that is the case, then pronouns are fiberglass. You can still use them to make shape, but they are not the stuff that stakes are made of, and you don't want to grab the wrong kind when you really need it. There are different types or functions of pronouns:

Personal:	*I, me, you, he, she, it, us, them*
Possessive:	*his, hers, mine, yours, theirs, ours*
Reflexive:	*myself, himself, yourself, themselves*
Indefinite:	*all, few, many, none, some*
Demonstrative:	*these, this, that, those*
Interrogative:	*what, how, which*
Relative:	*whichever, whoever, whatever, however*

ADJECTIVES

Adjectives: Descriptive words that modify nouns and pronouns.

Adjectives can be either descriptive (showing) or explanative (telling), and tend to identify, quantify, or elaborate the details of a noun or pronoun. If nouns and pronouns are the wood or fiberglass used to build the coffin (and verbs are the actions taken to put it together), then adjectives would be the flashy paint, the brass handles, and the velvety lining inside it.

Descriptive Adjective Examples:

I brushed the hair from the <u>creamy</u> nape of her neck and smelled her <u>cinnamon</u> scent.

Her <u>red</u> blood oozed from her veins.

It tasted <u>rusty.</u>

Explanative Adjective Examples:

She was a <u>beautiful</u> creature in life, but she would be an <u>exquisite</u> corpse.

When she rises, she will be a <u>terrible, horrifying</u> monster.

Adverbs

Adverbs: Descriptive words that modify verbs, adjectives, other adverbs, or clauses.

Adverbs are often words that end in "ly." Many adverbs, however, do not, such as "always" or "never." The most common adverb is "very"—I recommend you eliminate it from your vocabulary. Using "very" is a crutch you writers use very often and before you know it, you are very lost in your very boring and very unstructured writing, leaving your readers feeling very disappointed and like your writing isn't very good.

Adverbs clarify questions of condition. They may answer the "when" or "how often" an action takes place, or they may indicate the position of an action by answering "where" it took place. Here are some examples.

The vampire <u>quickly</u> leapt atop his coffin and bared his fangs <u>menacingly.</u>

He knew the torch-bearing townsfolk would arrive <u>very</u> soon.

<u>Luckily</u>, he remembered <u>yesterday</u> to buy ultra-absorbent dinner bibs for his guests.

Prepositions

Prepositions: Demonstrate relationships between nouns and pronouns.

Anything a vampire can do with a coffin indicates the spatial relationship between the vampire (noun) and the coffin (also a noun). Therefore, a vampire can be "inside" a coffin, "under" a coffin, "around" or "near" a coffin, or standing "over" a coffin.

Time relationships are demonstrated between nouns using prepositions like "during," "after," "before," "throughout," "until," and "past." Thus a vampire can be thinking of his coffin "during" a feast of blood "before" he returns to ground, but "after" he slaughtered the village.

Prepositional phrases are sometimes used to create *dependent clauses*, or parts of sentences that *depend* on the rest of the sentence to complete the thought. These phrases include the preposition, its object, and its modifiers.

At Blade's apartment, we realized we were going to die.

Before going to The Bronze, be sure to pack your holy water.

Conjunctions

Conjunctions: are connective words that link other words or phrases.

There are different types of conjunctions. Some work in pairs to demonstrate additional relationships, while some others coordinate equalities in words or phrases. There are still other types of conjunctions, but we'll focus on the basics. Coordinating conjunctions are the most commonly used, and they function by creating a link between two words or phrases of equivalence. Flesh and bones. Blood and organs. Garlic and holy water. Fangs and thirst. Vampires and werewolves.

FANBOYS is a popular acronym of the most common coordinating conjunctions. I always pronounce it "fang boys" in my head. It reminds me of my glory days in the

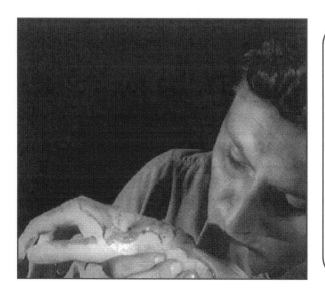

COORDINATING CONJUNCTIONS:
(Give Your Writing a Hand)

Flesh and Bone

Zombies and Brains

Witches and Broomsticks

Werewolves and Silver

Corpses and Coffins

but we'd rather not see—

Vampires and Sparkle

preparatory schools of England. When you have been a student as long as I have, you remember high school pranks as well as you remember the flavor of your first fang-paste. My early days, though, were resplendent. Oh, the havoc I sowed in those days before camera phones and the Internet. It is so much harder now to invoke carnage when the person sitting next to you is already uploading video footage of your midnight snack to his favorite social network. Ah, don't get me started. I am beginning to remember the teen angst that I finally outgrew during the French Revolution.

Where was I? Ah, yes. FANBOYS:

For, And, Nor, But, Or, Yet, So.

I have been hunted all night, <u>so</u> I must find a way to feed during the day.

I prefer A-Negative, <u>yet</u> all you taste like A-Positive. How disappointing.

I was in love once, <u>but</u> I ate her.

Correlative conjunctions function in pairs. They join two elements of equal value. When you use one part of the pair, you must use the second part later.

Neither/nor: I like <u>neither</u> blood banks <u>nor</u> donors for my meals.

Either/or: I prefer to drink the blood of <u>either</u> virgins <u>or</u> fast food workers.

Both/and: <u>Both</u> vampires <u>and</u> werewolves are born of an infected bite.

Sentences

Words, words, words are only as valuable as how they are strung together to create meaning for a reader. Stringing words together like some morbid marionette is the art of writing thoughts, completing ideas, creating clauses. To write a complete thought, a sentence must always have both a subject and a predicate. The subject is the object, person, place, or concept which is doing something or being seen. In short, subjects are nouns or pronouns. The predicate is the part of the sentence which elaborates about what the subject is, or does, or simply tells the subject to do something. Predicates hinge like the lid of coffins on verbs.

Subject + Predicate
Noun + Verb and modifiers
Vampires [noun] like [verb] blood [noun/modifier].

If both of these elements are not united, then the thought is incomplete and a fragment is present. A *fragment* is a dependent clause or statement that does not finish a thought. Conversely, if you have too many subjects and/or predicates, you end up with a run-on sentence. A *run-on* is a phrase or several phrases which demonstrate many distinctly completed thoughts.

The most common type of fragment occurs when a dependent clause (a phrase that requires more information for the entire thought to be expressed) is left to hang out there all by itself like a tasty maiden tied to a stake or a set of railroad tracks. Dependent clauses (also called "subordinate clauses") often contain both a subject and a predicate, but something is missing from them in much the same way Renfield was missing that elusive spark necessary to make him a fully functioning vampire out from under Dracula's thumb.

Fragments:

After we dug ourselves out of the ground.

Because I prefer red sauce to white.

When you bring holy water to a vampire bar fight.

Whatever reason the villagers had.

The above examples demonstrate incomplete thoughts. If you read them aloud, you can hear how your voice falters, expectant as it is to continue on after the phrase stops short. There is something missing. You are left questioning "what" or "why." To finish these thoughts, you need to pair it with an *independent clause,* which is a phrase that can stand all by itself because, alone, it is a complete thought.

Zombies, when they are able to utter coherent words at all (and not chomping on human innards) are likely to mumble in sentence fragments.

Completed Sentences:

After we dug ourselves out of the ground, <u>we ate a couple of bums in an alley.</u>

Because I prefer red sauce to white, <u>I drink blood fresh and undiluted.</u>

When you bring holy water to a vampire bar fight, <u>expect a blood bath.</u>

<u>The vampire's powerful hypnotic spell destroyed</u> whatever reason the villagers had.

In the examples above, you can hear the resolution of each idea introduced by the fragments. I often recommend to my classmates that they read their writing out loud to better spot fragments. Spotting run-on sentences is a bit like finding a vampire's reflection in a mirror if you don't read punctuation properly. That is, if you read a comma like it is a long pause (which is reserved for periods), then you won't necessarily catch your run-on mistakes.

Sometimes a writer doesn't end a sentence where it should, this could be caused by many things, like not knowing about sentence structure or just making a mistake, or maybe in the writer's mind these ideas are connected, all together like pearls on a necklace, a necklace that goes on forever and ever and wraps around the reader's neck and—.

Unlike vampires and zombies, writing must breathe.

A run-on, remember, is when there is too much going on in a sentence. There are too many subjects and too many predicates happening all at once for it to be functional.

Sometimes, writers create run-ons by using too many conjunctions. Other times, writers create comma splices, which is the combination of two independent clauses with a comma (a big "no-no" in the grammar world). Occasionally, writers simply spill one subject/predicate pair into another without noticing.

Run-On Phrases:

A werewolf will eventually die a mortal death, a vampire lives forever.

Ghosts cannot interact with the world they can haunt dreams and homes.

Coffins are not necessary vampires can live underground or in windowless houses.

In the statements above, if you read them without pausing (there is no punctuation telling you to pause, so that would be the proper way to read them), you will no doubt stumble over certain parts, your tongue twisting in your mouth as it tries to decode meaning from confusion. You probably experienced such a stumble when you encountered the words "a," "world they," and "necessary vampires." Am I right? Why do you suppose that is?

Corrected Run-On Sentences:

*A werewolf will eventually die a mortal death**;** a vampire lives forever.*

*A werewolf will eventually die a mortal death**, but** a vampire lives forever.*

*A werewolf will eventually die a mortal death**.** A vampire lives forever.*

*Ghosts cannot interact with the world**, but** they can haunt dreams and homes.*

*Ghosts cannot interact with the world**.** They can haunt dreams and homes.*

*Coffins are not necessary**.** Vampires can live underground or in windowless houses.*

*Coffins are not necessary**;** vampires can live underground or in windowless houses.*

*Coffins are not necessary **because** vampires can live underground or in windowless houses.*

Run-on sentences can be fixed by inserting a period between the two

> *A comma splice is rather like a gene splice between a zombie and a vampire. It is unacceptable under any circumstance and dealt with accordingly.*

independent clauses—that is, between the two complete thoughts. Other ways to fix them, as you can see, include inserting conjunctions, or if the ideas are related, inserting a semi-colon between the phrases. (It is not acceptable in formal writing to use a comma to link them; this would make it a comma splice, and thus a run-on sentence.) All of these are grammatically correct solutions—but it is up to you—the writer—to choose what kind of connection you want to make between your statements. Does your sentence need to end at a dead stop before moving on to the next? (Then a period is your best choice.) Or do you want your reader to experience the *connection* between the ideas, and thus, your sentences?

Also keep in mind sentence variety. If every sentence has the structure "subject-verb," the writing will feel very choppy and readers can lose interest and patience. Play around with how to connect ideas—or separate them—using punctuation marks and conjunctions. Play with sentence structure, sometimes opening with dependent clauses, or alternating between long and short sentences. Use sentences to create a rhythm in your writing.

> **Rhythm is important. Whether it is music, poetry, writing, or the pulse of blood through the neck of an innocent maiden.**

Paragraphs

If sentences are complete ideas, then paragraphs are complete realms of ideas. A paragraph, then, is like the coffin and all that it contains. Comprised of sentences which all revolve around one topic, paragraphs are like mini-essays or mini-chapters all devoted to a single subject. They can be woven together into a lengthier work, such as a story, or a chapter, or a book. And sometimes they can stand alone, like when you are writing a quick e-mail to a zombuddy or a co-worker at the local bloodbank.

In this sense, words comprise sentences which comprise paragraphs which comprise essays/stories/chapters/reports, and so on. The chief guiding principle for paragraphs is that all the components that make them up revolve around one concept and do not stray forth into tangents as this can cause the reader to lose your meaning.

Word → Sentence → Paragraph → Larger Work

There are no "rules" about how long paragraphs should be, but it's important to know how paragraphs affect readers. As with a stream of short sentences, a series of short paragraphs can move quickly, but it can also feel choppy. Long paragraphs can meander thoughtfully through a complex idea, but it can also feel like walking through a maze in a hall of mirrors—just when you think you've found the exit, it keeps going. Know the power of your paragraphs, and understand how they can help (or hinder) your writing.

In addition to the rhythm they can establish, paragraphs also have visual impact. Glancing at a page, and seeing how many paragraphs there are, can tell you a lot about the writing—how many main ideas it likely presents, how quickly it moves, how dense it is. And while most readers do not stop to count the paragraphs before they begin to read, the visual structure of the text does affect their reading experience.

Word Choice

Most vampires have a pretty strong sense of style. After hundreds of years of fashion, we generally have a better idea of what suits our personalities as well as our comfort. You have your newbies clad in red leather pants and trench coats with thick, black and white make-up painted on their faces. You have your sophisticated gentlemen and ladies in their velvet waistcoats, tailored satin shirts, and their perfectly manicured nails. You have your casual teen vampires in their tees and jeans with their mop of wild hair pointing like an anime comic character in gel-structured spirals.

Fashion is a choice, and to a vampire, it is brimming with opportunity.

Word choice, too, is a type of fashion, only in this case, it is an element of both grammar and style. You can either have silken ascots and pocket watches, or lime green polyester and beehives. Depending on the party, one works; the other is a clear mistake.

Word choice deals with proper spelling, commonly misused words and homonyms, jargon, denotation versus connotation, precise language, and clichés. Consider spelling first as it is the stitching used to hold a garment together. Commonly misused words would be a fashion faux pas—you've heard of PETA spattering fur coats with red paint to symbolize blood? Well, vampires who wear the

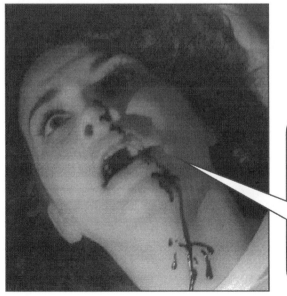

> *Had I known the fashion police was made up of vampires, I would never have worn white shoes after Labor Day.*

wrong clothes don't eat, so there's no blood spattering there. Homonyms can be misused, too. They are like a set of identically-cut t-shirts in different colors—you need a red shirt, but you accidentally grab a purple one. Jargon would be like the common wear of a clique or a uniform, and denotation versus connotation is similar to wearing the clothes you see plastered in high fashion magazines versus the clothes you actually see people in your neighborhood wearing. Precise language would be a tailored garment, while clichés would be a standard, boring crew-neck t-shirt that everyone else is wearing too.

A vampire has to look nice. How else do we get a dinner date?

Spelling

As with any rule, there are always exceptions. Vampires of one race spurt like a jar of jelly in the microwave when staked, and vampires of another race are paralyzed like stone when their hearts are pierced by

> **Zombees forgit how to spell wurds crectly aftur rizeng frum beeing ded.**

sharpened wood. Spelling is no different, but there are some basic rules that can occasionally help you out. Here's one of my favorites:

> *I before E except after C, except when it's "ay" like neighbor or weigh, or when it's weird and not very efficient:*

I before E:	*Fiend, Die, Fierce*
Except after C:	*Deceive, Conceit*
Except when it's "ay":	*Vein, Feign*
Or when it's weird:	*Weird, Forfeit, neither*
And not very efficient:	*Ancient, Species*

In addition, it helps to realize that language is founded on sound and, as such, phonetics can help you determine the spelling of a word. However, English is well known for being one of the most difficult languages to pronounce, so be wary of using phonetics exclusively to determine spelling.

Lastly, be aware that spell checkers (such as those found on most computer word processing software and some cell phones) are not foolproof. One of the foolish teens in my current rendition of high school honors English consistently misspells the word "definitely." Every time he goes to type it into his word processing program, he types it as such:

Definately

Of course, that is not the correct word, so when his spell checker (or his auto-correction feature) goes to correct it, it changes the word to this:

Defiantly

"Defiantly" is how strongly this person fights against my suggestion that he memorize spelling or use a dictionary—that is, he is "defiant" (or defensive and unlikely to follow the suggestion) about it, which is "definitely" (conclusively) a bad idea. Instead, he relies on a spell checker which occasionally fixes words incorrectly, or which skips over words spelled correctly but mistyped (such as typing "this" when you meant to type "the"—happens all the time). In the end, just make sure that you read over your text with your own eyes rather than submit to the whims of your spell checker.

Commonly Misused Words (Malapropisms) and Homophones

I once ate an entire town because its people said "irregardless" (which is *not* a word) when they meant to say "regardless." Malapropisms, or misused words, are all too common. No self-respecting vampire would ever confuse the meaning of two words, but humans are on this planet for a decidedly shorter period of time and, as such, don't always learn the proper usage or the precise definitions of things.

One form of malapropism is using an incorrect word that sounds similar to another word which would be correct. Another type of malapropism is when you confuse words which sound exactly the same as another word when spoken. Both of these examples of misuse can be especially confusing when using idioms, which is an expression whose meaning is not literal. If you're told to "keep your eyes peeled," you know that means to watch out for something, not literally peel your eyeballs (unless you happen to work

For all intensive purposes, a rain of terror is upon us and those zombies must get their just desserts, yes siree, Bob!

as a kitchen assistant in a restaurant catering to, shall we say, "specialty" tastes). Here are some idioms and their commonly misused versions:

Malapropism:	**Correct form:**
intensive purposes	intents and purposes
just desserts	just deserts
slight of hand	sleight of hand
rain of terror	reign of terror
tow the line	toe the line

Confusing words which sound identical but mean different things, such as "rain" and "reign" above, is a common mistake in writing. These kinds of mistakes slip past most spell-checkers because the word is spelled correctly—it's just the wrong one. Keeping a list of mistakes you commonly make in your writing or memorizing a list of commonly misused words and homophones is an effective way to combat these errors of meaning in your text. Take the list below (along with some tips and tricks I offer to help you remember which is which):

COMMON HOMOPHONES
words which sound alike, but mean different things

Altar: a place of worship
Alter: to change something

Deer: an animal (Werewolves eat deer)
Dear: beloved (Ella is my dear, darling sweetheart)

Lightening: lessening the level of darkness in something (like your hair)
Lightning: static electricity released usually during thunder storms.

To: toward (or part of an infinitive verb form)
Too: also
Two: the numeral 2

Very: a lot of, or many
Vary: diverse, or full of differences

Write: to form letters and make words, sentences, or stories
Right: to be correct
Rite: a ritual
Wright: a person who makes something (like a playwright makes plays)

Your: belongs to "you"
You're: a contraction (shorter version) of the words "You are"
Yore: the past, history

COMMONLY MISUSED WORDS
which may look similar, but do not sound alike

Accept: to receive (I accept your offering.)
Except: excluding (I will accept your offering except for the sewer rats—you keep those.)

Affect: to "alter" something—you can help remember this as both words begin with "a" (I was affected by the film and cried the whole way home.)
Effect: the "end result" of something—both begin with "e" (The effect of the film was depressing.)

Can't: contraction form of the words "Can not" (I can't get no satisfaction.)
Cant: empty language (If the guards had understood thieves' cant, they could have prevented the escape.)

Lay: to place something (She lays the doll on the bed.); or the past tense of "lie" (Yesterday, I lay in my crypt.)
Lie: to recline (I lie in my crypt when the sun is shining.)

Loose: the opposite of tight (My hair is loose and coming out of the braid.)
Lose: the opposite of win (I always lose a little blood when I'm hunting.)

Than: conjunction for comparisons (I am hungrier than a demon.)
Then: adverb to demonstrate timing sequence (First eat; then drink.)

That: identifying some<u>thing</u> (The vehicles that swarm the streets.)
Which: identifying nonessential information about a <u>thing</u> (Lilith's house, which was the darkest on the street, was illuminated by streetlamps.)

Where: identifying nonessential information about a <u>place/location</u> (Lilith's house, where everyone sleeps until dusk.)
We're: contraction form of the words "We are" (We're leaving.)
Were: past tense of the verb "to be" (The werewolves were hungry that night.)

Whose: identifying who owns something, or identifying nonessential information about a <u>person or living being</u> (Lilith, whose house is the darkest.)
Who's: contraction form of the words "Who is" (Who's Sookie? Anyone know her?)

Jargon

In the world of vampires, we take it for granted that you will know what we mean when we say we have a blood bond with our revenants. Of course, if you are not a vampire yourself or if you are unfamiliar with vampires, then you could not understand what is meant by either "blood bond" or "revenant." The former is a relationship, often telepathic and empathic, in which a maker (the vampire who turned the creature in question) and his child (the creature in question) communicate feelings and thoughts at great distances. The latter is a term we use for the most base vampires we create—those without thoughts of their own, similar to your zombies.

Jargon is best avoided. If you are part of a community, trade, vocation, or specialized field, you doubtlessly have words you use of which only you and your community know the proper meanings. Remembering who your audience is will help you avoid using words they will not understand. It is best to avoid jargon when writing outside of your "community."

> **It is best to avoid the use of jargon when writing outside of your intended community.**

Denotation versus Connotation

Denotation refers to the dictionary's definition of a word, whereas connotation refers to how the word is used conversationally. This is an important distinction. English is riddled with connotation which can vary by region and audience, but some words and phrases are universally used in a connotative way. Consider the cultural or connotative meaning of the following sentence:

I staked the vampire in his private place.

Now, before you go imagining that we have a band of vampire slayers out there who, shall we say, deliberately miss the heart, imagine the denotation of the sentence. "Private," according to the definition, means a personal or isolated place where others are not allowed. "Private place" or "private part," however, is used conversationally to refer to areas of the body many people are not comfortable talking about.

Denotatively, there is nothing wrong with the sentence listed above. It means that a slayer found a vampire's private location and drove a stake through his heart. At the same time, people reading this won't imagine that's actually what happened. Consider this alternative:

I staked the vampire in his hiding place.

Being aware of the cultural meanings of words (or "slang") can be a challenge, particularly for people who are just learning English. One way to determine if you are using a word properly is to refer to the *Oxford English Dictionary*, the crowned queen of our language. This dictionary, unlike some others, not only tells you the denotation, but also its connotation throughout history. Many words change meaning over time. The *Oxford English Dictionary* (or the *OED*) allows us to see the varying definitions of words as they are used conversationally and denotatively in various texts. You might also consider referring to a slang dictionary, as well, such as the popular *Urban Dictionary* found on the web.

Precise Language

You happen across an antique store where a wealth of old knickknacks and tchotchkes, baubles and trinkets are for sale. You find a dazzling old bottle and purchase it without question. As you are polishing the dust from its cool, metallic surface, suddenly a spiral of genie mist worms its way out the spout and you are faced with a wish-granting indentured servant. Who hasn't been there, am I right? Only, this is a once-in-a-lifetime opportunity. It won't happen again. You have three wishes. What do you wish for?

"Money."

"Wish granted," says the genie, nodding its head. Suddenly, a satchel of money lands in your lap followed by a knock at the door. You open the door, but not before you spread your fingers through the piles of cash in the satchel. At the door, you are greeted by a host of police officers who come to arrest you from robbing the

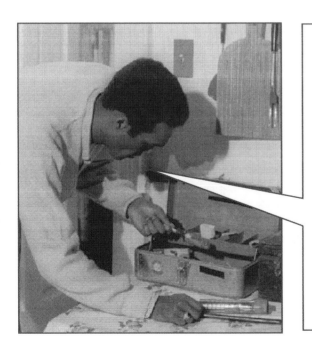

Proper tools are essential whether fighting off zombies or writing a thesis. Let's see. Here's a hammer to nail boards over the windows. And there's a cliché remover. Definitely need that.

nearest bank. With your fingerprints on the bag and the money, it looks like it is jail for you.

Why is this scenario so familiar? The correct answer is that whenever this happens to one of us, we have failed to use precise language. This failure allows the genie to interpret a meaning of its own when granting our wishes. In short, precise language is language which seals shut any window of personal interpretation, leaving only your intended meaning to pass to the listener or reader.

One way that we ensure our language is precise is to watch carefully for our use of basic verbs, such as "be" and "do." These verbs can be exchanged in many cases for more precise language.

Weak:	*The vampire coven **is** [a form of "be"] hunting the streets of New York.*
Better:	*The vampire coven <u>hunts</u> the streets of New York.*
Better:	*The vampire coven <u>stalks its prey on</u> the streets of New York.*
Better:	*The vampire coven <u>follows women as they exit taxi cabs or wander down dark alleys on</u> the streets of New York.*
Weak:	*The unsuspecting target **does** [form of "do"] her homework before leaving campus and walking alone in the dark to her apartment.*
Better:	*The unsuspecting target <u>completes</u> homework before leaving campus and walking alone in the dark to her apartment.*

Precise language is essential not only to our hapless wishers, but also to anyone who has entanglements with the law (whichever side) or healthcare or any other situation in which precision is vital. Laws hinge on grammar and word usage—that is often why they are so difficult to understand. The same holds true for the way many bills are written when you Americans go to the polls to vote. Precision is what allows writers to ensure there are no loopholes or blind spots that will allow criminals to escape the law. In healthcare, the same precision rules hold true: consider what would happen if your nurse forgot to mention the precise method of delivery of a medication that can be administered either orally or rectally, and I'm sure you are starting to see the importance of precise language. Choose your words carefully. It might just save your life, one day.

Clichés

These are words and phrases which have lost the power of their meaning as a result of how frequently they are used and heard by people. These phrases are as tired as the redundant tropes of your vampire fiction. Yes, we are immortal. Yes, we perish in the sun. Yes, we drink your blood. Yes, we die from decapitation and wooden stakes. Yes, we live only for mortal love and, even though we have thousands of years more than you, that mortal love is going to be an average woman or girl whom we would probably eat if given half the chance and who is somehow "special."

It's been done.

In the gist, that's a cliché. A story, idea, phrase, or concept so familiar that you just don't care anymore. It makes you tired to hear it. *That vampire is white as snow. Cedric Sullen fell in love with Ella because she thinks outside the box.* Blah, blah, blahbity blah. If you are writing clichés, chances are you are not writing well. Scan your documents for these tired phrases and bring them back to life with new words.

That vampire is white as snow is as pale as third-grade paste.

Cedric Sullen fell in love with Ella because she thinks outside the box thinks unconventionally, as if she were plucked from another time in history.

In short, clichés are deader than a doornail. It is best to avoid them like the plague.

Concluding Notes

Well, I suppose that is all I have for you. It's time for me to return to fifth period study hall, a delightful activity in which teenagers all sit around devising ways to trick the teacher into thinking he or she is reading a book when in fact he or she is sleeping, doodling obscene pictures on the desk, or reading social network updates on a cell phone. I, myself, will probably spend the hour reading people's thoughts, if it isn't too boring. After all, I've already read the textbooks a dozen times. What else is there for me to do? Perhaps write a book?

Writing Prompts for Chapter 12

1. Write your own theory of grammar. What is its purpose? Why is it important? How do you use it? What do you already know about it, and what do you need to know?

2. Create your own words and definitions. Write them into a story or poem and read it to a friend. Can you convince them your words are real?

3. Invent a new punctuation mark. What does it do? When is it used? Draft some rules and examples.

Writing Exercises for Chapter 12

1. **Parts of Speech:** Choose a sentence out of a book or from a website and diagram it. That is, write the part of speech of each word in the sentence over each word. Do this for several sentences. Look at the patterns the parts of speech form. Do you see any connections? Can you see any discernible patterns?

2. **Parts of Speech:** Find a copy of *Jabberwocky* and read it. This poem is comprised almost entirely of made-up words, but you should still be able to determine the parts of speech of each word. Diagram the words in the poem. What are the nouns? The verbs? The adjectives? How can you tell? Compare it to the patterns you found in the first exercise. Do you notice any similarities?

3. **Word Choice**: Dig up an old piece of writing, preferably something you wrote for school. Highlight all forms of the "to be" verb (be, am, are, is, were, was, been, etc.) and replace them with different verbs. Can you get rid of all of them? How does that change the tone of your writing?

4. **Word Choice**: Using online software, create a "word cloud" of a piece of your writing. What words do you use most frequently? Are there any common words or clichés? Can any commonly used words be replaced with new and different ones?

5. **Sentences:** Using what you know about punctuation and sentence structure, write the longest sentence you can. Can you write a 1-page sentence? A 2-page sentence?

6. **Sentences:** Go through a draft of your own writing with a critical eye for any

instance of fragment or run-on sentence. Correct each using the methods in this chapter.

7. **Paragraphs**: Try revising a piece of writing based on sentence variety. Pick a paragraph and play with sentence structure and length. Try alternating long and short sentences.

8. **Paragraphs**: Paragraphs are like building blocks. Put together, they create something larger than themselves. They can also be moved around to make new structures. Print out an essay you wrote for school. Cut it up based on the paragraphs, and try moving them around into new configurations. Think about your organizational choices and the connections between ideas. How many good combinations can you come up with?

−13−
The Dark Side of Publishing

or

You've Killed All Your Characters, So Who Do You Have to Resurrect to Get a Publishing Deal Around Here?

Antonia Cackle was a hard authoress to pin down. We ended up having to make a deal to get her to agree to write this chapter for us. A necromancer by trade, Madame Cackle holds power and dominion over all the other creatures in this book. With a wave of her wand, she can crumble the bones inside a vampire, halt a horde of zombies in their gobbling tracks, unwrap a mummy, or summon a ghost to do her bidding. Even some of the living are at her command as she holds sway over all creatures who have the misfortune to cross her path. It makes sense, then, that Antonia would write our chapter on publishing. Without further ado, we bring you the words of the greatest necromancer in history.

HAVE YOU GOTTEN all of the ingredients correct?

Have you mixed in your hopes and dreams and sprinkled them with the dust of the evasive Muse? And have you stirred in that special potion that mortal writers call "editing"? If you have done everything suggested in this tome, then it's time to bring your literary creation to life with a wave of your magic wand and the chanting of the magic word:

Publication.

Pardon me while I cackle for a few minutes and wipe the tears of laughter from the hollows of my cheeks.

Did you really think it would be that easy?

For a price, I could make that happen, but it is a price most would regret paying. A kidney is the fee for a poem or a short story, but a lengthier work will require a firstborn child or even your soul. William Shakespeare would never have finished *King Lear* if not for a few sacrifices sent my way. Edgar Allan Poe sacrificed so much that he eventually forfeited his life in later years. Using magic to attain publication is an option, but the cost is high.

For the mere cost of this book, however, I will share some of the trade secrets that are available to mortals who seek publication without the assistance of and cost associated with witchcraft. I do this only as I have now been promised three souls to do with as I wish in the future. Silly authors—they have no idea what they sacrificed when they signed that contract under the glimmer of a dark moon!

I will warn you: publication is not an easy task without the aid of a magic wand, potions, or spell books. But it can be done.

My first assumption (and no comments here or I'll turn you into a braying animal that shoos away flies with its tail) is that your work is finished, edited, and polished to sparkling sheen. Its pages should be stained with blood from the hard work you poured into this endeavor. If this is not so, then you are not ready for the next step.

> **Publication is not an easy task without the aid of a magic wand, potions, or spell books. But it can be done.**

I'm fond of repeating myself, what with the chanting and all, so please allow me to reiterate what I just said:

If this is not so, then you are not ready for the next step.

Are you starting to hear the importance of this? Why else would I repeat myself in a book? You could simply reread the line again and again until it lifted off the page and took root in your ear canal like a tiny worm. I repeat it because I need you to hear it.

So often, new writers believe that once they've completed the first draft of their manuscript, their hard work is done. All that sweat of creation, the labor of writing, is over. Surely they've written a masterpiece. The inspiration that swirled around them like magic fairy dust was so potent it made them feel light as wings. With all that fairy dust floating around, of course they believe they've created something magical—and that may be true.

But will people read it?

If there is even a single mistake, typo, error, resource cited incorrectly, even something seemingly as trivial as a missing comma, your efforts could all be for naught. And errors of grammar, mechanics, and spelling are merely cosmetic mistakes—what about mismanaged scenes? What about characters whose hair is red in chapter one, only to be black in chapter 13 because you lost track of important details? What about the missing steps between your character being in a car then suddenly sitting in someone's home without any transition between events? Did you really think that the enchantment would enable you to write perfectly on the first try?

Foolish mortal.

The real work is still ahead of you. Writing is the easy part. Writing is the *fun* part. What comes after writing is editing, revising, re-drafting, and revisioning. These processes can go on and on. You pour over your words, knitting the needles of language together over and over until the words are woven snugly, laying across your lap just so. To achieve this serendipitous beauty, many writers enlist the services of an editor prior to submitting their work to prospective agents or publishers, but an editor doesn't do the work for you. He or she (or it) will merely point out areas that are weak or unclear or disconnected so that you can do the work of revising. It is *your* work, after all, isn't it?

Only after you have invested laborious hours improving your work, relentlessly stripping away the unnecessary lines until your work shines like a bleached skeleton— only then will a publisher or agent take your work seriously. Remember, if you submit your work too early, you may burn bridges with publishers and agents who find your work laughable or, at the very least, deem you too unprofessional for them to waste their time on you in the future. How, then, will you ever make it to that next step?

Of course, the next step can mean many things.

If you have simply written an essay for your Necromantic Literature class or a report for your boss at Dark Harbinger Interment Services, then you have no need to seek publication in the literal sense. By the very nature of being a student or an employee, you may assume that every time you hand work into a teacher, professor, or boss, it becomes figuratively published. You don't want to be the one laughed at over the water cooler because you misspelled "mastication," do you? Or the one your boss fires because you sent a report to the board of directors on her behalf in which you accidentally used the malapropism "he's a wolf in cheap clothing," and now she's the laughing stock? If you'd only assumed that your work was being published, perhaps you wouldn't now be lying in your cold grave turning with the worms at my necromagical disposal?

Funny how things work.

I can see through my magic crystal ball that most of you have something you'd like to see in print; that is, you'd like to see your work published in journal, magazine, or book format.

Getting published? Hey, no worries. That's easier than vanquishing a lone zombie in some rural cemetery.

They say everyone's got a book they are working on, right? Now, whether you've written a piece for the *American Journal of Mad Scientists* explaining just how rigor mortis reverses when the dead become reanimated, or have just finished the great American novel, the process has very similar steps.

The first step, as I have already stated, is perfecting your work. Polish, polish, polish until it gleams sickly green in the moonlight. Then—and only then—ship it off. But to where?

The second step involves doing some research. Blow the dust off the cover and crack the spine; it's time to seek out publishers and agents. The world of publication and literary representation is a small one. If you arouse anger in an agent because you wasted his or her time, it won't be long before everyone in the community has heard of you. Well, maybe it's not quite that dismal, but you should at least assume that it's possible and act accordingly.

> **Polishing your work is similar to polishing that dusty old lamp you found in the sand. Nothing special will happen until you put a little elbow grease into it.**

So what does this all boil down to? You need to know exactly what a publisher publishes and what an agent represents *before* you send them your manuscript. That means you'll have to do some research. Look the publisher up online. Do they publish books with stories similar to yours? Have they published authors from whom you have drawn inspiration? Does the agent expressly state in her submission guidelines that she only reads the genre in which you have written? If so, you are in luck. You might be able to submit to this publisher or agency.

More often than not, however, publishers specialize. It will be a waste of time—yours and theirs—if you submit your work of horror to a publisher that exclusively specializes in romance novels. Similarly, it is counterproductive to waste your time, effort, and attention seeking literary representation from an agent who detests horror and only represents middle-school children's books. Again, you don't want to waste their time. Chances are, they work with people who might consider you book, and they do have a lot of lunches over which they talk shop. Don't be on their naughty list when those lunches happen.

Once you have found a list of publishers or agents to whom you would like to submit your work, make sure that you understand the nuances of their unique submission requirements. Failure to submit work in precisely the format, method, and timeline requested by a publisher or agent is a mortal sin that will bury your manuscript six feet deep instantaneously. Your inability to follow submission guidelines also implies two things about you to prospective publishers and agents: you are unprofessional and you can't follow directions. And if you can't follow directions, how will you manage to live up to your end of a publishing contract?

You won't.

Therefore, if the publisher tells you in her guidelines that you must submit all your stories printed in crayons on large sheets of construction paper rolled into a scroll and attached to the ankle of a carrier pigeon, then your only question should be: "what color crayons?" If an agent declares that he will only look at your manuscript (or, "MS" in the publishing business) if you include it as email attachment in a particular file format with a specific message in the subject line, then you reformat your document to adhere to these requirements and follow the specified submission protocol with your submission email.

The third thing you need to do is query the publisher or, in some cases, an agent. A query is simply a question—something that you ask before you make presumptions. In the world of publication, this method of "query" has certain expectations—that is, agents and publishers will expect your queries to follow certain guidelines. Sometimes, those guidelines will be in the submission guidelines you've already so fervently studied. If they are not, you'll find that most publishers and agents follow a similar script.

Before creating a query, you need to research the publisher or agent to see (1) if the agency is currently open to queries and/or submissions, and (2) what process you'll need to follow to formally submit your manuscript. It is always wise to be familiar with the types of stories selected by the publisher or agent. If you are submitting to a magazine or journal, it's a good idea to purchase a few issues to get a feel for the voice, style, tone, and genre the publishers look for in their stories. The same goes for book publishers. Are you sure they are interested in your writing genre? You wouldn't send a full-length, 80,000-word manuscript (the usual length of a short novel in the publishing industry) about zombies who love to put two scoops of viscera on their brain flakes to Little Golden Books press, would you?

Once you have determined that the publisher/agent actually works with the style or genre you wrote and is accepting queries, don't make the mistake of assuming they also want to see your actual article, short story, or book. Many companies simply want

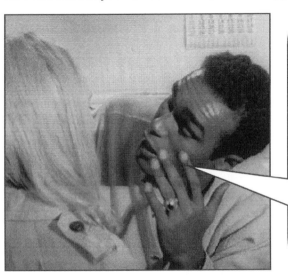

Aren't you listening? I guarantee that Little Golden Books will not be interested in 28 Days After the Snowy Night of the Return of the Living Evil Dead Residents.

a query prior to reading or considering anything for publication because they don't have the time to read through a hundred manuscripts a day. Some will ask that the query be accompanied with your work (or a sample of your work if it is a longer piece), but pay close attention to what's specified in the submission guidelines. Don't send them the entire boiling cauldron when all they want is the newt's eyes.

Most publishers are open to email queries. Whereas this was once taboo, it is now pretty much accepted practice. While there certainly are still paper-and-pencil publishers who prefer to review everything in hard copy, that is no longer the norm. The amount of paper saved by accepting email submissions amounts to a small forest, and digital submission and response turnaround makes the submission process faster and more efficient for everyone involved. If you don't already have a copy of your work saved in a digital format (be it a thumb drive, disk, or on the cloud), you'll need to do this before you attempt to submit. Even the paper-and-pencil publishers will eventually need a digital copy of your work.

> **If Stephen King had a difficult time finding a publisher for *Carrie*, then it may not be reasonable for you to expect a publisher to hand you a contract and a six-figure signing bonus on your first try.**

The query itself is a stage you might be stuck in for some time. Consider that Stephen King had practically given up on *Carrie*, even chucking the manuscript in the trash at one point, after receiving rejections to queries. We're talking about the *King* of horror here, giving up on his masterpiece (*Carrie,* for Lucifer's sake) because he was so discouraged. Indeed, it might never have been published at all if not for the intervention of his wife, Tabitha, who encouraged him to keep trying. Querying can be a discouraging business. Be prepared for lots of rejections before you find a publisher or agent willing to bite (and I'm not talking about your neck, either). Some publishers might reject your inquiry out of hand, without even seeing a sample of your work. Other publishers might request the complete manuscript or first three chapters of your novel. Whatever the case, it all begins with a query, and queries all follow a fairly distinct formula.

Because time is money to publishers and agents, you must get to the point quickly. After you block out the frame of the letter (your name and contact information, followed by theirs, the date, etc.), you begin the query by jumping right into what makes your work so special. Consider the first line of your query letter to be the most important—that's where you hit them with a teaser. A hook. If a publisher or agent isn't "hooked" instantly by your first line, he or she might never read the rest of your letter, let alone request to see a sample of your work.

Here is an example of a query letter that a member of my coven recently sent to that esteemed press, Broomsticks & Batwings:

W.W. West
369 Yellowbrick Lane
West Village, OZ 45432
wwwest@ozmail.com

July 12, 2012

Ms. Luella Eastwick
1313 Eye of Newt Lane
New York, NY 66666

Dear Ms. Eastwick:

Samantha is a young (although perhaps not as young as people think) attractive witch with a problem. She has fallen in love with a mortal.

That, however, is more of a problem than one might think: in order to marry the dashing Mr. Stevens, Samantha must promise to forgo the use of her magical powers and join the ranks of housewives and soccer moms in the quiet suburban neighborhood of Westport.

However, as much as she loves her husband, leaving behind the powers of magic is much more difficult than one might imagine, especially when an interfering mother enters the scene and is not exactly fond of Samantha's chosen mate.

Now, a little about me. I am a member of the Witch Writers Association of America, affiliated with the regional chapter in Salem, Massachusetts. I've been a finalist in numerous contests, receiving first place in the recent Morgan La Fey Awards and an honorable mention in the Death to All Munchkins Halloween writing contest. I hold a degree in Ancient Spellcasting as well as an honorary degree from San Francisco Witches and Warlocks Academy, where I was an acquaintance of the Halliwell sisters, whom I believe you have worked with in the past.

Per the instructions on your website, I am enclosing the first three chapters of my novel and a synopsis along with a SASE for your convenience. Thank you for your consideration. I look forward to an opportunity to share the entire manuscript with you soon.

Sincerely,
W. W. West

You will notice that my friend kept the query intentionally short. It jumps right into the good stuff about the work in question, and it also mentions the submission guidelines—this is a good idea because it reminds the publishers or agents that you actually followed directions, including the important step of providing a SASE (a self-addressed, stamped envelope with enough postage to return whatever you sent them), if required. Remember, you are not writing another book here—you just want to grab the reader's attention in the hope that they will want to see more of what you've written.

Also, notice that Ms. West did not send it to one of the powerhouse publishers out there. She sent it to a

> **Witches may enjoy reading the *Book of Shadows*, but most zombies are much more comfortable with books such as *See Jane Run (and Stumble)*.**

smaller house, the lesser-known Broomsticks & Batwings. It is a fact that there are just a few major publishing companies left to contend with, but the good news is that there are plenty of smaller presses out there willing to work with fledgling authors. Whether you write short stories, novels, or non-fiction, it is to your benefit to investigate these companies. Good resources include *Writer's Marketplace* (available both in print and online), Duotrope, and Preditors and Editors, just to name a few. Or, for a small down payment, I can arrange to have your manuscript accepted by any publisher in the world. I've worked with more than one author willing to trade their soul for just that privilege.

If you thought writing was hard work, try getting published. It is not impossible, but it requires an entirely different set of skill sets. So does self-publishing.

Self-Publishing

The good news is that you don't necessarily have to deal with traditional publishers or expose yourself to the pitfalls associated with witchcraft to get ahead. ("Sparkly" vampires? Yep, a spell casting gone awry was responsible, and teenage girls across the world now suffer from a misconception that vampires won't rip off their heads and drink blood from their skulls. I think it was a problem with substituting liver of gnat for tongue of bat. Either that, or the witch creating this spell used her BeDazzler to stir the contents.)

But be forewarned: there's no turning back once you've gone the route of self-publication. Most traditional publishers won't be interested in work that has been published previously. Many times, publishers want to buy the right to be the very first people to feature your writing. If you've self-published a manuscript, it may kill your chances of subsequently finding a publisher willing to pay top dollar for the privilege of bringing that work to print.

In addition, there are thousands of "self-published" authors in the marketplace, saturating the online market with their work—and not all of the material out there is of good quality. Many times, self-publishers forego the route of hiring a professional editor to work with their material, and the final product suffers accordingly as a result.

Remember, just because you wrote something doesn't mean it is ready to be published. It also doesn't mean that it's any good. An editor's job is to make sure that the manuscript it is not only good enough and ready for publication, but also that it is free of typos and grammatical errors—things you likely missed when conducting your own edits. If you could spell it right, you probably would have done so the first time through, right? Spell checkers only catch about a quarter of your mistakes—it doesn't notice when you insert a correctly spelled word that happens to be wrong for the context. There are plenty of poorly written, self-published books out there. Don't let yours be one of them.

While poorly written books are bad enough, another problem with self-publishing is that many authors pay to have their book printed. This often carries a financial burden that isn't incurred when books are printed by traditional publishing houses. Publishing with a traditional publisher (regardless of the medium) can give you a feeling of success, validating that your work is valuable to someone other than yourself. Self-publishing can't do that in the same way, as many authors learn.

Still, I've already established that publishing is a tough industry. You can go years without ever hooking even a small press willing to publish your work. Many authors turn out of necessity to the industry of self-publishing, but caveat emptor. There are spiked traps everywhere. Be aware there are lots of scam artists out there hoping to cash in on gullible authors—and not all of them are witches or warlocks. These charlatans are a breed much viler than any witch, vampire, werewolf, or zombie you will ever encounter. Most of these "publishers" offer a free or inexpensive method for publishing your work, but then offer all kinds of à la carte add-on features that are usually not worth the price of a bat's wing or lizard gizzards. Whether you are going with a small publisher or one of the services offered by the major bookstores,

Self-publishing comes with its own unique handful of problems. Anyone have an aspirin? This headache is killing me.

make sure to read the small print. Understand what you are signing up for. What does a book cover design cost you? Are they offering you cover templates that will look like a dozen other books? What does editing cost you and how good is their editing service? Where are their books distributed?

Some companies that offer you self-publishing options include: Amazon (CreateSpace), Barnes & Noble (PubIt!), Lulu, and Smashwords. Some of these companies publish in both print and electronic format, while some only focus on e-publications. Do your research. Make sure you are comfortable navigating their layout and utilizing their content management controls. Also make sure that you are prepared to market your book yourself, and that you understand what the terms of service are before you sign up for any form of self-publishing.

> **Anyone with a computer can publish to the Internet, but that doesn't mean everyone should.**

Web Publishing

Another flavor of self-publishing is web-based publishing. The World Wide Web is a magical device. When I was just a girl in the South of Italy studying the effects of my potions on fresh cadavers, the Internet was barely dreamt of. Back then, we used carrier ravens and telepathy to get messages across great distances, though with considerable more effort. Today, instantaneous communication to the far reaches of the world happens at the push of a button.

Pushing that button, though, has its drawbacks. For instance, few people realize that there are consequences associated with posting something to the web. It doesn't matter if you failed to sign a lengthy contract or if your writing never appears in print (many publishing houses specialize in only publishing eBooks, anyway)—if you publish to the Web, the manuscript has still technically been published.

That means, if you post a comment to your Spitter Feed—something unique and clever and completely your original creation—the idea is now published. You could go so far as to copyright that idea. Copyright law is expansive and covers several areas, but generally speaking, the moment you write something, you own that intellectual property (so long as you didn't write it *for* someone else who has domain ownership of your intellectual property—all very confusing, isn't it?).

This also means that things published on the web will have an equally difficult time eventually finding a home with a traditional publisher who requires first publication rights. Your blog is a publication. So is your listserv, your forum, your feed—all publications. Most websites are free of charge (some subscription sites exist, true enough, and certainly some sites allow you to receive donations from patrons), but if you post your work to a domain that can be viewed by anyone anywhere at any time, then why would anyone pay to read the same thing in an eBook, journal, or bookstore?

They wouldn't need to. Why buy the donor when you can get the blood for free, sweetie?

This also applies to works in progress, as well. Consider a spell I was working on for quite some time. I was trying to develop an incantation that would allow all the terra cotta soldiers in the Chinese Emperor's tomb to awaken like golems and destroy the world. Naturally, I needed feedback for a spell of this magnitude. Not that I'm an amateur, mind you, but I'm simply smart enough to recognize that all writing—including enchantments—needs a fresh pair of eyes and a solid edit before the spell is ready to be cast.

In the digital age, feedback is easily gotten. All you have to do is post your work either online or to the cloud and share it with your coven. Of course, this was before I knew about the cloud. It was some time back, and I was a little green (still am, I suppose). So, I posted my work to a blog and asked my sisters to critique it. I thought surely my work was safe there. Who else would find my obscure blog on the web?

The answer?

Only *everyone*.

When I'd finally perfected the spell, I was ready to sell it to a power-hungry oil executive in Dubai. I was quite surprised to receive a very curt (and very short) rejection letter, indicating that the oil executive was backing out of the bargain we'd struck. Why? Because he'd come across my spell online, where it was published and available for anyone to see, he no longer felt the need to pay me for it.

I'd love to turn that power-hungry oil executive into a sniveling salamander and cast him onto a bed of hot coals, but oil executives seem to have powerful protective amulets that render them impervious to even the darkest arts (or the United Nations).

But heed my example and avoid making the same mistake I did: if you publish

First, I'll cut this line out of your manuscript. Then this one. And this one. Ha, ha, ha! With all those little red editing marks, doesn't it look like your manuscript is bleeding?

anywhere on the Web, you are still publishing your work. Whether you post it to a blog, a newsfeed, a listserv, or a website you created, you are published.

If you still choose to go the Web publication route, be careful of editorial mistakes. Nothing screams "amateur" like a typo, or induces people to make fun of you like a misspelled word. So approach your Web publishing with the same level of diligence that you would a traditional print publication—scour it with a polishing stone until all the imperfections are buffed out, and then (and only then) hit "submit" on that tool bar. Especially if you are trying to make a living (or a dying) as a writer.

Publishing Academic Writing

Academic writing is usually a demon of a different color. Professors, researchers, and others in higher education are hard pressed by the institutions that employ them to publish. Plucky students inspired by a few kind comments from an instructor may seek to find a home for their papers. Scientists publish findings to demonstrate their own professional development, and technologists publish research to stay current. As a result, academic writing generally requires a different cauldron, a few handfuls of spider web, and a widdershins wand swirling as opposed to the deosil flourish for *other* types of publication.

> **Academic writing usually requires more attention and polishing than other styles of writing. A couple of eyeballs and a dash of newt mixed with a quick stir will not get the job finished or in proper form.**

Scholarly writers tend to specialize in highly esoteric forms of study much the way spellcasters specialize in various genres of the arcane. We have weather witches highly skilled in calling down the rain; you have meteorological students that study rainfall patterns over the Gobi Desert. We have necromantic witches whose focus of study is to create zombies from the newly dead; you have medical students who have honed their study on the decomposition patterns of exposed corpses. The further one travels in their course of study, the more elite their subjects of expertise become. I once knew a witch who was revered all across the land for her ability to conjure a boil on the inside of an enemy's left nostril.

Given this level of specialization that comes with academic writing, the first step to academic publication is identifying scholarly publishers that specialize in similar areas of academic focus as that of the paper you wish to publish. Because academic writing is intended for an audience of scholars and is intentionally written to be analytical, argumentative, and research-based (as opposed to entertaining), publishers in the academic sector are looking for very different things than, say, *Zombie Today* magazine. While your research about the extent to which urban-dwelling zombies are evolving problem-solving skills might be a gripping read for many people, academic publishers will be inclined to publish it based on its enlightening content and sound research or findings over its entertainment value.

Another key difference between academic publishing and other forms of publishing is that academic publications go through a process of peer review. Imagine that you have just concocted a potion that can cause its drinker to shrink to the size of an apricot. You see practical uses for aspiring zombie chefs looking for the newest hors d'oeuvres to serve at the next Undead Happy Hour. You wouldn't just start selling the snake oil to every undead hipster that crosses your path without sharing it (and testing it) with your necromantic friends, now would you? Peer review is a method by which all of your magical work is checked and double-checked by other master witches and wizards in the field. The same holds true for peer-reviewed writing: every article, essay, or book that is published by an academic publisher has been reviewed by one or more experts in that field. Peer review validates the research being presented and helps to ensure that new publications are accurate, original, innovative, and relevant to the field. Personally, I only ever cast peer-reviewed spells myself. It's how I keep my bony figure.

Finding an academic publisher that specializes in your area is not as hard as it might seem. Most academic publishers tend to operate out of universities (e.g. the University of Chicago Press) and publish everything from scholarly websites, blogs, and digital projects to journals, monographs (books by a single author on a single subject), and anthologies. As I dimly recall, I believe my very own *Necronomicon Ex Mortis*, a scholarly tome of great historical and mystical significance to my trade, was published out of Miskatonic University, my alma mater. Ah, how I miss my youthful college nights spent wailing at the sea and bloodletting my dorm mates to raise the

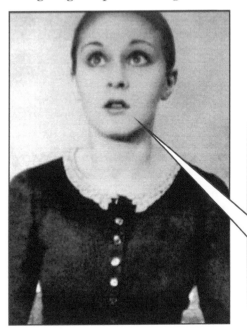

Elder Gods from the briny deep. Those were the days. In fact, I think I published my own first paper with Miskatonic University Press. It was a treatise on the proper application of leeches during a bone-setting ritual.

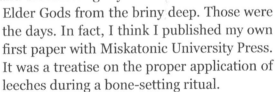

Sir, I'm so sorry you had all that trouble when you read out loud from my dead-summoning book on Halloween, but didn't you read the disclaimer on the title page?

And that reminds me: to seek out opportunities for academic publishing, start with your own campus—many colleges, universities, and even departments or programs publish the work of their students and faculty. There are many journals published in every field, each with a slightly different audience, purpose, and ranking. Top-tier journals will be highly competitive in terms of publication and you will need to demonstrate your powers of prose and critical thinking to make the cut—and I'm not suggesting a literal cut, mind you. That *almost* never works to get you published. What does sometimes work, though, above and beyond threats of bodily injury, is casting a wide net. When submitting your work, select a range of journals to submit to.

Once your article has been submitted for publication, it goes through the review process. In most instances, the managing editor will decide whether to allow your submission to go through this process. While you are waiting for the verdict, this would be a good time for a bonfire and a skyclad spiral dance or two. Perhaps even a small sacrifice. Unicorns are fantastic for this, but I wouldn't recommend narwhals. Everyone knows horned sea creatures are pure myth. *Wink.*

If selected, multiple reviewers will read your article, make comments, and make recommendations to the editor about whether it is worthy of additional consideration for publication (these recommendations are typically: "yes," "yes with revisions," "revise and resubmit," or "no"). The peer review process can take months or even years, factoring in the time associated with revising and resubmitting your work.

Be prepared, though. Academic publishing can take a very long time. It is appropriate to have a score of mummies on hand to perform the necessary rituals of longevity, perhaps extending your life another, oh, say a hundred years or more? At least for the first round of peer review. Perhaps another hundred for the second.

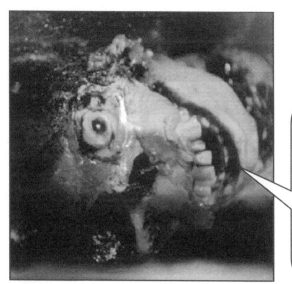

Marketing Your Writing

Unless you find yourself being scooped up by a major publishing house, learn to accept the possibility

I sure wish I'd taken that whole "publish or perish" thing more seriously.

that you will spend the rest of your mortal years convincing anyone who'll listen to buy your book. Self-publishing or publishing through smaller publishing houses often means that the burden of getting your work noticed falls squarely upon the author's shoulders. Now are you beginning to understand why so many desperate writers come to me for help?

To market your book, you absolutely need to have a website and actively employ social media. These are the necessary tools of self-promotion that all writers must utilize in this day and age. In fact, many writers who freelance find that their résumé is much less effective than having an established web presence. A blog, social network newsfeed, or website all serve to demonstrate your writing expertise and professionalism (or lack thereof) to prospective publishers, readers, and employers— so adeptly using these tools is a must.

In addition to web-based mediums, consider other avenues of marketing. If you went to a high school or a college, contact the alumni board and see if they will mention you and your book in their newsletter or campus magazines. If you live in a city, see if your city has a print magazine and send them a press release. If you write within a specific genre, find magazines that cater to that genre and place an advertisement in them. Offer to do interviews, send your book to reviewers, and ask for radio and video spots with your local news access points. Everything helps.

And remember, there's no such thing as "bad" publicity. People are just as likely to buy your work if they hear it's terrible (sometimes even more likely, as everyone wants to see for themselves what all the howling is about) as they will be if they come across a wonderfully positive review. Don't worry about bad reviews or criticism—it's all publicity for your book.

Often, budget is another factor to be considered. How can you garner the most attention for the investment of money and time you are willing to sacrifice? Will the window cling featuring the cover of your book that you had custom made for your car's rear window make as much of an impact for $45 as the printed press release you mailed (by old fashioned postal services, no less) to dozens of newspapers in your region?

Press releases are, perhaps, the easiest free way to publicize your work. They are form letters that contain all the key information necessary to show an editor or publisher your news, so they can decide whether or not to run the story. Not every press release will be printed, and publishers make no guarantee that your press releases will ever see print—after all, it's free marketing for you when they could charge you for ad space. So if you want to maximize the chances that your press release will be noticed and taken seriously, make sure to follow the basic guidelines presented below.

You will find an example of a press release used for marketing purposes on the next page. We'll reuse Ms. West's manuscript from the cover letter we looked at previously.

Contact: W.W. West
Phone: (207) 555-6666
Book: *Bewitched, Bemused, and Bewildered*

For Immediate Release

Local Witch Publishes Self-Help Novel for Interspecies Marriages

Salem, MA (November 13, 2011): Witches and humans comingling in matrimonial bliss is the subject of W.W. West's newest novel, *Bewitched, Bemused, and Bewildered,* published by Broomsticks & Batwings in October of this year. The book chronicles the tale of a beautiful, young witch, Samantha, who falls hopelessly in love with a mortal man and marries him against her mother's witchy instincts. Hilarity and hijinx ensue when their very different worlds collide in this compelling novel of humanity, witchery, and tomfoolery.

This book is certainly relevant to our current political climate in which litigators and lobbyists try to determine the fate of interspecies marriage. A hot-topic in the news lately, the question has arisen as to whether witches should be allowed to marry mortals at all. This novel explores the possibilities of just such a marriage—the good and the bad. It's an inside look into an interspecies relationship.

Bewitched, Bemused, and Bewildered is available in trade paperback at all your favorite brick-and-mortar book sellers around the globe, and it is also available for purchase from your favorite eBook vendors. A portion of the proceeds from this book will be donated to the Witches in Wichita Foundation as well as the Incantation Project, which helps inner city youth develop the sorely needed vocational skills of resurrecting the dead and cooking human ears.

End.

Notice how the sample jumps right into the glory before explaining what makes the story particularly relevant, useful, or interesting to the public at large? It closes with the details necessary to actually market the book—in particular, how and where to buy it. In addition, it explains how buying it will have a positive impact on the world by donating to a charity, a solid marketing tactic that not only sells more books, but helps others who are in need.

Press releases are not the only way to market a book, but they are a useful method for helping to spread your marketing message and call attention to your book across the widest prospective audience possible. After all, if no one reads your book because no one has heard of it, what was the point of selling your soul to me to have it published in the first place?

Writing Prompts for Chapter 13

1. Imagine you are starting your own horror publishing company. Draft a list of your own specific submission guidelines. What will you take, and what will you reject? How do you want things delivered, and what will you do if they are not delivered the way you want them?

2. If you've tried to publish before and received a rejection letter, imagine now that you are writing a reply to the rejection. The publisher will never see it (because you are going to burn it after you write it—and don't save it, for hell's sake). You can write anything you want. Go.

3. Write a paragraph or two about why you deserve to be formally published.

Writing Exercises for Chapter 13

1. **Polish:** Find a piece of writing you have written that you believe is ready for publication. Before you zip it off to a publisher, find an editor willing to read it either for a fee or as a favor (perhaps an old teacher or a friend could help you). Ask them to comment on places where you need to make changes.

2. **Polish:** Try reading your writing backwards to catch typos or grammatical mistakes.

3. **Research Publishers:** Take a piece of writing you'd like to publish and do a quick web search for publishers who might consider your work. Make a list of all the publishers (and agents, if you like) that review the sort of work you have written.

4. **Submission Guidelines:** Find six separate publishers on the web. They should be completely unique and not imprints of the same publishing house. (An imprint is a "section" of a publisher that focuses on one or two genres.) Review the submission guidelines for each publisher. Note similarities and differences. Note how many of them say they do not accept simultaneous submissions (which means you cannot submit the same story to more than one publisher at the same time). Begin to tailor one of your pieces to match the guidelines of one publisher.

5. **Query Letter:** Research a list of query letters online for books or stories you yourself have seen published and enjoyed reading. Make notes about any unique features or qualities you find between the letters. Next, craft your own letter and try to incorporate some of those same features and qualities.

6. **Marketing:** Make a list of as many ways as you can possibly think of to market your book—that is, ways you can get the word out that you've published something.

Afterword from the Authors
(WHAT'S LEFT OF THEM, ANYWAY)
or
"In the Velvet Darkness of the Blackest Night"
or perhaps
"Not With a Bang, But a Whimper"

Y OU LAST SAW our three intrepid writers holed up in an apartment facing a zombie blitzkrieg, a setting sun, a dying laptop, and a publication deadline. You'd probably like to hear that at the last possible moment, the United States Armed Forces swept into the city, annihilated the zombie horde ascending the fire escape, and rushed the trio of writers to a safe house on a tropical island riddled with fresh pineapple and coconut cocktails.

But that's not what happened.

Stan was the first to go. With his sledgehammer in hand, he wedged himself against the wall between the two windows that opened onto the fire escape. He took the first zombie with a smash to the skull as if he were playing Whack-a-mole at Jokers at his grandkid's birthday party. But when the second zombie crashed through the window behind him and wrapped its arms around his waist, Stan didn't have time to bring the hammer back around before the creature took a chunk of meat out of his forearm.

At the sound of crashing glass, Rachel retreated behind the Feng Shui tower of canned goods and was immediately flooded with an ironic sense of calm. It didn't last long though, as a blue-jumpsuit clad zombie crashed his meaty fist through the tower and all that Feng Shui magic evaporated in an instant. He grabbed hold of her red hair and yanked her scalp toward his gnashing teeth. Like iron pincers, they pierced her skull and penetrated the fleshy gray matter of her brain in a log-flume-ride spray of blood, killing her instantly.

When the first zombie crashed through the window, it was Araminta who fled through the front door of the apartment, laptop clutched to her chest like a high school textbook in a teen romance. With the stairs pulverized, she had nowhere to go but up. So that's what she did. She ran up four flights of stairs before she found an apartment with an open door and flung herself inside. Bolting it shut behind her, she scrambled to open the laptop and save the final document before sending it to the printer at the stroke of midnight.

Relief swam through her as a smile lifted the corners of her mouth.

"It's done," she said with a sigh. "Now I can—"

But Araminta never finished her thought. As she backed away from the laptop, she failed to notice the creature shambling up behind her. Once a 90-year-old shut-in with blanched white hair and folds of wrinkles hanging from her jowls, the woman had long ago lost her teeth. When the zombie virus took her, her dentures had been sitting in a glass by her bed. It never occurred to the zombie to put the teeth back in her mouth. Not even as she gummed away at Araminta's shoulder with supernatural tenacity.

It took a while, but her steel-trap jaws finally managed to break some bones. She used her fingers to dig into the flesh and pull out some meaty bits before Araminta lost consciousness.

All three of our authors died. But not for long. Look out your window now, if you dare. You might just see them wandering the streets below, hands outstretched before them. They call out for brains—the brains of writers.

Writers like you.

WORKS REFERENCED OR CONSULTED

Film and Television

Army of Darkness. Dir. Sam Raimi. Universal Pictures, 1992.

The Cabinet of Dr Caligari. Dir. Robert Wiene. Decla-Bioscop AG, 1920.

Dawn of the Dead. Dir. George Romero. Laurel Group, 1978.

Dawn of the Dead. Dir. Zack Snyder. Universal Studios, 2004.

Dracula. Dir. Francis Ford Copploa. Perf. Gary Oldman, Winona Ryder. American Zoetrope, 1992.

The Evil Dead. Dir. Sam Raimi. New Line Cinema, 1981.

Evil Dead II. Dir. Sam Raimi. De Laurentiis Entertainment Group, 1987.

The Hunchback of Notre Dame. Dir. Wallace Worsley. Perf. Lon Chaney. Universal Studios, 1923.

Indiana Jones and the Temple of Doom. Dir. Steven Spielberg. Paramount Pictures, 1984.

Interview with the Vampire: Vampire Chronicles. Dir. Neil Jordan. Warner Brothers Pictures, 1994.

Queen of the Damned. Dir. Michael Rymer. Warner Brothers, 2002.

Re-Animator. Dir. Stuart Gordon. Empire Pictures, 1985.

The Return of the Living Dead. Dir. Dan O'Bannon. MGM/UA Home Entertainment, 1985.

The Rocky Horror Picture Show. Dir. Jim Sharman. Twentieth Century Fox, 1975.

Salem's Lot: The Movie. Dir. Tobe Hooper. Warner Home Video, 1979.

Shaun of the Dead. Dir. Edgar Wright. Universal Pictures, 2004.

Teen Wolf. Dir. Rod Daniel. Wolfkill, 1985.

True Blood. Home Box Office (HBO). 2008. Television series.

The Vampire Diaries. CW Television Network. 2009. Television series.

The Walking Dead. American Movie Classics (AMC). 2010. Television series.

Works of Fiction (Novels, Poems, Zines, Plays, and Songs)

Anson, Jay. *The Amityville Horror: A True Story*. New York: Pocket Books, 1977.

Austen, Jane and Seth Grahame-Smith. *Pride and Prejudice and Zombies*. Philadelphia: Quirk Books, 2009.

Baum, L. Frank. *The Wizard of Oz*. New York: Puffin Books, 2008.

Burroughs, William. *The Western Lands*. New York: Penguin, 1988.

Coleridge, Samuel Taylor. "Christabel." (1816). *The Norton Anthology of English Literature: The Romantic Period*. Eds. Stephen Greenblatt, M. H. Abrams, Jack Stillinger, and Deidre Shauna Lynch. New York: W. W. Norton & Company, 2006.

Dark Moon Digest: The Horror Fiction Quarterly. Issues 1-6. Dark Moon Books, 2010-2011.

Dickens, Charles. *A Christmas Carroll and Other Stories*. New York: Modern Library, 1995.

Eliot, T. S. "The Hollow Men." 1925. *The Complete Poems and Plays, 1909-1950*. Orlando, FL: Harcourt Brace & Company, 1971.

Faulkner, William. "A Rose for Emily." *Selected Short Stories of William Faulkner*. New York: Random House, 1993.

Gilman, Charlotte Perkins. "The Yellow Wall-Paper." *The Yellow Wall-Paper and Other Stories*. Ed. Robert Schulman. New York: Oxford University Press, 2009.

Ginsberg, Allen. "Howl." *Howl and Other Poems*. San Francisco: City Lights Publishers, 2001.

Haddon, Mark. *The Curious Incident of the Dog in the Night-Time*. New York: Vintage Books, 2004.

Harris, Charlaine. *Dead Until Dark*. New York: Ace, 2001.

Irving, Washington. "The Legend of Sleep Hollow." *The Complete Tales of Washington Irving*. Ed. Charles Neider. New York: De Capo Press, 1998.

Jackson, Shirley. "The Lottery." *The Lottery and Other Stories*. New York: Penguin Classics, 2009.

King, Stephen. *Carrie*. New York: Doubleday, 1974.

---. *It*. New York: Signet, 1980.

---. *The Stand*. New York: Anchor Books, 1978; 1990.

Kirkman, Robert. *The Walking Dead, Book 1*. Art by Tony Moore, Charlie Adlard, and Cliff Rathburn. Berkeley, CA: Image Comics, 2011.

Lovecraft, H. P. "Herbert West – Reanimator." *Necronomicon: The Best Weird Tales of H. P. Lovecraft*. Ed. Stephen Jones. London: Victor Gollancz Limited, 2009.

Matthews, Araminta Star. *Blind Hunger*. Largo, FL: Dark Moon Books, 2011.

Meyer, Stephenie. *Twilight*. New York: Little, Brown, and Company, 2005.

Milton, John. *Paradise Lost and Paradise Regained*. New York: Signet Classics, 2010.

Poe, Edgar Allen. "The Raven." *Complete Stories and Poems of Edgar Allen Poe*. New York: Doubleday, 1984.

Rolling Stones. "Sympathy for the Devil." *Beggars Banquet*. London Records, 1968.

Shakespeare, William. *Antony and Cleopatra*. London: Arden Shakespeare, 2006.

---. *Hamlet*. Open Source Shakespeare. George Mason University, 2003-2012. <http://www.opensourceshakespeare.org/views/plays//playmenu.php?WorkID=hamlet>

Shelley, Mary. *Frankenstein*. Ed. J. Paul Hunter. New York: W. W. Norton & Company, Inc., 1996.

---. *The Last Man*. Ed. Morton D. Paley. Oxford: Oxford University Press, 1998.

Stevenson, Robert Louis. "Strange Case of Dr. Jekyll and Mr. Hyde." (1886). *Strange Case of Dr. Jekyll and Mr. Hyde and Other Stories*. New York: Oxford University Press, 2006.

Swanson, Stan. *Forever Zombie: A Collection of Undead Guy Tales*. Daytona Beach, FL: Dark Moon Books, 2009.

Stoker, Bram. *Dracula*. Mineola, NY: Dover Publications, 2000.

The Tale of Sinuhe and Other Ancient Egyptian Poems, 1940-1640 BC. New York: Oxford University Press, 2009.

Williams, William Carlos. *The Collected Poems of William Carlos Williams. Volume I: 1909-1939*. Eds. A. Walton Litz and Christopher MacGowan. New York: New Directions, 1991.

Woolf, Virginia. *Orlando*. London: Wordsworth Editions Limited, 1999.

Wordsworth, William. "The Affliction of Margaret." *The Complete Poetical Works of William Wordsworth*. Ed. Henry Reed. Philadelphia: Porter & Coates, 1851.

Writing on Writing

Addonizio, Kim and Dorianne Laux. *The Poet's Companion: A Guide to the Pleasures of Writing Poetry*. New York: W. W. Norton & Company, 1997.

Adler, Mortimer and Charles Van Doren. *How to Read a Book: The Classic Guide to Intelligent Reading*. New York: Simon & Schuster, Inc., 1972.

Aristotle. *Poetics*. Trans. Joe Sachs. Newburyport, MA: Focus Publishing, 2006.

Bernays, Anne and Pamela Painter. *What If? Writing Exercises for Fiction Writers*. Second edition. White Plains, NY: Longman, 2003.

Bovée, Courtland and John Thill. *Business Communication Essentials*. Third edition. Upper Saddle River, NJ: Pearson Prentice Hall, 2007.

Booth, Wayne C., Gregory G. Colomb, and Joseph M. WIlliams. *The Craft of Research*. Chicago: University of Chicago Press, 2003.

Bullock, Richard, Maureen Daly Goggin, and Francine Weinberg. *The Norton Field Guide to Writing with Readings and Handbook*. Second edition. New York: W. W. Norton & Company, 2009.

Burke, Jim. *The English Teacher's Companion: A Complete Guide to Classroom, Curriculum, and the Profession*. Third edition. Portsmouth, NH: Heinemann, 2007.

Cleaver, Jerry. *Immediate Fiction: A Complete Writing Course*. New York: St. Martin's Press, 2002.

Dixon, Debra. *GMC: Goal, Motivation and Conflict: The Building Blocks of Good Fiction*. Memphis, TN: Gryphon Books For Writers, 1996.

Drury, John. *Creating Poetry*. Cincinnati, OH: Writer's Digest Books, 2006.

Elbow, Peter and Pat Belanoff. *Sharing and Responding*. New York: McGraw-Hill Higher Education, 2000.

Faulkner, Grant. "How to Start a Novel? Write the Whole Thing in a Month." *National Writing Project*. August 2008. 27 February 2012. <http://www.nwp.org/cs/public/print/resource/2665>

Fry, Stephen. *The Ode Less Travelled: Unlocking the Poet Within*. New York: Gotham Books, 2005.

Gage, John. "Asking Questions, Generating Ideas." *The Shape of Reason: Argumentative Writing in College*. Boston: Allyn and Bacon, 2001.

Graff, Gerald and Cathy Birkenstein. *They Say, I Say: The Moves that Matter in Academic Writing*. New York: W. W. Norton & Company, 2010.

King, Stephen. *On Writing: A Memoir of the Craft*. New York: Pocket Books, 2000.

Knost, Michael. *Writers Workshop of Horror*. Chapmanville, WV: Woodland Press, 2009.

Kremer, John. *1001 Ways to Market Your Books: For Authors and Publishers*. Taos NM: Open Horizons, 2006.

Lamott, Anne. "Shitty First Drafts." *Bird by Bird: Some Instructions on Writing and Life*. New York: Anchor Books, 1994.

Lane, Barry, Gretchen Bernabei and Robert Rhoeme. *Why We Must Run With Scissors: Voice Lesson in Persuasive Writing*. Third edition. Shoreham, VT: Discover Writing Press, 2001.

MacNair, Wesley. Personal Interview with Araminta Star Matthews. Fall 1999.

Nuts & Bolts: A Practical Guide to Teaching College Composition. Ed. Thomas Newkirk. Portsmouth, NH: Boynton/Cook Publishers, 1993.

"Overcoming Writer's Block." Penn State Graduate Writing Center. 2011. 5 January 2012. <http://composition.la.psu.edu/resources/graduate-writing-center/handouts-1/Overcoming%20Writers%20Block%20Fall%202010.pdf>

Pellegrino, Victor C. *A Writer's Guide to Transitional Words and Expressions*. Wailuku, HI: Maui Arthoughts Company, 1999.

Poe, Edgar Allen. "The Philosophy of Composition." (1846). *The Portable Edgar Allen Poe*. Ed. J. Gerald Kennedy. New York: Penguin Books, 2006.

Rossen-Knill, Deborah F. and Tatyana Bakhmetyeva. *Including Students in Academic Conversations: Principles and Strategies of Theme-Based Writing Courses Across the Disciplines*. New York: Hampton Press, Inc., 2011.

Ruggiero, Vincent Ryan. *Beyond Feelings: A Guide to Critical Thinking*. Seventh edition. New York: McGraw Hill Higher Education, 2004.

Sexton, Adam. *Master Class in Fiction Writing: Techniques from Austen, Hemingway, and Other Greats*. New York: McGraw-Hill, 2005.

Viders, Sue, Lucynda Storey, Cher Gorman and Becky Martinez. *10 Steps to Creating Memorable Characters*. New York: Lone Eagle Publishing Company, 2006.

Vogler, Christopher and Michele Montez. *The Writers Journey: Mythic Structure for Writers*. Third edition. Studio City, CA: Michael Wiese Productions, 2007.

Woolf, Virginia. *A Room of One's Own*. Orlando, FL: Harcourt, 1929.

Writer's Market: Guide to Getting Published. Cincinnati, OH: Writer's Digest Books, 2010.

Zinsser, William Knowlton. *On Writing Well: The Classic Guide to Writing Nonfiction*. New York: HarperCollins, 2006.

Non-fiction/References

Asimov, Isaac. *Yours, Isaac Asimov: A Life in Letters*. New York: Doubleday, 1995.

Backstein, Karen. "(Un)Safe Sex: Romancing the Vampire." *Cineaste*. 35.1 (Winter 2009): 38-41. MasterFILE Premier.

Baker, Catherine. *Your Genes, Your Choices: Exploring the Issues Related to Genetic Research*. American Association for the Advancement of Science, Science + Literacy for Health Project: 1999. Web. 3 Nov. 2011. <http://www.choicesandchallenges.sts.vt.edu/modules/pdf/yourgenes.pdf>

Bell, George E. *Writing Effective Sentences*. Boston: Allyn and Bacon, 1993.

Boffey, Philip. "Rare Disease Proposed as Cause for 'Vampires.'" *New York Times*. 31 May 1985, p. 15. Web. 3 Nov. 2011. <http://www.nytimes.com/1985/05/31/us/rare-disease-proposed-as-cause-for-vampires.html>

Brooks, Max. *The Zombie Survival Guide: Complete Protection from the Living Dead*. New York: Three Rivers Press, 2003.

Bulfinch's Mythology: The Age of Fable, The Age of Chivalry, Legends of Charlemagne. Ed. Richard Martin. New York: Harper Collins, 1991.

Centers for Disease Control and Prevention. "How is Rabies Transmitted?" Atlanta, GA: CDC, 2011. Web. <http://www.cdc.gov/rabies/transmission/index.html>

---. "Zombie Preparedness." Atlanta, GA: CDC, 2011. Web. <http://www.cdc.gov/phpr/zombies.htm>

Efthimiou, C.J. and S. Ghandi. "Cinema Fiction vs Physics Reality: Ghosts, Vampires, and Zombies." *Skeptical Inquirer*. 31.4 (2007): 27-40.

Eller College of Management. "Educating Future Social Media Professionals." The University of Arizona, 2012. <http://insite.eller.arizona.edu/outreach/index.asp>

Fox, Michael. "Animism, Empathy, and Human Development." *Between the Species*. (Summer/Fall 1995): 130-140.

Gee, Joshua. *Encyclopedia Horrifica: The Terrifying TRUTH! About Vampires, Ghosts, Monsters, and More*. New York: Scholastic, Inc., 2007.

Goss, L.W. "Rabies-Hydrophobia." *Experiment Station, Circular No. 9*. Kansas State Agricultural College. (1910). Web. <http://www.ksre.ksu.edu/historic publications/ Pubs/sc009.pdf>

Gottlieb, Richard. "The European Vampire: Applied Psychoanalysis and Applied Legend." *Folklore Forum* 23.2 (1991): 39-61.

Jakobsson, Ármann. "Vampires and Watchmen: Categorizing the Mediaeval Icelandic Undead." *Journal of English and Germanic Philosophy*. 110.3 (2011): 281-300.

Lunsford, Andrea. *The Everyday Writer,* Fourth edition. Boston: Bedford St. Martin's, 2009.

Maberry, Jonathan. *Zombie CSU: The Forensics of the Living Dead.* New York: Citadel Press, 2008.

The Malleus Maleficarum of Heinrich Kramer and James Sprenger. (1487). Trans. Montague Summers. (1928). Mineoloa, NY: Dover Occult, 1971.

---. Trans. Montague Summers. Ed, Marc J. Driftmeyer. Reanimality. July 2005. Web. 2 Nov. 2011. <http://www.reanimality.com/founders/mjd/writings/magickmalleusMaleficarum.pdf>

Mann, Thomas. *Essays of Three Decades.* New York: A. A. Knopf, 1947.

Melton, J. Gordon. *The Vampire Book: The Encyclopedia of the Undead.* Detroit: Visible Ink Press, 1999.

The Oxford English Dictionary, Second edition. Oxford: Oxford University Press, 1989.

Pinker, Steven. *How the Mind Works.* New York: W. W. Norton & Company, 1997.

"Rabies." *A.D.A.M. Medical Encyclopedia.* U.S. National Library of Medicine. PubMed Health. 10 February 2011. Web. October 27, 2011. <http://www.ncbi.nlm.nih.gov>

"Rhodopis." *The Dictionary of Classical Mythology.* Ed. Pierre Grimal. Oxford: Blackwell Publishers, 1996.

Robinson, Mary. "Memoirs of Mary Robinson. Written by Herself." (1800). *Revolutions in Romantic Literature: An Anthology of Print Culture, 1780-1832.* Ed. Paul Keen. Peterborough, Ontario: Broadview Press, 2004.

Russell, Jamie. *Book of the Dead: The Complete History of Zombie Cinema.* London: FAB Press, 2005.

Sabesta, Judith Lynn. *Weavers of Fate: Symbolism in the Costume of Roman Women.* University of South Dakota. (n.d.) Web. 3 Nov. 2011. <http://www.usd.edu/arts-and-sciences/upload/Harrington-Lecture-Sebesta.pdf>

Siddique, Sophie. "Haunting Visions of the Sundelbolong: Vampire Ghosts and the Indonesian National Imagery." *Spectator.* Special Issue: *Axes to Grind: Re-Imagining the Horrific in Visual Media and Culture.* Ed. Harmony Wu. 22.2 (Fall 2002): 24-33.

Simmons, Ernest J. *Chekhov: A Biography.* Chicago: University of Chicago Press, 1962.

Sureau, Pierre. "History of Rabies: Advances in Research Towards Rabies Prevention During the Last 30 Years." *Reviews of Infectious Diseases.* 10.4. (1988): S581-S584.

Strunk, William and Elwyn Brooks White. *The Elements of Style.* London: Longman, 1999.

Tufte, Edward R. *Envisioning Information.* Cheshire, CT: Graphics Press, 1990.

Urban Dictionary. 2011. <http://www.urbandictionary.com/>

Welford, Mack. "American Death and Burial Custom Derivation from Medieval European Cultures." *The Forum.* (Sept./Oct. 1992): 11-14. Web. 2 Nov. 2011. <www.nyu.edu/ classes/gmoran/WELFORD.pdf>

Wilde, Oscar. "Review." *Pall Mall Gazette.* 4 August 1886.

Winnubst, Shannon. "Vampires, Anxieties, and Dreams: Race and Sex in Contemporary United States." *Hypatia.* 18.3 (Summer 2003): 1-20.

Wood, Robert E. "Taking Up the Past: Hamlet and Time." *Journal of Dramatic Theory and Criticism.* (Spring, 1988): 21-40. <http://www.opensourceshakespeare.org/ views/plays/play_view.php?WorkID=hamlet&Scope=entire&pleasewait=1&msg= pl#a1,s1>

Woodward, Ian. *The Werewolf Delusion.* New York: Paddington Press, 1979.

Further Reading: Research, Writing, and Publication

CreateSpace (Amazon) offers free tools for self-publishing and distribution: <https://www.createspace.com/>

Duotrope's Digest, a free online resource for writers of fiction and poetry: <http://duotrope.com/>

Lulu, self-publishing book printing, and eBook publishing: <http://www.lulu.com/>

"On Memoir, Truth and 'Writing Well.'" *All Things Considered.* NPR. 13 April 2006. Radio. 21 December 2011. <http://www.npr.org/templates/story/story.php? storyId=5340618>

Online Writing Lab at Purdue University: <http://www.owl.english.purdue.edu>

Preditors and Editors, guide to publishing and publishing services: http://pred-ed.com/

PubIt! (Barnes & Noble) allows you to self-publish NOOK books: <http://pubit.barnesandnoble.com/pubit_app/bn?t=pi_reg_home>

Research and Documentation Online (Diana Hacker and Barbara Fister) gives guidelines for finding and evaluating sources: <http://bcs.bedfordstmartins .com/resdoc5e/>

Smashwords: eBooks from independent authors and publishers: <http://www. smashwords.com/>

Writer's Marketplace (available both in print and online): <http://www. writersmarket.com/>

Image Sources

13 Ghosts. Dir. William Castle. Columbia Pictures, 1960.

Atom Age Vampire. Dir. Anton Giulio Majano. Mason Distributing Corp., 1963.

Attack of the Giant Leeches. Dir. Bernard L. Kowalski. American International Pictures, 1959.

The Brain That Wouldn't Die. Dir. Joseph Green. American Pictures International, 1962.

The Cabinet of Dr. Caligari. Dir. Robert Wiene. Decla-Bioscope, 1920. Goldwyn Distributing Company, 1921.

Creature from the Haunted Sea. Dir. Roger Corman. The Filmgroup Inc., 1961.

The Devil Bat. Dir. Jean Yarbrough. Producers Releasing Corporation, 1940.

Dracula. Dir. Tod Browning and Karl Freund. Universal Pictures, 1931.

Frankenstein. Dir. James Whale. Universal Pictures, 1931.

The Golem. (Der Golem). Dir. Paul Wegener and Henrik Galeen. Deutsche Bioscop GmbH, 1915.

Horror Hotel. Dir. John Llewellyn Moxey. Trans-World Film, 1960.

The Hunchback of Notre Dame. Dir. Wallace Worsley. Universal Pictures, 1923.

The Mummy. Dir. Karl Freund. Universal Studios, 1932.

Night of the Living Dead. Dir. George A. Romero. Image Ten/Laurel Group/Market Square Productions, 1968.

Nosferatu the Vampyre. Dir. Werner Herzog. 20th Century Fox, 1979. 518 Media, 2005.

Nosferatu. Dir. F. W. Maunau. Film Arts Guild, 1922.

The Phantom of the Opera. Dir. Robert Julian. Universal Studios, 1925.

Plan 9 From Outer Space. Dir. Ed Wood. Valiant Pictures, 1959.

Shubi. "A Necronomicon made by a Lovecraft fan." 29 August 2004. *Wikimedia Commons.* <http://commons.wikimedia.org/wiki/File:Necronomicon_prop.jpg>

Supernatural. Dir. Victor Halperin. Paramount, 1933.

The Vampire Bat. Dir. Frank R. Strayer. Majestic Pictures, 1933.

Werewolf of London. Dir. Stuart Walker. Universal Pictures, 1935.

White Zombie. Dir. Victor Halperin. United Artists, 1932.

The Wolf Man. Dir. George Waggner. Universal Pictures, 1941.

NOTE TO READERS

As we will likely update *Write of the Living Dead* with subsequent editions, input on typographical, grammatical and other errors is appreciated. We would also be grateful for any suggestions you might have for additions to this book that you feel writers would find useful. You may send an email to WotLD@darkmoonbooks.com or visit the Dark Moon Books' website (www.darkmoonbooks.com) to fill out a comment sheet.

Author Biographies

ARAMINTA STAR MATTHEWS

Author of Dark Moon Books' *Blind Hunger*, a zombie apocalypse book for young adults, Araminta Star Matthews earned her BFA in Creative Writing from the University of Maine and her MFA in the same field from National University. In addition to writing, Araminta teaches writing and literature courses at colleges in Central Maine, Methods of Teaching English for the Maine Educators Consortium in concert with Endicott College's Graduate Program, and English and career development courses as a certified teacher for the second largest adult education facility in Maine. In her spare time, she is a pop culture enthusiast, a gamer, and an avid fiber arts and paper crafter. She lives in Maine with her hyperactive whippet, Devo, and her life partner, Abner.

RACHEL LEE

A voracious reader her entire life, Rachel Lee earned an MA in English from the University of Maine and now teaches academic writing and research at the University of Rochester where she is pursuing her Ph.D. In addition to tutoring undergraduate and graduate writers, she also works for the William Blake Archive and has published articles about electronically editing the strange, multi-media works of the poet-artist, William Blake. She has always been attracted to the dark and supernatural in the arts, and perhaps that's what drew her to the Romantic period of literature, a period dedicated to mysticism, nature, and metaphysics. In her spare time, she cares for her aging pug and writes her dissertation on the printing revolution of the Romantic period.

STAN SWANSON

Author of five books (including *Forever Zombie*, a horror short story collection), Stan Swanson has been in the publishing business for more years than he cares to recall. His other "occupations" have included singer/songwriter, retail store manager, newspaper editor, graphic artist, and web designer. He started his own publishing company (Stony Meadow Publishing) in 2006 and added the Dark Moon Books imprint in 2009. In 2010 he created and began publishing *Dark Moon Digest*, a horror literary quarterly which has been hailed as one of the best new horror magazines to appear in years. His hobbies (which he has little time to enjoy) include playing guitar, writing young adult novels, watching horror movies and playing video games.